Trout Streams
of Wisconsin &
Minnesota

Beth Christensen on the Lower Kinnickinnic

Trout Streams of Wisconsin & Minnesota

Jim Humphrey

and

Bill Shogren

A Fly-Angler's Guide to More than 150 Rivers and Streams

2ND EDITION

BACK COUNTRY

Backcountry Guides
Woodstock, Vermont

An Invitation to the Reader

With time, access points may change, and road numbers, signs, and landmarks referred to in this book may be altered. If you find that such changes have occurred near streams described in this book, please let the author and publisher know, so that corrections can be made in future editions. Other comments and suggestions are also welcome. Address all correspondence to:

Fishing Editor
Backcountry Guides
P.O. Box 748
Woodstock, VT 05091

Library of Congress Cataloging-in-Publication Data

CIP data for this title is available from the publisher.

Some of the material in this book has appeared in different form in *Fly Fisherman, Midwest Fly Fishing, Minnesota Sportsman, Outdoor News, Minnesota Trout,* and *Mainstream* (the newsletter of the Twin Cities Chapter of Trout Unlimited).

Published by Backcountry Guides, a division of The Countryman Press, P.O. Box 748, Woodstock, VT 05091

Distributed by W. W. Norton & Company, Inc., 500 Fifth Avenue, New York, NY 10110

Cover and text design by Bodenweber Design
Cover photograph by Joyce Humphrey
Interior photographs by the authors unless otherwise credited
Stream improvement drawings in chapter 1 courtesy Wisconsin Department of Natural Resources. Hook removal drawing in chapter 1 provided by O. Mustad and Son (USA), Inc.
Maps by Mapping Specialists, Ltd., Madison, Wisconsin © 1995, 2001 The Countryman Press

Printed in the United States of America

10 9 8 7 6 5 4 3

ACKNOWLEDGMENTS

Cheerful and honest thanks are accorded to the many friends who have generously or accidentally contributed to this work, especially the late Dick Frantes, the Acerbic Angler, who fished more Minnesota and Wisconsin streams—and who was skunked on more, by his own admission—than any other fly-fisher. Dick shared his triumphs and failures of more than 35 years. Al Farmes and John Schorn are fishing partners, environmental champions, and better fishermen than either of us.

Bob and Ginnie Adams, Mike Alwin of Mitchell's Fly Shop, Jack Ambuhl, Darrell Anderson, Joe and Jim Balestrieri, Wayne Bartz, Gordon Bentley, Judge Robert Bowen, Gale Brooks, Greg Breining, Herb Buettner, Jay Bunke, Loren Carver, Ellen Clark, Ed Constantini, Jim Curry, Royce Dam, Curt Dary, Ron Erlandson, the late Dave Ewart, Tim Faricy, Dave Fass, Jim Franczyk, DuWayne Fries, Aaron Gabriel, Professor Clarke Garry, Chuck Goossen, John and Vicki Goplin, John Gosz, Carl Haensel, Pat Hager, Dick Hanousek, Chris Hanson, Ken Hanson, Bill Haugen, Tom Helgeson, Dr. Mary Henry, Gary Horvath, Duke and Bridget Hust, Vern Imgrund, Jon Jacobs, Paul Jaeger, Skip James, Louis Jirikowic, Mickey Johnson, Charlie Johnston, Dr. Art Kaemmer, Mike Klimoski, Dr. Will Koukkari, Andy Lamberson, Dan Larson, Ted Mackmiller, Ron Manz, Craig Mason, Joe Michl, Bob and the late Jean Mitchell, Pete Mitchell, Ray Newman, Elliot Olson, Perry Palin, Jay Paulson, Steve Payne, Shawn Perich, Dave Peterson, Tracy Peterson, Robert Pils, Bob Reynolds, George Rogers, Sandy (Sandra) Rolstad, Steve Roth, John Rowell, Bill Schad, Mike and Connie Schad, the late Dr. Ivan Schloff, John Schorn, Dorothy Schramm, Bill Schuessler, Dick Schwartz, Dick Shira, Chris Shogren, Gary Sobotta, Eric Sorenson, Bob Talasek, Jim Tamte, John Vollrath, Dick Wachowski, John (Duke) Welter—all have contributed wittingly or unwittingly to our education. Others of equal skill and acumen have demonstrated on stream for our benefit. If we have failed to mention your name, forgive us.

We have also gleaned much from the writings of Gary Borger, W. Patrick McCafferty, Caucci and Nastasi, Ernest Schwiebert, Drs. Edmunds, Jensen, and Berner, Dr. W. L. Hilsenhoff, Swisher and Richards, and Dr. Tom Waters.

The professional fish managers and researchers of the Minnesota and Wisconsin Departments of Natural Resources who have patiently answered our sometimes naive questions are legion, but on some of them we have leaned most heavily: Bill Thorn, Mark Ebbers, Dick Hassinger, Bruce Gilbertson, and Jack Wingate of the Minnesota DNR; Bob Hunt, Ed Avery, Scot Stewart, Marty Engel, Max Johnson, Frank Pratt, and Larry Claggett of the Wisconsin DNR. To them, thanks and admiration for their devotion to the future of trout fishing.

Others of the Wisconsin and Minnesota DNRs are Deserae Bushong, Jim Cox, Peter Eikeland, Paul Eiler, Dennis Ernst, Chris Frieburger, Russ Heiser, James Holzer, John Huber, Tom Jones, Lee Kerner, Lee Meyers, Rick Nelson, Jeff Roth, Don Schliep, Jim Talley, Ron Theis, Dick Thompson, Tom Thuemler, Dale Togson, and Gene VanDyck. Our friend, Dean Hansen, Ph.D in entomology and columnist for *Midwest Fly Fishing,* has graciously reviewed our section on hatches and emergence charts.

We salute other friends, and strangers, who have labored to ensure scientific management and improved habitat for trout; and give thanks for the many environmental organizations and their volunteers.

DEDICATIONS

For Joyce Eloise Reed Humphrey, best friend, partner, photographer, and wife.
—Jim Humphrey

To my father, Alton G. Shogren, who on a snowy opening day in 1950 took me to Elk Creek near Eau Claire, Wisconsin, where I caught my first trout.
—Bill Shogren

GOOD COMPANY

To the list of distinguished presidents-fishermen cited in our profile of the Brule River of Wisconsin we can add the name of that good and gentle man, Jimmy Carter, a committed fly-fisher for trout.

We may also go back to the roots of our collective history for an endorsement of the noble sport. George Washington, our greatest president, during a break in the Constitutional Convention on Monday, July 30, 1787, fished for trout near Valley Forge on the evening stream.* Later he noted in his diary that he went fishing for perch near Trenton "with more success." So be cheered. If the trout don't rise for you, know that you are in good company.

*See *Miracle at Philadelphia*, Catherine Drinker Bowen

Contents

PREFACE TO THE SECOND EDITION

In this second edition we have revised many of the original stream profiles to reflect the latest information and observations, and have added profiles of more than 30 streams for a grand total that exceeds 150. We have corrected a few errors, embellished some maps, improved the syntax, and mentioned in passing other unprofiled streams that may merit the attention of explorers. We have added several tactics with the hope that they will lead you to discoveries on your own. We have revised descriptions of the two states' rules and regulations, with the usual caveat that you will have to read the regulations booklets when you buy your licenses. Regulations change annually, and sometimes it seems oftener than that.

Since the publication of the first edition, our opportunities to fish for trout early and often have been liberalized by the states' Departments of Natural Resources, although other restrictions have been added, such as no-kill or slot limits. We have not played much with the historical background included in the first edition, probably because no revisionist historian has seen fit to challenge us. Although this edition is packed with information, there are yet gaps in our understanding and information. We'd like mayfly emergence charts for every stream; we'd like to know more about the subtler effects of low-head dams and beaver dams; the relationships between heron populations and trout numbers; the most productive pools on every stream that we have visited! And why the Hex have diminished on the Upper Kinnickinnic of Wisconsin.

Even since completing this revision for our editors we have uncovered useful or fascinating information: Wisconsin leads the nation in miles of Class I high quality trout streams with naturally self-sustaining trout populations (3,500 miles); Minnesota has 92,000 miles of waterways, of which 27,000 miles have been ditched to improve agriculture; 40 percent of the trout stream mileage flowing through private lands in southeastern Minnesota is already under easements and open to fishers; it is probable that the water access law in Wisconsin (which allows anglers to wade the streambeds without challenge from landowners) was decided in a lawsuit brought by Mr. Frank Wesley Wade, a Civil War veteran, against a private club on the Willow River of Wisconsin in 1896. The Wisconsin Supreme Court decided in his favor in 1898. Although the access law was expanded by the Wisconsin Legislature in 1999 to include bank-walking to the high-water mark, another powerful group is attempting to send trout fishers back to the dark ages when the water belonged to the landowner.

Other questions and advice pique our interest: The Rush River of Wisconsin, a superb river for big trout, is running cooler and there is more natural reproduction of brown trout, and the Hex hatch on the Straight River is appearing earlier now than it did a decade ago. Jeff Weiss, a fisheries specialist with the Minnesota DNR, noted that "not many anglers fish these (southeastern Minnesota) streams after May 31." He also noted that the catch rate of trout reported in his creel survey was "surprisingly high" at 1.9 trout per hour. Another Minnesota report from the DNR wonders why so few anglers are fishing for brook trout on the North Shore streams. So many questions; so few answers.

The other day an angler stopped by while we were practice-casting in the backyard. He was looking for help, but in the course of our exchange he mentioned that his friends had found a "honey hole" on a stream we have tramped over but decided not to profile because we had not thought it worth our time. Occasionally a friend will introduce us to a secret pool or a productive section of a marginal stream, and then ask us to hold it a secret. What a dilemma! Our discovered secrets are shared with you, but some promises to others must be kept.

Minnesota and Wisconsin are states of extraordinary beauty, progressive ideals, and a healthy respect for the environment. We have said that the folks are friendly. One anecdote will suffice. We were examining the astounding improvements on the Tomorrow River, when a farmer stopped his tractor and invited us to fish his easement. He added that his neighbor would probably invite us also if we asked.

In this book we have saluted our fishermen-presidents, and have tipped our hats to the ladies, Dame Juliana Berners, 1492, and Mary Orvis Marbury, 1892. And we close here with advice from two notable authors. Izaak Walton (1593–1683) said, "Doubt not that angling will prove to be so pleasant that it will prove to be, like virtue, a reward to itself." And from a predecessor of Dame Juliana, Geoffrey Chaucer (1343–1400): "As no man is born an artist, so no man is born an angler."

This is not a scientific treatise, although inevitably some arcane terminology must be employed because trout fishing is part science, even if mostly art. The neophyte, the occasional trout fisher, and the expert will all find something useful. It is a handbook for fly-fishers who want to expand their horizons while they explore the graceful trout streams of Wisconsin and Minnesota. We know these streams, have parked at the bridges and in the Department of Natural Resources parking lots, have waded long into the interiors, have planted trout, and have electro-fished and helped debrush several. We have fished most of them; on a few we have only walked the banks. Sometimes we have caught trout, too.

The streams that we have chosen to showcase are personal choices. Some sections of streams are so beautiful that the catching of trout is less important than the sound of moving waters and the play of light and shadow among the trees. In truth, this book is not for meat hunters. We have not included any superproductive streams that happen to meander through the town dump.

Several of our rivers are big and brawling, requiring cautious exploration in belted waders and with the support of a staff. Others may be fished in hip boots with short, delicate rods and gossamer leaders. A few should be fished in prayerful attitude from the banks.

It is not difficult to obtain county maps or U.S. Geological Survey maps that reveal those thin blue threads of streams that run through unfamiliar country. The Wisconsin and Minnesota Departments of Natural Resources produce excellent maps of most designated trout waters, but the peripatetic fisher on vacation in strange territory is traveling blindly if he or she relies solely on those publications, as good as they are. That stream that appears so inviting on the map and in the imagination may be only a trickle during the heat of August. Or the stream may be posted against trespass, or that fire trail is be meant for four-wheel-drive vehicles only. Many headwaters creeks are too narrow or brushy to allow for even the most accurate of presentations. And sometimes the hike in from the road is too exhausting or too long for the day fisher.

We have had help and advice from countless friends from Trout Unlimited, from the Federation of Fly Fishers, and from the dedicated professionals of the states' Departments of Natural Resources. Additional information has been gleaned by watching, or reading the works of, more accomplished anglers. While help was always welcome, we have not always accepted the advice. Egregious mistakes are our own.

Reasonable people will aver that one stream is better than another. We've had fishers tell us that a stretch of river is dead. Others have enjoyed the best fishing of their lives there a week later. One experienced angler insisted there were no Hex or brown drakes on his river; a second expert gave us time frames for both emergences. Taxonomists may disagree over the classification of a mayfly. Many of us have a decided preference for best length and weight of rod for use on our midwestern streams. Everybody has his secret "meat fly" that is better than all others.

We have tried to report factually on the character and fishability of these fine streams, but conditions change from year to year—flash floods may alter watercourses or scour aquatic life, dams may be removed and improve the habitat for trout, beavers may impound free-flowing streams, drought can reduce flows to a trickle. Streams may alter their character by reason of logging, farming, development, or neglect along their corridors. Certain species of aquatic insects may decrease in number or disappear. Fishing regulations will change as the fisheries researchers acquire new knowledge, or as politicians inject their personal prejudices into the process. A dozen other factors can affect trout fishing in a stream between the time of research and publication of the information.

We may have missed a notable hatch of mayflies because we weren't there at the right time, or our superb experience on a stream may have been the result of happenstance—sheer luck, if you will.

Inevitably, some errors have crept into our maps or travel directions. Roads and bridges can be rerouted between the times of our surveys and publication. Road names may be changed by fiat of county commissioners. When you find a grievous error, please write to the fishing editor of Countryman Press. We'll try to do better next time.

Sometimes the "I" used in our reports is Bill telling the story, sometimes Jim. The "we" may be a composite of overlapping experiences. We don't care for the "Me and Joe" stories any more than you do—tales of how me and Joe caught big fish—but often we must use the personal pronouns to give you the "feel" of a stream or sense of place.

In the course of our far-flung explorations, we have gone headfirst down a steep bank on the Root River, snared by barbed wire. We have stepped off a bank cover to submerge ourselves and a new microcassette recorder. We have braved snow and sleet and the doldrums of midsummer. All for you!

We've been confronted by a surly badger in southwestern Wisconsin, and Paddy or Beverly Beaver has put down our trout on numerous occasions. Too often we've had to pull stakes before the possibilities of a grand stream were exhausted. But someone has to do the grub work, you will agree.

We have encountered a young barred owl crying for its mother, and the mother replying with her seven hoots from the vastness of the woods. We've had a bear and her cub cross our path, and had wild turkeys run from us. We've seen moose, the rare "cross fox," a fisher, and coyotes, and have heard the howlings of a wolf pack on spectral nights.

We've had otter kits, paws on a log and peeping over, watching us while we watched them. We've seen sandhill cranes, and white flies patrolling at dusk, trailing their banners.

We've had triumphs and failures, from the secret streams of southeastern Minnesota, through the green and gentle lands of west central Wisconsin, to the primitive tangles of northeastern Wisconsin and the North Shore of Minnesota. Alas, we have not yet encountered a mountain lion. And we missed by a week or so the chance to fly-fish for a hippopotamus in the Mecan River.

We've dined on superb but inexpensive fare in many friendly supper clubs, and have lunched alfresco at streamside on mushrooms and magnificent Wisconsin cheese, with a split of chenin blanc to wash them down—even while trout were rising.

The air is pure, the folks are friendly, and the landowners are cooperative (mostly). The scenery is often spectacular, and the trout will test your acumen and skill. Paradise!

Wisconsin and Minnesota may be unsung in the fly-fishing annals, but if you like the thought of 3,000 trout streams and more than 12,000 miles of designated trout waters, come fish with us.

1 | Introduction to Wisconsin and Minnesota Trout Fishing

The Land and the Seasons

This is an immense land of more than 135,000 square miles—a ragged square some 400 miles north to south and another 400 east to west. Its population of 10 million is spread thinly through the vast conifer forests, bogs, and lakelands of the north and along the major waterways, but is more heavily concentrated where the land is intensively farmed in the southern half. From the spate rivers of the Arrowhead Country along the North Shore of Lake Superior to the spring creeks of southwestern Wisconsin, there is a spectrum of waters and scenic delights for every fisherman, even a couple of "mountains" rising to 2,000 feet. The topography is generally flat or rolling, except for the pitches from the escarpment of the North Shore and the drop through hardwood forests in the coulee country of the lower Mississippi River.

In the north are huge state forests, national forests, wildlife areas, Native American reservations, the wilds of the Boundary Waters canoe country, and, in the northwest corner of Minnesota, the shallow valley of the Red River of the North. A surveyor's anomaly produced the Northwest Angle, which intrudes into Canada to include a piece of the Lake of the Woods. This is the most northerly point in the Lower 48.

There is perhaps more fresh water at the surface here than on any comparably sized area on earth. In surface area, Lake Superior is the largest body of fresh water in the world; Lake Michigan is not far behind. Some 25,000 lakes and countless ponds attract hordes of fishers for warm-water species. Among those lakes are more than 300 that are managed for stream trout on a "put-grow-take" basis.

To the south are the cornlands of Iowa and Illinois. The western third of Minnesota is part of the Great Plains region. To the east is the Upper Peninsula of Michigan, which should logically be part of Wisconsin, and the long

Bill Shogren on a Wisconsin spring creek

southward thrust of Lake Michigan into the heartland of the Midwest. Two waterways dominate both history and topography—the Mississippi, which originates in Minnesota, and the Wisconsin River, the hardest-working river in the United States, which bisects much of the state of Wisconsin north to south, and then fishhooks into the Mississippi close to the Illinois border. Curiously, rainfall can flow north into Hudson Bay, east into the Great Lakes, the St. Lawrence, and finally the Atlantic Ocean, or south into the Gulf of Mexico.

More than 600 Minnesota trout streams are concentrated along the North Shore of Lake Superior and in that great shaggy southeast triangle between the Mississippi and the Iowa border. Wisconsin has 2,500 trout streams spread generously, some flowing north into Superior, some east into Green Bay on Lake Michigan. Many others are tributaries of the St. Croix and the Mississippi, or of the Wisconsin River in the coulee country. A surprising number of streams meander through state forests or wildlife management areas. Three rivers have been designated Wild and Scenic Rivers by act of Congress, and three others are similarly protected by state law. Thousands of miles of streams are under easement to the states' Departments of Natural Resources, offering easy access and the illusion that you are fishing through the original wilderness.

Temperatures in the upper Midwest run to extremes, from 90 degrees Fahrenheit in August to 30 below during the winter. There is no distinct rainy season; of the approximately 30 inches of annual precipitation, a somewhat larger proportion falls in June and July. Sudden spring snowmelt may discourage fly-fishers for weeks at a time in the northern streams, but the southern streams are usually in good shape on regular opening weekends in mid-April in Minnesota and the first week of May in Wisconsin. Both states offer early seasons on certain streams, but such concessions to trout fishers may change from year to year.

Although far from the Atlantic seaboard, this interior country was opened early to exploitation by explorers, traders, and priests. In 1634, a mere 27 years after the settlement of Jamestown in Virginia and only 14 years after the Pilgrims floundered ashore near Plymouth Rock, Jean Nicolet canoed into Green Bay on Lake Michigan, paddled up the Fox River, and, legend has it, reached the Mississippi over the portage to the Wisconsin River. Twenty years later, Medard Chouart and Pierre-Esprit Radisson coasted along northern Wisconsin to the western end of Lake Superior. On May 17, 1673, Father Marquette and Louis Joliet left civilization at the Mackinac Straits to follow Nicolet's water trail into the Mississippi as far south as the Arkansas River in what is now the state of Arkansas. In 1680 Father Louis Hennepin reached St. Anthony's Falls in what is now downtown Minneapolis. That same year Daniel Greysolon, the Sieur du Lhut, labored up the Misakota and traversed the portage into the St. Croix, a major tributary of the Mississippi. The Ojibways' Misakota was the Dakota's Nemetsakouat, which the English called Burntwood and the French Bois Brûlé; now it is known as the Brule, a premier trout and steelhead stream in northwestern Wisconsin. With our usual American practice of modifying difficult names or words for ease of pronunciation, or sometimes as a cartographer's misspelling, du Lhut became Duluth, now Minnesota's gateway to the North Shore.

There is a trout stream for every traveler. A few, like the Wolf, are wide and wild. Some pitch down in fury through channels carved in stone; some wind softly through groves of sighing trees. Many open into green pastures where the air is sweet and jewelweed adorns the banks.

The Fishes

Any attempt to delineate fully the complicated life histories or biological diversity of the salmonids now present in midwestern waters is beyond the scope of this book. In prehistoric times, only two species of char inhabited the area now known as Wisconsin and Minnesota. They were the lake trout, *Salvelinus namaycush,* and the brook trout, *S. fontinalis.* You see the problem already—taxonomically these are not even trout! Because fish biologists were rare during the early days of the exploitation of the continent, the original ranges of native salmonids remain subject to conjecture. It is generally agreed that lake trout occupied all the Great Lakes, except Lake Erie, and a few large, deep, northern inland lakes left behind by the retreating glaciers some 10,000 to 15,000 years ago. The brook trout, also called speckled trout, or "specs" in midwestern parlance, are thought to be indigenous to the northern Great Lakes and many of their tributaries, to Ontario's Lake Nipigon, to the spring-fed streams of the St. Croix watershed of Wisconsin, and to a few spring creeks of southeastern Minnesota, northern Iowa, and possibly southwestern Wisconsin. The Nipigon brook trout, which are still carefully segregated from the Lake Superior population, are considered a separate race or population.

During the late 1800s, European brown trout, *Salmo trutta,* and rainbow trout, *Oncorhynchus mykiss,* were introduced into the waters. Within the past 25 years, several popular species of Pacific salmon have been imported, together with the Atlantic salmon, *Salmo salar,* and planted in tributaries of the Great Lakes.

In the spring of 1884, brown trout eggs from Germany were reared in the Northville, Michigan, hatchery and viable fry were deposited into the Baldwin River, a tributary of the Père Marquette. Eggs of Loch Leven brown trout arrived in the United States from Scotland in 1885; additional shipments from Germany, Scotland, and England followed. Progeny of the various shipments were soon inextricably mixed and distributed widely. Even that first German shipment of eggs may have included two subspecies or races of brown trout—one a lake resident, the other a riverine inhabitant.

In 1887 Wisconsin imported 1,000 European brown trout eggs and raised them in the Bayfield hatchery. That was only the beginning of a multitude of plantings from various sources, most often from mixed hatchery strains. A few were planted in Lakes Michigan and Superior, where they have reproduced and contribute to the fishery. Hatchery-raised browns were distributed widely in inland rivers. Hundreds of first-class Wisconsin streams now provide superb fly-fishing for naturally reproducing browns; marginal streams must be stocked. Introduced into Minnesota's Root River system in 1888, browns have since established "wild" populations in many streams, although some marginal streams still require supplementary stocking to maintain a quality fishery. Brown trout have become the salmonid quarry of choice for legions of midwestern fly-fishers.

The history of the rainbow is even more richly obscure. Rainbow trout were imported from the Pacific coast before the turn of the 20th century. As early as 1872 they were stocked in private ponds in Wisconsin. In 1883 they were introduced into Lake Superior by the province of Ontario. In 1885–1886, 600,000 were distributed throughout the state of Wisconsin. By 1887 they had been planted in tributaries of the Root River in southeastern Minnesota. Subsequently, they were planted extensively in rivers and lakes throughout the region. Rainbows have become a successful fixture in the Great Lakes and many of their tributaries, where they are known as "steelhead," but in inland streams they have rarely developed reproducing populations. Anecdotal evidence suggests that rainbows in inland streams tend to drift downstream in response to instinct. Another case can be made that rainbows disappear because they are easier than browns to catch and keep.

The populations, races, or strains of rainbows imported into the Midwest were innumerable. Since then they have been bred and crossbred to the point that their histories and separate genetic characteristics have become diffused.

And that leads us inexorably to the consideration of the proper taxonomic identification of our several species of trout. We tiptoe with trepidation through the minefield of subgenera, subspecies, populations, stocks, strains, races, and even "nations." Most ichthyologists agree, somewhat reluctantly, that all American brown trout are one species, *Salmo trutta,* composed of many different races, populations, or strains. Some brown trout, however, are anadromous, going to sea, or in this case to a large lake, such as Lake Superior or Lake Michigan; others spend their entire lives in the stream. Are they different subspecies, strains, or races?

The rainbow provokes similar speculation. At one time we traced the origin of the Irwin strain of rainbow trout, discovering after some effort that it was named for a hatchery. The Irwin strain supposedly has lost its anadromous behavior. Dr. Lauren R. Donaldson of the University of Washington, creator of the popular strain of rainbow that bears his name, is reported to have said, "We like to think our results compare with the poultrymen's development of the broad-breasted turkey." The Donaldson, once popular with fish managers, has been replaced in Minnesota by the Arlee strain of rainbow, which is easier to breed. Lately the Minnesota DNR has introduced an element of wildness into the Plymouth Rock (someone had a sense of humor?) strain of brown trout by taking milt of wild browns from two southeastern Minnesota streams. The Wisconsin DNR hatcheries produce Irwin strain rainbows and the St. Croix strain of browns.

It appears after close reading of the literature that the term "strain" is most often applied to domesticated trout, namely hatchery stock. "Population" is a useful term to describe a group of trout within a species that has marginally distinctive characteristics. Probably none of our browns or rainbows are wild trout in the sense that they are direct descendants of an originally imported discrete population. So when we refer to wild trout in the pages that follow, take it to mean trout and char that have successfully reproduced over several decades or seasons without a continuous infusion of hatchery strains. Fortunately, both the Wisconsin and Minnesota Departments of Natural Resources have moved the protection and propagation of wild trout to the top of their priority lists.

Most fly-fishers, we suspect, will be satisfied to know that they are fishing brooks, browns, or rainbows without questioning the particular lineage of their quarry.

The Streams and Rivers

In this book we profile more than 150 trout streams, from pristine brooks to potent rivers, and we mention in passing many more that may inspire the inquisitive instincts of fly-fishers. These streams are not necessarily the best that you might choose, if you could wade the 12,500 miles of designated trout waters in more than 3,000 streams. But rest assured that we have included a baker's dozen of the premier fly-fishing streams in each state. For every profiled stream, we identify the DeLorme map page number, the county or counties through which the stream flows, nearby cities or villages offering food and lodging, and travel directions.

We have observed, sometimes loosely, a number of criteria in our selection. The habitat should be suitable for the reproduction of at least one of the trout species present, or, if reproduction is marginal, for the overwinter survival and growth of planted trout. The stream should be wadeable, at least in part, with variations from deep pool to riffle and run. There must be room for a fly-caster to practice her or his art, and to capture a few trout of larger-than-average size. The stream should be esthetically pleasing, a subjective evaluation that might be characterized by adjectives such as "enchanting," "beautiful," "quality water," and the like. Of least importance is the need for an extraordinary population of trout, although many of our streams exceed the magic number of 1,000 trout per mile.

In general, on all Wisconsin and Minnesota trout streams you will find your best fishing where the Departments of Natural Resources have purchased blocks of land or leased easements along the streams. The public lands are marked on some maps by overprinted blocks of green, on others by a leaping trout, and by various symbols on Department of Transportation county maps. Public Fishing Grounds are often, but not always, signposted. Easements are often clearly delineated by fencing parallel to the river and 66 feet from the centerline of the river. Publicly controlled sections of river are most likely to have been improved by bank stabilization, in-stream structures, and intermittent debrushing.

It is possible to fish for stream trout on certain streams in southeastern

Minnesota as early as January 1, and on many Wisconsin streams as early as the first Saturday in March.

Maintaining a trout stream over the years is labor intensive and hugely expensive. The DNRs have neither the money nor the manpower to keep all of the streams tailored for fly-fishing. Some public stretches now will be cramped by brush and fallen snags, or beavers will have interrupted the flow. It's a shame to see some of our beautiful streams degraded by time and neglect—nearly unfishable—and yet the trout will live out their lives unmolested, and maybe that's one way of assuring the continuation of a discrete native stock.

WISCONSIN

Wisconsin has more than 2,600 designated trout streams encompassing more than 9,500 miles of water. It leads the nation in miles of high-quality streams with natural reproduction (3,500 miles). Southeastern Wisconsin has only a few streams, and there's a big void north and west of Stevens Point, where warm-water streams predominate. Milwaukee County has no natural trout streams, although there are anadromous trout and salmon runs through the city. At the other end of the scale Marinette County in northeastern Wisconsin lays claim to 196 trout streams. For the convenience of traveling fly-fishers, we have arbitrarily divided the state into six sections, although the southeast section includes few streams with resident trout.

Beginning in 1980, the state applied a classification system to all its trout waters and, with few exceptions, statewide bag and size limits were established. Class I streams were high quality with significant natural reproduction. Class II required supplemental stocking of hatchery trout. Class III streams were of marginal quality. Classes I and II comprised 81 percent of total mileage.

Although those 1980 classifications are still useful to establish a historic benchmark, they are no longer specifically applicable to any particular stream. Streams change. They may become better or worse for all of the reasons we enumerated earlier. We know that there has been an improvement in overall quality since the survey of 1980, and that further improvement is likely over the next several decades.

In 1990 the DNR promulgated a new category system designed to "maximize the potential many Wisconsin streams have for producing trout."

Wisconsin fish managers had identified a number of problems that prevented Wisconsin trout fishing from being as good as it could be. Many streams produced satisfactory numbers, but the trout weren't as large as anglers would like. Stocked fish were caught too soon after being planted, thereby depleting the streams and effectively shortening the season. Fish growth and public access were poor on many small streams. Too many large trout were being caught and killed. In some streams natural reproduction was poor because the breeding stock was fished out. On the other hand, the report concluded that there was great potential for improved fishing.

Wisconsin streams are distributed widely and are diverse in structure. Water quality is generally excellent, and forage food and habitat are adequate. Angler surveys revealed that the quality of the outdoor experience was more important than the number of trout creeled. And high on the list of factors that determined quality was the chance to catch and release an occasional trophy.

To allow the new category system to be evaluated, it was to remain unaltered for five years through 1994. Fish managers reviewed each stream in their areas and assigned a rating of Category 1 through 5 to each, "based on trout growth rates, reproductive success, fishing pressure, location in the watershed, habitat, long-term fish survival, water quality, and other factors. Classifying streams this way statewide would make it possible for fishery biologists to manage streams for specific types of trout fishing."

Category 1 streams have no minimum size but do enforce a bag limit of 10 trout, of which only 5 may be either browns or rainbows. Category 2 has a minimum of 7 inches and a bag limit of five. Category 3 has a 9-inch minimum, bag limit 3. Category 4, minimum 12 inches for browns and rainbows and 8 inches for brook trout; bag limit of 3 in total. For Category 5, special regulations, size and bag limits vary by specific stream. Some 50 streams were assigned to Category 5 in 1990.

Since 1994 there have been annual minor changes in regulations for some streams. Categories have changed; trout mileage has been added or subtracted on a few streams.

In 1997, after extensive debate, the Wisconsin DNR introduced an early season beginning March 1 and continuing to the regular opening on the first Saturday in May. The early opening was approved year by year through 2000. Catch-and-release with barbless artificial lures was required. The opener did not apply to spring ponds, or to sections of a handful of streams.

Some responsible and vocal individuals and factions opposed the early season because they believed that eggs or fry could be damaged by wading anglers, particularly in the fragile streams of northeastern Wisconsin. Proponents cited studies that indicated no damage to redds or fry. So controversial was the discussion that the state council of Trout Unlimited chose neutrality. Because of continuing differences, in 1999 the Wisconsin Natural Resources Board revisited the question.

With a Solomon-like compromise, in the fall of 2000 the Natural Resources Board authorized a permanent early season, beginning on the first Saturday in March and ending after the April Sunday that precedes the regular opening on the first Saturday in May. That five-day hiatus presumably will allow the trout a few days' respite; or perhaps it allows weary anglers a few days to prepare for the regular season.

However, not all of Wisconsin's 72 counties open early. In general, the northeastern quadrant of the state is excluded due to the more fragile nature of the habitat. Roughly, the counties east of US 51/39 and north of WI 23 are excluded. Forty-nine counties open early; Bayfield, the 50th, opens except for a section of the upper White River. The Pine River in Florence County, sections of the Peshtigo, the Pine and the Rat in Forest County, and the Wolf in Langlade open early. And there are numerous other opportunities for early trout fishing within the proscribed area. The 2001 regulations guide listed 11 additional counties where specific streams or stream sections opened early. The bag limit for trout during the early season is zero, and barbless hooks are required.

If it should occur to you when reading the regulations guide that the regulations seem complicated, remember that they are designed to give you more opportunities to fish for trout, not less.

And what of the future? You can bet your boots there will be changes designed to improve the quality of your experience in Wisconsin.

MINNESOTA

Minnesota has more than 3,300 miles of trout water distributed among 651 designated trout streams. Although there are streams throughout the state, the concentrations occur in the secret streams of the southeast and in the Arrowhead region above the North Shore of Lake Superior. In eight counties of the southeast that open early there are approximately 632 miles spread over 156 streams (although some streams may be counted in more than one county). Three Arrowhead, or North Shore, counties share 268 streams and much of the remainder of the 3,300 miles.

There have been somewhat fewer changes in regulations and classifications in Minnesota than in Wisconsin. In Minnesota, statewide, the traditional or regular stream trout season begins on the first Saturday closest to April 15 and closes after the last day of September—but there are many exceptions.

First off, beginning in 1999 *all* trout streams in eight counties of southeastern Minnesota are open from April 1 to the regular opening day for catch-and-release with barbless hooks. And all these streams are catch-and-release with barbless hooks between September 15 and 30, inclusive.

Since 1987, when the state DNR issued its Long Range Plan for Fisheries Management, significant miles of quality waters have been placed under special regulations. Eight streams of southeastern Minnesota are under special regs during the regular season. The regulations vary by stream, but all require the use of barbless hooks.

Twelve stream sections in the southeast are also open January 1 through March 31 for catch-and-release with barbless hooks. Included are four sections on the several branches of the Whitewater River, part of the South Branch of the Root River, Hay Creek near Red Wing, Beaver and East Beaver Creeks, and others.

Because the regulations are complicated, you are advised to study your annual *Minnesota Fishing Regulations* booklet. Rules for taking stream trout in lakes, and trout and salmon in the North Shore counties and Lake Superior tributaries, are even more abstruse.

Bill and Jim are among many who have enjoyed fly-fishing for trout in the North Star State, even as early as the first week of January. On a clear winter day when the sun is shining, the ambient temperature is in the high 20s, and the brown trout are rising to midges—join us on the Cliff Pool in Whitewater State Park, or on the pastures of Hay Creek where you might play tag with a bull. Oh, frabjous day! In March tiny blue-winged olives may appear; more rarely, a fall of tiny black stoneflies may cause the trout to rise. No need for you to rise early: Practice your art between 11 AM and 3 PM.

The Minnesota DNR is also active on other fronts. Extensive habitat improvement continues. Approximately 3 miles of stream corridors are

Dr. Art Kaemmer fishes on Hay Creek in southeastern Minnesota on a late winter day. This was a productive day for Griffith's Gnats and Black Ants!

improved each year through cooperative efforts with angling groups, landowners, and other government agencies. Since 1987, 700 miles of stream have been identified or improved as trout habitat, and a few streams have been added to the list of designated trout waters. The DNR notes in its *Trout Fishing Access* brochure that "According to more than 2,400 DNR fish population surveys, the trout population in southeastern Minnesota has tripled since 1970 and the average number of browns more than 12 inches long increased from 26 per stream mile in the 1970s to 55 in the 1990s."

Fly-fishing for trout is better now in Wisconsin and Minnesota than it was 20 or even 30 years ago. This is due in part to the application of habitat improvements and sophisticated regulations.

But regulations are not a panacea. They are only one tool in the hands of the keepers of the streams. Special regulations, categories, or classes are not the answer to acid precipitation, siltation from eroded fields, and thoughtless lumbering and grazing practices. Nor are they the solution to irresponsible applications of pesticides and herbicides, leaking chemical dumps, leaching landfills, and degraded waste disposal systems. Improved habitat is the number one priority of every fish manager. A clean environment ought to be the goal of all anglers.

Fly-fishers shouldn't expect miracles from the regulations. We must continue to protect and improve the environment for both humans and trout. We must also limit our kill, not kill our limit.

Catch-and-Release

Catch-and-release of trout by fly-fishers has been practiced for decades. And recently anglers for other species have also come around to the idea that the release of a trophy allows it to be caught more than once. Catch-and-release makes possible the catch of a trophy trout several times in a season, thereby sharing the pleasure of the chase among several fishers; or it may permit released trout to grow larger where the habitat will sustain additional numbers of big fish. A big female, if released, can spawn thousands of eggs.

If you wish to join the legions of fishers who practice catch-and-release, here's how to release your trout. (Catching them is another story.) First, crimp down the barb of your fly. We do not always carry a net. Play the fish quickly. When it ceases its airborne antics, grab the leader, clamp the rod under your arm or between your knees, and pull in the fish hand over hand. Run your hand up under its belly and cradle the trout gently, keeping it in the water. Turn it belly-up and back out the hook. If the hook is embedded inside the mouth, instead of in the lip as is usually the case, pick the hook out with a forceps. If it is too deep and difficult to remove, cut the leader short. Right the trout and hold it lightly until it powers its way out of your hand. If it tips on its side, indicating a state of exhaustion, gently move it forward and back to flush water through its gills, pumping lifesaving oxygen into its system. Release the fish in quiet water. You'll get the hang of it soon enough. With luck and skill you may come back next week to re-create the thrill of the catch and the release.

Precise instructions such as these are always subject to qualifiers, or to dispute. So you may prefer to use a net in those mythic waters where all the trout are huge. If you choose to net your trout, get one of the new shallow-netted catch-and-release nets. Do not play the fish to exhaustion. Lead the trout into the net. Clamp the rod under your arm or between your knees. Use one hand to cradle the trout in the net (still in the water), and the other to back out the hook. If you aren't reasonably ambidextrous, you may have to transfer the net from one hand to another.

And while we are about it, let us get some acidulous comments off our chests. We have seen fishers derrick a fish out and flop it on the bank to admire. We have seen them dangle their lip-hooked catch at eye level to count the spots. A recent Canadian study demonstrated that mortality of trout increases dramatically with time spent out of water. Even brief exposure to air—30 to 60 seconds—can cause eventual death. Therefore, release your trout in the water.

Too many Saturday-morning TV shows have filmed smiling anglers sticking their fingers in the gills of fish and then congratulating themselves on being practitioners of C&R. Gills are too fragile to allow for such harsh treatment. Another common visual that causes us pain (and the fish damage) is that of a bass angler with thumb and forefinger clamped like a vise on the fish's mouth, the body hanging limply at right angles to the clamp.

Catch-and-release is here to stay, we hope. It's an efficient and enjoyable practice that will help extend our sport well into the 21st century. The sizzle of fresh fish in a pan is transitory; the remembrance of a fine fish released to freedom lasts forever.

There is a new method on the horizon as well. The idea is to use flies with hooks snipped off at the bend so the fish don't get hooked. To a good percentage of fly anglers, feeling and seeing the strike (fooling the trout) is the big thrill. The landing of the fish is secondary. For these people, the hookless fly is another alternative.

Habitat Improvement

During the period from 1920 to 1980 the miles of cold-water trout habitat nationwide decreased by as much as 50 percent. Since 1980 we have lost more miles due to an expanding population; mindless development in the watersheds; chemical pollution; fence-to-fence farming; decreased groundwater flow due to irrigation; grazing, which tramples the streambanks; clear-cutting of forests; filling of wetlands; and a thousand other ills that soil, water, and air are heir to.

For example, at the turn of the 20th century there were at least seven native brook trout streams in the Twin Cities of Minneapolis and St. Paul, Minnesota. In the greater metropolitan area there were many more than 14. We are now engaged in a reconstruction and defense of Eagle Creek, which joins the Minnesota River at Savage. As late as 1960 Jim Humphrey used to shoot over there from Bloomington to relax with a brace of brilliant brookies after a hard day in the office. Brown's Creek in Stillwater is also undergoing rehab.

Another anecdote will serve to illustrate the losses. In the 1950s Dick Frantes, a plumber by trade, was employed as an inspector for the gas company. One memorable day he was working in the subbasement of a downtown St. Paul commercial building. And there he found, in a concrete channel, a free-flowing stream, one of the early trout streams, that had been paved over in the 1920s, or perhaps earlier.

We won't belabor the point. Every reader must mourn the loss of one of her or his favorite streams. There is hope for the future, however, because the environment has become a cause for many Americans. Aroused and articulate citizens are holding politicians' feet to the fire on behalf of clean air, clean water, and protected trout streams.

Trout fishers have decided that they ought to protect the streams that remain, regardless of what may occur in the wider world. And so we arrive at a discussion of trout stream rehabilitation and improvement. The subject is complicated, the material available for study is extensive, and the oppor-

Brush bundles

tunity to get your hands dirty restoring a stream is there for those who care.

We quote from "Wisconsin Trout Stream Habitat Management" on the last page of the *Trout Fishing Regulations and Guide:* "Habitat management focuses on the stream channel and its banks. The idea is to create conditions favorable for trout by adding something to the stream or modifying what's already present.

"Trout need certain environmental conditions, called habitat, to survive and flourish. Cold water, plenty of oxygen, sheltered places to hide and rest, and abundant supplies of insects and forage fish are the most important. For streams supporting wild trout, add gravel beds for spawning, water swift enough to sweep silt from developing eggs, and half a dozen other factors just beginning to be understood.

"Leave out one of these conditions and you may still have a trout stream, but it probably won't produce to capacity. Leave out many more and you can forget about the trout. They won't be there."

All is not lost. Scientific habitat improvement can enhance the streams that remain. The techniques are many. This is not an attempt to describe all of them, nor to imply that they can be applied indiscriminately. Our experience is pretty much limited to cutting brush and pulling deadfalls from the streams on winter days—as long as the windchill factor is not worse than minus 20 degrees.

The appropriate technology to be applied is best left to the professionals who know what will work, and where. We review a few examples here to give you a taste of the possibilities, and to show how you can recognize them on the stream.

Riprap is usually easy to spot. It's a jumble of broken rock lining the bank, most often on an outside curve of a stream. Riprap stabilizes the bank and provides cover for trout in the interstices among the huge blocks or boulders at the base of the pile. The streambank should be sloped at a 30-degree angle and grassed. (For an example of riprap, see the photograph accompanying Timber Coulee Creek in "Southwestern Wisconsin.")

Riprap is most often used in agricultural areas where cattle have eroded the banks. It is often possible to deliver quarry blocks to the pastures with heavy equipment when the ground is hard. In some cases where heavy equipment can't approach the stream, smaller stones can be carried by boat to interior sections of the river. It may take a sharp eye to spot the improvements there after a year or two.

Bank covers, often called "cribs," may be even more difficult to identify if they've been in for several seasons. These are wooden shelves or platforms set into the bank, then covered with a layer of rock, and topped with small stones and sod. Typically, they will create a cave 2 or 3 feet wide, 8 or more feet long, and perhaps as much as a foot deep. Trout hide from predators

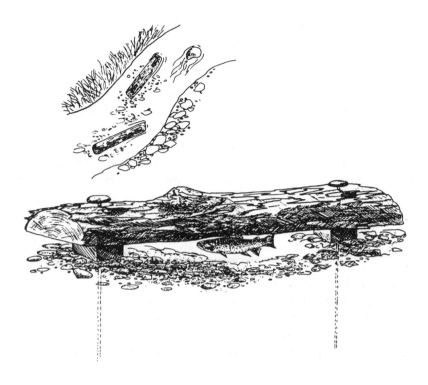

Half-log. Inset shows position of half-logs in stream.

back in the shadows, but venture out to feed at the edge of the cover. Such covers may be built in the stream, but many newer ones are assembled on land and then carried to the stream and anchored with reinforcing rods. Variations on the bank covers are called "lunker structures" or "skyhook covers."

Brush bundles and brush mats narrow the stream, collect sand and silt, and provide space for young trout to hide. Half-logs are simple, economical structures used to provide hiding, resting, and security cover for yearling and older trout in reaches of stream having sparse in-stream cover. Dozens of them have been pounded into the bed of the Willow Race in west central Wisconsin. You are likely to discover them when you tear your waders on the bent reinforcing rods, but waders are cheap compared to the opportunity to catch numbers of brown trout.

Other structures include log or rock sills to create plunge pools; Hewitt ramps, which are artificial waterfalls designed to add oxygen and create pools; and sand traps. Fencing and gravel crossings for cattle are frequently needed to protect a stream. Old wing dams are encountered often. Some wing dams on the upper Kinnickinnic of west central Wisconsin date to the days of the Civilian Conservation Corps, but are still serviceable.

Stream improvements are long lasting but labor intensive. The initial cost is expensive. Professional fish managers must design and supervise the installation, and many hired hands or volunteers are needed to do the bull work.

No good result comes cheaply in this world. Stream improvements may be the wisest investment to secure the future of trout fishing on your home stream.

A fine reference for those interested in learning more about habitat improvement is *Trout Stream Therapy* by Robert L. Hunt, a former fisheries research biologist with the Wisconsin DNR (University of Wisconsin Press, 1994).

Play It Safe

We note elsewhere in this book that our profiled streams are neither intimidating nor, save for a few, dangerous. But there's no point in ruining a good outing for lack of preparation and care.

Only a handful of our rivers are wild and rough—the Wolf, Bois Brule, Peshtigo, and some on the North Shore—but a stout wading staff is always useful to pull or prod yourself out of sucking silt, to negotiate steep and slippery banks, and to probe for drop-offs. We have rescued a fellow angler

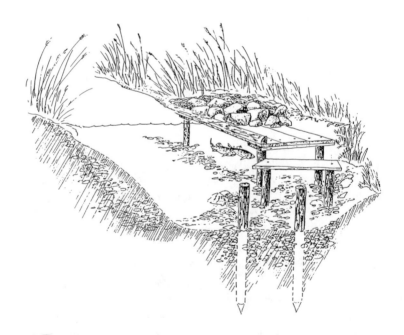

Side view of traditional bank cover structure showing construction stages

Brush mats

from a slow and sinking death on a trout lake, when he took one step too far, by throwing our staff to him. He pried himself out.

Our longtime staff is an aluminum ski pole 4 inches short of armpit height, slung over the shoulder on a shock cord front to back. It has saved us from dangerous falls on numerous occasions.

Felt-bottomed boots and waders are recommended, except on ice. On late-night excursions, carry two flashlights, or at least one that you've checked out. Both Bill and Jim have suffered because their flashlights failed, or because they stayed too long after sunset without a light.

Turning to domestic and wild animals, there is a lot more "bull" than truth about the danger of bulls in pasturelands, but we remember one episode above Bucksnort Dam on Trout Run that set our hearts to pounding.

Bears, badgers, coyotes, wolves, moose, skunks, cougars (aka mountain lions, panthers, and pumas), bobcats, and lynx will leave you alone if you leave them alone. You're not at a petting zoo. Don't stand between a mother bear and her cubs, and don't store your provisions in your tent if you camp out. You probably won't see a wolf, coyote, or cougar that has drifted down from Canada and elected to stay because it likes the provender, but if you are lucky you may hear one howl or growl on a misty night. Moose have been known to run right over a visitor during the rutting season. Badgers are beautiful creatures that inhabit southwestern Wisconsin, but they are surly; when they begin to hiss, keep your distance. You must know the swaggering skunk, which doesn't care who you are or how exalted is your position in the world of men.

Snakes. Don't stick your hands in the crevices of limestone cliffs on the lower Kinnickinnic or in the bases of towers in the coulee country of south-eastern Minnesota and southwestern Wisconsin. It's an old dodge to warn neophytes about the rattlers along a particular stream in order to keep them (the neophytes, not the rattlers) out of a favored fishing hole, but we haven't encountered a rattler yet. Not yet.

Our friend Felix Rondeau told us how he fell asleep on his private trout stream in northern Minnesota and awoke a couple of hours later, 300 yards downstream, carried by Minnesota mosquitoes. He surmised that three of them had lifted him. That's a tall story; it would have taken at least four to transport our old friend.

Ticks. Yes, we have them. If you push your way through heavy cover, inspect yourself at evening's end. A few cases of Lyme disease have been reported in western Wisconsin. A spray of insect repellent on your boots or waders, on the sleeves of your shirt, and on your trout vest will provide pro-tection. Several of our friends have taken a series of shots to prevent the disease.

There is barbed wire lying like snares in farm country, and barbed hooks around anglers. We twice removed hooks from our pal Dick Frantes, utiliz-ing the monofilament loop technique that has been widely publicized. Loop heavy mono around the bend of the embedded hook. Press down on the eye of the hook. A quick yank on the loop in a straight line with the shank will free the barb with little damage. (See illustration.) It works. Dick continued fishing for hours and with no ill effects. You can, of course, avoid the trau-ma by pressing down the barbs of your hooks with pliers.

The greatest danger in the Midwest comes from driving your car at high speed at night and plowing into one of an overpopulation of deer. We almost wiped out a deer, the front end of our car, and perhaps our lives on Interstate 94 opposite 3M headquarters, not far from downtown St. Paul. We can still hear those hooves scrabbling at the pavement as the deer veered off. We and the deer were lucky. Luck runs out for thousands of Wisconsin and Minnesota drivers every year. In northern Minnesota your nighttime opponent might be a moose, with disastrous results.

To add interest and danger, in the summer of 1996, 40 elk were intro-duced into the Clam Lake area of Wisconsin, where they are thriving. In 1997 drivers killed 44,210 deer on Wisconsin roads, confirming the need for caution.

In 1998 three curious encounters with bears were recorded. In one a bear came up on a cabin porch and carried away a small dog. In the second a frightened bear knocked down a hiker who was in his way. More seriously, a

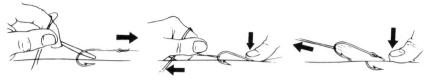

1. Loop heavy mono-
filament around the bend
of the embedded hook.

2. Press down on the eye
of the hook.

3. A quick yank on the
loop in a straight line with
the shank will free the
barb with little damage.

Above: the loop method of hook removal

bear pulled the tent of a sleeping Boy Scout into the woods. The boy was bitten through the tent and required surgery. His father and other Scouts drove off the bear. It was reported that the lad had chocolate wrappers at his side, which underscores the need to stow food out of the reach of marauding wildlife.

Maps

Every explorer of our far-flung trout streams will need at least two current maps of his area of interest. No one map will suffice because no single map illuminates all of the detail, and all will contain errors. Streams and roads will be misnamed or renamed, the blue lines of streams will run in the wrong places, older maps may not include new roads, and trails may have disappeared. Many original and colorful road names have been replaced with numbers, we think to enable crews to locate 911 emergency scenes; with that no-doubt-needed change, however, some of our history disappears together with the historic names.

We have used the DeLorme page numbers under the name of each stream in this book because the finely detailed DeLorme atlases, 16 by 11 inches in book format for each state, are widely available at sports shops and magazine counters. The DeLorme *Minnesota Atlas and Gazetteer* divides the state into 77 sections; the Wisconsin book contains 81 sections. Both are available by mail from DeLorme Mapping, P.O. Box 298, Yarmouth, ME 04096, phone 207-846-7000.

The Milwaukee Map Service, Inc., 959 North Mayfair Road, Milwaukee, WI 53226, phone 1-800-525-3822, sells a series of four excellent maps of Wisconsin, which name most of the minor roads and block out in green many of the public lands. This is an invaluable aid to fishers who are looking for sections of streams that have received habitat improvement. Find it in fly shops and map stores.

Wisconsin trout fishers should be sure to obtain the *Wisconsin Trout*

Fishing Regulations and Guide when they buy their licenses and trout stamps. This 8½-by-11-inch brochure maps all significant designated trout streams in the state and color-codes the trout waters by category. This one is a must for Wisconsin fishers. Unfortunately, some license sellers may forget to give it to you.

Minnesota fishers will want "Trout Streams of Southeast Minnesota," a large folded map showing the designated trout streams of the six southeastern counties overprinted in blue. It can be ordered by mail, free, from the Minnesota Department of Natural Resources, Section of Fisheries, Box 12, DNR Building, 500 Lafayette Road, St. Paul, MN 55155, phone 651-296-3325 or (toll-free in Minnesota) 1-800-MINN-DNR. This one contains a wealth of supplementary information—miles of good water, trout species, and shoreline ownership. Don't leave home without it. A companion map, "North Shore Fishing Guide," may be ordered by those who plan to fish the North Shore streams of Lake Superior.

Minnesota now offers, by mail from the DNR for $2, a remarkable brochure, *Trout Fishing Access in Southeastern Minnesota*, which locates all of the streams in color, showing miles of trout waters, habitat improvements, easements, and public lands. Order this from DNR Regional Headquarters at 2300 Silver Creek Road Northeast, Rochester, MN 55906. You can also pick up the book at the St. Paul headquarters, at area fisheries offices, and at some state parks.

Minnesota also produces for sale a series of 51 Public Recreation Information Maps (PRIM), which show parks, forests, trails, canoe routes, water access sites, designated trout streams, wildlife management areas, and more. They are available from the DNR gift shop at the St. Paul headquarters as well as from regional offices, state parks, and major sporting and map stores.

County maps are available from the Departments of Transportation of both states, and at many map stores and sports shops. These large-scale maps, half an inch to the mile, are useful but do not give the names of minor roads.

Many counties and communities in both states produce instructive touring maps that we have found useful. State park, wildlife area, and national forest maps will round out your tackle. We obtain our state park and wildlife area maps at entrance kiosks; national forest maps are available for a modest charge at any ranger station within the forest.

Minnesota state park maps are free by mail from the DNR Information Center, 500 Lafayette Road, St. Paul, MN 55155, but with a limit of 10 items. Information on Wisconsin state parks is available from the Bureau of Parks and Recreation at 608-266-2181.

Because of space limitations we have not been able to provide a map in this book for every stream profiled. We have included maps of the big rivers and of some of the smaller streams that we consider particularly appealing. Where appropriate, we have indicated preferred access points with an arrow. Our maps are composites, drawing on the various sources described above and illustrating, we trust, those elements that will make for a most success-ful experience for you.

In keeping with the technological age, both states now have web sites that will lead you to voluminous information on fishing for trout, including the downloading of southeastern Minnesota stream maps exactly as they appear in the DNR's brochure. Minnesota: www.dnr.state.mn.us. Wisconsin: www.dnr.state.wi.us.

Ah! Technology. We've got communications galore. We get e-mails on our computers and we visit web sites. Click one and we can be told where to go, what to use, and at what hours. We have even heard of two-way radios on trout streams. It goes something like this: "Hey, Joe, I have a blue-winged olive hatch up here; what's happening down there?" It seems a bit too easy.

Don't get us wrong. We are for progress, but we also think there is value in paying your dues.

There are so many variables in this game of trout angling. So much has to be learned and enjoyed from experience, from trial and error. In our rush for quick information we miss out on the discovery and wonderment of the event.

Easy access to fishing information has caused overcrowding on major rivers during major fly hatches. Too many beginning anglers think that fol-lowing the crowd is the whole experience. During these overcrowded times we steal away to those little "veiled treasures" and peacefully catch gorgeous trout in beautiful solitude.

Trespass and Navigability

If you can get into a stream from a bridge or by crossing public land, you are usually safe from challenge, but if you find a fence across the stream, common sense dictates that you request permission from the landowner to proceed beyond the fence. Most landowners are accommodating in our part of the world and permit angling in their stream sections. A few may disagree with the concept of navigability. If a canoe can be maneuvered through a stream during high water, the stream is considered to be a public waterway, but you must stay between the high-water marks. This is still a murky sub-ject; some disputes as to navigability wind up in court.

Stream sections that run through state, national, or county lands are open during the regular trout season, except in a few sanctuaries. Many other streams have signposted easements where the DNR has purchased or leased a corridor on one or both sides of a stream. Wisconsin posts most of its easements with small green-and-white PUBLIC HUNTING & FISHING GROUNDS signs. Minnesota marks fewer easements. Unfortunately, some signs have fallen or have been deliberately removed. A very few easements have been acquired by public-spirited organizations such as Trout Unlimited.

But what if there are no posted easements on your trout stream? If there's a well-defined path along the stream, you may assume either that the landowner doesn't object or that there's an easement. If fencing parallels the stream about 66 feet from the stream centerline, it usually indicates a public easement. When approaching a bridge, we always scan the open fields for a well-made fence that follows the stream meanders. Look for neat bracing at the corner posts, indicative of careful DNR construction.

Fishing easements permit anglers to walk the streambanks within the fenced corridor, but camping, hiking, trapping, hunting, and other uses are prohibited.

Respect the landowners' rights. Don't break down fences, don't cut or disfigure trees, and take your litter out with you. Above all, close the gates behind you. We know of a few farmers in southeastern Minnesota who now refuse permission to cross their lands because of litter left behind by trout anglers.

Hunters have poked a gun barrel into a hornet's nest in southeastern Minnesota by failing to ask permission to hunt private land, or by leaving their trash behind, or by breaking fences. Recently we saw an angler cross a field that had that day been prepared for planting. This is a negative if we want to remain friends with the owner. In 1996 Minnesota's trespass law was strengthened to make it easier for farmers to pursue trespassers. With the movement of city dwellers to their bits of heaven in the country, we are seeing more NO TRESPASSING signs. We are warned to tread cautiously lest access to our precious streams be forbidden.

Wisconsin produces a mixed bag, if we may steal a metaphor. The land is being gobbled up by ex-suburbanites who bring their greensward and riding mowers and KEEP OFF signs with them. But in 1999 the state legislature passed a law that allows anglers to follow a stream through private land, provided they keep below the high-water mark, "the point on the bank or shore where the water is present often enough to leave a distinct mark." We will all become lawyers eventually. You may not cross private land to get to the stream without permission. Find a bridge, a DNR easement, or ask permission.

2 | Hatches, Tactics, and Tackle

The Trout Foods

What do trout eat? Trout eat everything. At times trout are such gluttonous consumers that food will be oozing out of their vents while they are taking more in at the front. At other times they lie quiet, seeming to be interested in nothing edible. One researcher reported that trout may obtain as much as 70 percent of their *annual* dietary needs from the *Hexagenia* mayfly alone, which may account for some streams being notably poor producers except for some weeks before and during the Hex hatch.

When actively feeding at the surface, trout are renowned in literature and lore for being selective, which means that often they will target some insignificant species of insect to the exclusion of all other foods. A common occurrence on midwestern streams is the evening rise of small trout to tiny midges. Trout will feed fearlessly at rod tip distance, ignoring both your presence and your larger artificial. If you change to a #20 or #22 midge pupa or dry fly, there is still no guarantee that they will accept your offering. Your fly may be too different in silhouette against the night sky, or be just a size off, or fail to duplicate the peculiar action of the natural. You might conclude that trout are fickle and fussy as well as gluttonous, and you'd be right on the money.

Trout feed on at least 10 different orders of aquatic insects, plus several orders of insects that are associated with the riparian environment. Fortunately for us, only those genera or species that are important to the trout's diet have been replicated by fly-tiers. Otherwise we'd be carrying thousands, rather than only hundreds, of patterns.

Trout also feed on chubs, shiners, sculpins, and sundry small fish, plus crayfish, scuds, leeches, and other swimmers and crawlers. Worms are a favorite. Big trout have been found to have snakes and mice in their stomachs. Trout have been observed by Joe Balestrieri in southwestern Wisconsin thrusting their heads into a mass of weeds to dislodge snails. Naturally, fly-tiers have exercised their imaginations in the creation of swimming mice, snails, and even articulated worms!

From the menu of aquatic insects, trout take the winged stages of mayflies, caddisflies, and midges—and, less often in our area, stoneflies—on the surface. Terrestrials such as beetles, ants, inchworms, leafhoppers, and grasshoppers are taken in the surface film as well. The larvae or nymphs of mayflies, caddis, stoneflies, and crane flies, together with scuds (freshwater shrimp), leeches, and minnowlike forage fish, are taken subsurface. For smaller trout, the primary sources of protein are the several stages of the mayflies, caddis, midges, and stoneflies, as well as scuds. Large trout require a more substantial diet.

Mayflies present the classic challenge to fly-fishers. When the Hendrickson, *Ephemerella subvaria,* is emerging from southeastern Minnesota and southwestern Wisconsin streams from approximately mid-April to mid-May, trout may restrict their feeding to the nymphal form escaping from the bottom or to the winged dun on the surface. Either an artificial nymph or a dry fly that closely resembles the naturals will be demanded. Similar conditions occur throughout the season when the sulphurs, brown drakes, or Hex are predominant emerging species. Tiny blue-winged olives may be encountered all season long on our streams, but that doesn't guarantee that trout will feed on them continuously.

Caddisflies pose fewer problems of selectivity for fishermen. Caddis hover over our streams from May through the season's close. The pupa rises to the surface, pops out as an adult with wings, and flies to nearby brush. Mating usually takes place on vegetation or on the ground. After mating, the female bounces on the surface of the water to release her eggs or swims down to deposit them on the stems of waterweeds. Trout take caddis at all stages, but only a handful of artificial patterns is necessary to trick them.

Stonefly nymphs crawl out to some convenient rock, molt, and fly. A day or two later, but rarely observed in our area, the females of some species may buzz on the surface while releasing eggs. Trout feed chiefly on the nymphs migrating through the shallows, so your mayfly nymphs will do double duty for the nymphs of stoneflies.

Scuds (freshwater shrimp) hang out in the weeds and patrol the margins of streams all season long. When swimming they look like arrows, or perhaps javelins. There are scud patterns, but bristly mayfly nymphs are a satisfactory substitute. Leeches are always slinking around and are replicated by the Olive Woolly Bugger. Ants, beetles, inchworms, and other terrestrials fall or are blown to the surface during the warm months and are seized by trout opportunistically. Artificial flies need not precisely match the natural, but size and (sometimes) color are important. One or two standard fly patterns will fairly represent several minnow forms. The Muddler is a sculpin when weighted; dry it is a grasshopper kicking on the surface.

Trout feed down deep, in the mid-depths, and on the surface. The literature of trout fishing has long romanced the rise of trout to specific mayfly hatches. Matching the hatch is a fascinating exercise and worthy of a lifetime of study, but remember that trout take most of their protein from underwater life-forms. So study the hatch charts, but fish deep.

MAYFLIES

Because most fly-fishers for trout soon become entranced with the identification, replication, and dating of the times of emergence of significant mayflies, it seems necessary to devote a few paragraphs to these Ephemeroptera.

The mayfly begins as an egg; sooner (or later) it becomes a larva or nymph that crawls, burrows, or swims on the bottom of the stream. After a number of instars, which are the periods between the molts of the exoskeleton, the nymph usually swims to the surface. Some species crawl to the shore. It then flies into the brush or trees, if a trout doesn't pick it off as it is swimming up. After as little as an hour or as long as a couple of days of resting—even longer with some species—the dun, or subimago, slithers snakelike out of its shuck, unfolds glassine wings, and joins a crowd over the stream for the mating ritual. There are, as always, exceptions to this process. Some duns molt immediately; one species of female dun doesn't molt.

In the final adult stage, the imago, also called the spinner, develops long legs and tails, hyaline wings, and a shiny body that appears to be lacquered. The male grabs a female. They mate. The female deposits her eggs on the surface, or drops them like bombs, or crawls down along a stem to deposit her eggs underwater. She then dies, usually with wings outstretched in what is known as the spentwing position.

The above is a truncated explanation of the marvelous process. Professional entomologists would doubtless take exception to our version. But in a careful reading of the scientific literature of mayflies you'll often run into qualifiers such as "generally," "usually," "sometimes," "often." Seldom will you find the word "always," because mayflies, like humans, do not always act predictably or invariably. Nor do entomologists like the use of the word "hatch," which is more accurately applied to something coming out of an egg. They prefer "emergence," and who is to blame them?

Fly-fishers have several opportunities to match the various stages of the mayfly life cycle—nymphs crawling on the bottom or swimming up, emerging duns with forewings rising like sails, females touching down to drop their eggs, and finally spentwings. Some anglers tie flies to represent each stage!

Stenonema/Stenacron

Let's get the numbers out of the way. There are more than 600 species of mayflies north of Mexico. Many of them are not native to our region, and only a few are found in sufficient numbers to trigger the attention of trout or trout fishers.

Approximately 150 species occur in Wisconsin, many of which are rare. (See W. L. Hilsenhoff, *Aquatic Insects of Wisconsin*, 1995.) Our guess is that there are fewer in Minnesota due to the more limited habitat, and many of them are not important to trout or trout fishermen. That makes your job more manageable.

In our charts of significant mayfly emergences we have relied on our own observations and identification, and on the reports of reliable observers. In some stream profiles we have named and dated specific mayfly emergences. Otherwise the "Generalized Emergence Chart" will be a guide, but only a guide. In some cases we have missed significant emergences. Even the most definitive text, *The Mayflies of North and Central America,* by Edmunds, Jensen, and Berner, notes the problem that some mayflies may become active when entomologists are home in bed. Similarly, some heavy hatches appear at night when anglers are sitting around the cabin with drink in hand, telling lies to one another.

Hatches also change over time. Anecdotal evidence suggests that the predominant hatches on some of our streams are now composed of smaller species of mayflies, and fewer of them, due to deteriorating water quality or, rarely, improving water quality. Fencing, for example, may eliminate cattle droppings, which enrich the water and produce some larger mayflies. On many streams the major hatches are *Baetis,* called tiny blue-winged olives, or *Tricorythodes,* called tricos; and midges, which are not mayflies but true flies.

Emergence dates may also change from year to year. Weeks of cold weather may delay a hatch; warm weather may accelerate the emergence. Other factors known only to God may affect hatch times. In short, emergence charts were not brought down from the mountain by Theodore Gordon, the patron saint of American fly-fishers, or even by Swisher and Richards, nor were they chiseled into tablets of stone or marked with a stylus on wax.

CADDISFLIES

According to Dr. Hilsenhoff, there are probably 275 species of caddisflies (Trichoptera) in Wisconsin. Margaret Monson, also an entomologist, estimates 280 species in Minnesota. Without being unduly scientific we could divide caddisflies into two major groups: those with a portable case and those without.

The casemakers may have a rough tube fashioned of plant materials or rock particles, which are stuck together with a substance the caddisflies produce themselves.

Those without a portable case are either free-living or live within a fixed retreat behind a catch net that they spin.

All begin as an egg, which hatches into a larva, which pupates, and then eventually swims or floats to the surface to become an adult winged caddisfly. Trout will eat the casemakers, but we've had our greatest success with a Green Caddis Larva, which represents the free-livers; with a soft-hackle that looks like a pupa rising; and with an Elk Hair Caddis on the surface. Although we may get an argument from some fly-tiers, the color of the adult at the surface is much less important than the size of the artificial.

STONEFLIES

Stonefly nymphs clamber among the rocks and "scatter like rats" (Ann Haven Morgan in her wonderful old book, *Field Book of Ponds and Streams,* 1930) when you pick up a rock.

Stoneflies (Plecoptera) are vulnerable as nymphs when they are heading to the shore through the shallows, but we have not often found trout feeding on the egg-laying adults at the surface. Sometimes we have found trout feeding on the adults of the early black stoneflies on Hay Creek in southeastern Minnesota in March. Dean Hansen also reports activity on the Kinnickinnic in March.

FLIES AND MIDGES

This very large order of aquatic Diptera, two-winged true flies, includes many families that are of no interest to trout fishers, although trout may occasionally feed on blackflies, punkies, and no-see-ums. Two families are important—the crane flies and the midges.

Two crane flies afford some interesting opportunities. The larva of the giant crane fly (which we describe in our profile of the Rush River in Wisconsin), when replicated by a yellowish Woolly Worm, may entice very large trout. In our profile of the Kinnickinnic of Wisconsin we describe how John Schorn tied into a batch of trout when fishing a soft-hackle, a representation of the pupa of the *Antocha* genus, which was swimming to the surface. The *Antocha* is frequently mistaken for a mayfly, because in flight the long legs dangling behind look like tails; but the presentation to trout is a very different case. Observation is all-important.

Midges, of the family Chironomidae, are omnipresent on our streams all season long and represent a consistent food source for trout. We have taken trout with a Brassie on the bottom or a Griffith's Gnat on the surface on innumerable occasions when nothing else would satisfy them. We have noted one occasion, on the North Branch of the Whitewater, when the trout were stuffed with midge larvae.

Midges are tiny, #26 and #22—even as minuscule as #32—but their presence is too often overlooked by anglers who are casting a #12 Adams. Be advised and be warned.

Even smaller midges and other true flies appear in clouds on our streams. Dick Frantes called them "number 50 dandruff," but if trout are feeding on them, you might as well wind up and go home.

We include two charts, with the caveat that they do not represent perfection.

Other trout foods include the early black stonefly, found as early as March in the southern range; the carpenter ant, in the middle of May; the water boatman in March; the little yellow stonefly or little golden stonefly, toward the end of May; and the giant brown or giant black stoneflies, which appear on many northern rivers. In central Wisconsin, on the Tomorrow River, for example, they will emerge on or about June 1. The black cricket will be chirping during the hot months.

The hatch charts are only a rough guide, sometimes spot-on, sometimes off by as much as two weeks. Hatches may also be interrupted by weather. You may meet a heavy hatch of brown drakes on June 5th, but none in the air on the 6th and 7th. On the 8th they may fly again.

The Artificials

As Izaak Walton wrote, "There are twelve kinds of flies to angle with, which makes up a jury of flies likely to betray and condemn to death all the trout in the river."

But that was England then, and this is the United States now. England has but 50 or 60 species of mayflies; Wisconsin alone has 150. Still, there is a grain of truth embedded in the wisdom of Walton. More than 2,000 fly patterns have been named by their American creators, but many are merely minor variations of historic patterns. The famous Pass Lake of the Midwest, one upon which we rely, is only a slight change from the Trude of western waters. And so, out of our vast experience of fishing the waters of the United States, from the Midwest to the Far West, we have hit upon a Terrific Twenty.

To the newcomer to fly-fishing, the choice of flies is a mystery wrapped in an enigma. It's a daunting puzzle that turns some people off before they really get into the sport.

Some anglers carry as many as 200 different patterns in their fly boxes. Others, out of desperation or despair, have reduced their flies to a mere handful of patterns.

There is a middle ground. The 20 patterns that we call the "Terrific Twenty" will serve you well throughout the Midwest, and the West, too, for that matter, all season long.

Trout take flies—mayflies, caddisflies, et al.—and terrestrial insects at the surface with a visible rise, the most exciting game in town. But trout feed primarily below the surface on the nymphal forms of various aquatic insects and on crustaceans such as scuds, cress bugs, and crayfish. Large trout fatten on minnows, leeches, and crayfish. Our 20 artificials are reasonable approximations of all these trout foods, except perhaps crayfish. Hundreds of species of aquatic insects take wing from the surface as adults, far too many to replicate, but 12 patterns of dry flies should cover the variety of forms and spectrum of colors displayed by mayflies, caddisflies, midges, and even some common terrestrials.

The Adams is a match for the darker species of mayflies encountered in April and May. The Light Cahill will substitute for the pale mayflies of summer. The Tiny Blue-Winged Olive, #16, #18, and #20, is an exact stand-in for many important species of mayflies and midges throughout the season. The Trico, #20, #22, and #24, is a dead ringer for *Tricorythodes,* which blanket many of our streams early mornings beginning toward the end of June and lasting into September. The White Wulff, #8, is a generic substitute for any large night-hatching mayfly, including the fabled *Hexagenia* of July and the *Ephoron* of August. The Brown Bivisible is an all-purpose, bouncy, fast-

Naturals	Jan	Feb	Mar	Apr	May	June	July	Aug	Sept	Artificials
Baetis (14 spp.)			XXXX	XXXX	XXXX	XXXX	XXXX	XXXX	XXXX	Tiny Blue-Winged Olive #16 & #18.
Paraleptophlebia (7 spp.)				XXXX	XXXX				XXXX	Dark Blue Quill, Slate-Winged Mahogany Dun, Blue Dun, all #14 & #16.
Ephemerella subvaria				XXXX	XX					Dark Hendrickson, Adams, Red Quill (M), Brown Hen Spinner (F), all #14.
Ephemerella (18 spp. in 5 subgenera)					XX	XXXX	XX			Light Hendrickson, Sulphur, Light Cahill, Dark Slate-Winged Olive, all #14 & #16.
Stenonema vicarium					XX	XX XX				March Brown, Gray Fox, Dark Cahill, Ginger Quill, all #12.
Ephemera simulans					XX	XXXX				Brown Drake, March Brown, Chocolate Dun, all #12.
Stenonema/Stenacron (10 spp.); mainly spinner falls						XX	XXXX			Light Cahill, Sulphur, Ginger Quill, all #14.
Heragenia limbata & H. atrocaudata						XX	XXXX	XX		Hex, Green Drake, White Wulff, all #8, #10, & #12.
Tricorythodes atratus & T. stygiatus						XX	XXXX	XXXX	XXXX	Trico, Tiny White-Winged Black, Tiny Gray-Winged Olive, all #18 & #20.

Species						Common names / sizes
Pseudocloeon (8 spp.) [now *Plauditis*]			xx	xxxx	xxxx xxxx	Small Yellow Mayfly, Blue-Winged Olive, Minute Gray-Winged Olive, all #20, #22, and #24.
Isonychia (6 spp.); mainly spinner falls				xx	xx xx	White-Gloved Howdy, Slate Drake, Mahogany Dun, all #12.
Ephoron leukon & *E. album*				xxxx		White Wulff, Trailer, White Fly, all #10 & #12.

Note: Each x represents approximately one week.
Potamanthus (cream fly) and *Siphlonurus* (gray drake), mid- to late-season hatches, are limited to the northern half of the range. As you travel north, the hatches may appear days or even weeks later.

Naturals	Jan	Feb	Mar	Apr	May	June	July	Aug	Sept	Artificials
Midges	....	....	xxxx	xxxx	xxxx	xxxx	xxxx	xxxx	xxxx	Dry: Tiny Blue-Winged Olive, Griffith's Gnat, #18 to #24. Nymph: Brassie and Dark Mottled Grayish Olive, #20.
Baetis species	....	....	xxxx	xxxx	xxxx	xxxx	xxxx	xxxx	xxxx	Dry: Tiny Blue-Winged Olive #18 & #20. Nymph: Gold Ribbed Hare's Ear #18 & #20.
Paraleptophlebia debilis			xx	xxxx	xxxx					Dry: Dark Blue Quill, Slate-Winged Mahogany Dun, Blue Dun, all #14 & #16. Nymph: Dark Grayish Brown #16.
Ephemerella subvaria				xxxx	xx					Dry: Dark Hendrickson, Adams, Red Quill (M), Brown Hen Spinner (F), all #14. Nymph: Dark Hare's Ear, Wiggle Nymph, Pheasant Tail, all #16.
Ephemerella spp. plus subgenera Drunella, Attenella, etc.					xx	xxxx				Dry: Light Hendrickson & Light Cahill, #14 & #16. Nymph: Gold Ribbed Hare's Ear #16.
Pseudocloeon spp. [now Plauditis]							xxxx	xxxx	xxxx	Dry: Small Yellow Mayfly, Blue-Winged Olive, Minute Gray-Winged Olive, all #20 & #22. Nymph: Yellowish Green or Pale Olive #20.

						Description
Tricorythodes spp.					xx xxxx	xxxx	Dry: Trico, Tiny White-Winged Black, #20 to #24. Nymph: Any black-bodied #20 to #24.
Caddisflies (various)		xxxx	xxxx	xxxx	xxxx	xxxx	Dry: Tan, Olive, or Speckled Caddis, all #14 to #20. Nymph: Green Raggedy Caddis Larva, Peeking Caddis #16.
Crane fly: *Antocha* spp.			xxxx	xx			Dry: Blue-Winged Yellow #12. Nymph: Yellow Sally, we, #14.
Grasshoppers				xxxx	xxxx	xxxx	Hoppers, #12 and #14.
Scuds		xxxx	xxxx	xxxx	xxxx	xxxx	Tan, Pink, Olive, Brown, Purple, #12 to #16.
Leeches			xxxx	xxxx	xxxx	xxxx	xxxx	Black, Olive Woolly Bugger, #8 to #12.

Note: Each x represents approximately one week. Dots (....) indicate minor activity.
Stoneflies are not important in southeastern Minnesota.
Epeorus vitreus is a minor mayfly hatch: April and May emergence. Dry: Gray-Winged Yellow Quill and Light Cahill. Nymph is dark amber #14.
Stenonema/Stenacron spp.: Minor mayfly hatches. June 15≠July 30. Dry: Sulphur and Light Cahill #12. Nymph: Gold Ribbed Hare's Ear #14.
Potamanthus, cream fly, is reported mid-July through August.

water fly. The Elk Hair Caddis is an adult caddis; on a #20 hook it is also an emerging midge. The Pass Lake, with its back-slanted calftail hair wing, is both a caddisfly and a mayfly in process of unfolding its wings at the surface. It is a superb attractor, even when allowed to sink. Not least, everybody uses the fanwing or hairwing Royal Coachman at some time during the season. Like nothing else on earth, it is a proven pattern for pounding up trout when they are not feeding on the surface.

The Black Ant is for the slow days of summer when inept ants are falling from overhanging brush. An anomaly: The Ant will often take winter trout when other offerings are refused. Perhaps trout mistake the black body for a rising midge, or for the adult of the tiny early black stonefly. We know one expert who uses an ant pattern exclusively. A Black Beetle is also a choice morsel during the warm months.

The Griffith's Gnat, #20, invented by a founder of Trout Unlimited, is a dry fly that has given us our best catches over several winters on the Whitewater of southeastern Minnesota, including a 13½-inch rainbow trout. It's useful whenever midges are hatching, which is year-round on our streams.

JIM HUMPHREY

Royal Coachman flies

The Gold-Ribbed Hare's Ear, Green Caddis Larva, Pheasant Tail, Brassie, and Brown Woolly Worm are sinking patterns that duplicate the underwater stages of many aquatic insects. A Pink Scud should be fished over and through weedbeds on overcast days and at night.

The Muddler is a grasshopper kicking on the surface in July or August, or a minnow when weighted and swimming in the middle depths. For big, stream trout, or for rainbows from the lakes in the fall, the leechlike Olive Woolly Bugger has no peer.

You will want many of the Terrific Twenty in more than one size. Where a size for a dry fly is not specified, buy #14. A #16 is about right for the Gold-Ribbed Hare's Ear, Green Caddis Larva, and Pheasant Tail. A #20 Brassie replicates midge larvae. Scuds are #12 and #14. The Brown Woolly Worm, Muddler, and Woolly Bugger should measure about 1½ inches and be tied on a #8 or #10 long-shanked hook.

No doubt you will add one or two killer flies of your own as your experience unfolds.

Because Bill has had so much fun this year with a Hornberg fished dry on the surface or just under the film, I suppose we could add that. Other anglers swear by a Green Beetle. We've had success with a crayfish pattern, if you can find one with claws that don't collapse on the retrieve. Oh, Lord! We have violated our precept already. Well, perhaps you'll wind up with a Thrifty Thirty. We began with Perfect Thirteen some years ago, and here we are with a Terrific Twenty.

Since issuing the first edition we have fished many more places, and the original streams many more times. We have never claimed to be consistent, dogmatic, or purist. We learn as we go and steal secrets from our friends. Dorothy Schramm, an expert fisher, casting instructor, and tier, recommends a Rusty Spinner for use during mayfly spinner falls. Why didn't we think of that? The Prince Nymph, for some unknown reason, has proven effective during the early season on southwestern Wisconsin streams, such as the Big Green and Timber Coulee. Backswimmers are usually reserved for trout lakes, but we have seen them sculling the shallows of the Middle Branch of the Whitewater on a winter's day.

The beadhead nymph or beadhead soft-hackle is now one of the most popular flies here; with good reason. Reluctant, but nevertheless convinced, Humphrey carries three sizes of brass beads and strings one or more of them on the tippet ahead of the unweighted fly as needed.

As a matter of courtesy and fair trade, it is always a good idea to buy a few flies recommended by a local fly shop in your area of interest. You'll get a warmer reception to your questions.

The Tactics

There is no way we can elucidate all of the tactics that we have learned by experience and from reading the magazine articles and books about trout fishing. What follows here are a few of the tactics that we have gleaned by experiment and observation over many years and that we think may be especially helpful to you on Wisconsin and Minnesota streams. We hope you will add your own and contribute to the literature of our sport.

DOUBLE YOUR CHANCES: THE STRIKE INDICATOR AS LURE

Ray Bergman, author of that classic text, *Trout,* used a large and bushy dry fly tied very short about 4 to 6 feet above his sunken fly when he was fishing nymphs upstream. His "dobber," or "float," was tied with a highly visible palmered hackle. Bergman said, "The purpose of this dry fly is to give you something to watch for indications of a strike." He didn't say how often trout struck his floating indicator!

A famous angler of our day uses a tiny, streamlined cork as an indicator. It is strung on the leader and painted some bright color. A world-class fly-tier strings on an inch or so of fluorescent fly line, hollowed and slipped up the leader. Others opt for a piece of bright spun fur knotted above the blood knot where the tippet joins the leader. Skip James, keyboardist with the St. Paul Chamber Orchestra, threads a short segment of fluorescent chartreuse poly through a slip knot in the leader. Skip "frizzes" out the ends and applies floatant.

For several seasons Jim's strike indicator was a 1-inch, fluorescent orange-and-chartreuse streamer (with hook) linked to the leader by 3 inches of mono that was a size larger than the leader at the connection. (As an aside: The dropper mono stub must not be thinner than the leader, else the indicator will wind around the leader.) Quite often the heaviest trout would take the strike indicator like leopards leaping. And that should tell us something.

If you are determined to use a strike indicator, why not hide a hook in it and double your chances? Crimp the barb if the use of more than one fly on the same cast induces guilt feelings.

Swim the indicator itself through the most desirable water and let the point fly flutter underneath. On big streams that are broken by surface boulders, cast the indicator up against the rocks. You will know that the point fly is working down below in the dark and secret places.

Fishing upstream with this combination on smooth, clear water over beds of eelgrass is difficult, but you can get through by floating an emerger in the film on the point.

We don't pretend that this two-fly combination is easy to manipulate. You'll have to work out the balance between the sizes and air resistance of the indicators and point flies. The combinations are endless, bounded only by your imagination and experience. A two-toned streamer may be tied sparse and small. It will eventually sink, even if greased, but will still be visible at considerable depth in clear water. You could use grasshoppers, bivisibles, Irresistibles, Humpys, or other similar floaters for your indicators, if you prefer to follow in the footsteps of Ray Bergman. Jim's latest indicator is a "Parafluor," a #12 or #14 parachute dry fly tied with a moss-green or chartreuse fluorescent poly wing. Its visibility, even in poor light, is outstanding. The parachute will support considerable weight and combines well with a #16 Gold-Ribbed Hare's Ear.

There is only one difficulty with this method of two-fly fishing. The mind wanders; you begin to visualize the searching action of the deep-swimming nymph. That's sure to be the moment when the best trout of the day slams your indicator. Concentrate on the indicator: Watch for that telltale twitch, dart, or sideways lurch, or for its sudden disappearance in an explosion of spray.

A strike indicator won't always produce extraordinary results, but if you use it creatively, you will double your chances.

(Note: When you add a 3-foot tippet to a tapered leader, leave a 5-inch section of leader extending beyond the surgeon's knot. If you use an indicator fly, the tying stub is already in place. If you are fishing with a single fly, the stub causes only an occasional tangle.)

GRASSHOPPERS AND OTHER SUMMER FARE

Fly-fishing for trout can try the patience of a saint during the doldrums of summer. An early-rising trout fisherman may find tricos mating and falling spread-eagled at 68 degrees early mornings on many midwestern streams; but that may be very early indeed. You rise before sunup, arrive on the stream at dawn, hope springing eternal that the tiny white-winged blacks will show themselves. Or you may search among a selection of streams for the late-evening hatches of the white fly or the Hex. But if none of the above show, what then?

Throw an artificial grasshopper in the heat of the day. On one July day under bright sun with air temperature at the boiling point, I caught and released seven brown trout, the largest of which tipped an honest 11 inches, all taken on a #12 Green Hopper. It required 16 strikes to hook the seven, all between the hours of 11 AM and 2:30 PM. That scenario has been repeated again and again, other days, other years, other streams.

You can't fish just any stretch of trout stream, though. Find a meadow section, or one that borders a farm field, where grasses bend to water's edge. It need not be a long section because your progress, wading upstream, will be slow and remarkably stealthy.

Almost every stream will have a hopper section—most quite short—where the DNR or volunteers from TU have brushed the banks to permit grass to develop.

So a hot, dry summer is not all bad: The hoppers are out in force, and even lethargic trout have to eat. Hoppers, in truth, represent a luscious, easy meal.

Strikes will often occur explosively, usually close to the bank, often under the bend of the grass. Roll casts and sidearm casts will come into play—even the bow-and-arrow cast on occasion. But don't neglect to pattern the full width of the stream. Trout on the hunt may lie in the middle, even if they are exposed to predators. Sometimes their desire for a listless hopper trapped in the film overcomes their native wariness. Cast into the tangles of fallen branches, the "sleepers," and work the slicks below and up through the narrows. There is a hot pocket immediately upstream from the narrows.

There are alternatives if hoppers don't produce for you within 15 or 20 minutes. Carpenter ants, leaf worms, black beetles, crickets, and other summer fare may entice trout out of hiding.

OH, THOSE TRICOS!

Tricorythodes mayflies appear early mornings on most trout streams from East Coast to Far West. Although they are tiny, they constitute a significant portion of trout diets from the third week of June through September, and even into October if the season is open. There are 30 species in the genus in Central and North America; 6 of them are located in the Midwest, of which Dr. Hilsenhoff lists 2 in Wisconsin. Artificial dry flies designed to replicate the naturals are tied on light-wire hooks from #20 to as small as #24. The thorax is generally black; the upright-winged duns are tied with a white feather wing, or occasionally with blue dun hackle sans wing. Spentwings, whose wings lie outstretched on the surface, are tied with white hackle tips or translucent poly yarn.

That's almost enough of the technical stuff. Fishing the tricos, sometimes known as "the white curse," can be a study in frustration, but also a triumph of art and technique if an angler arrives at the propitious moment, picks out a feeding trout, and successfully offers it a fake.

Tricos emerge late at night or very early in the morning, most often before sensible anglers are awake and brooding over their morning coffee. But there are times when the hatch appears after daybreak. A doctoral thesis reports that the males emerge after sunset and continue throughout the night, but that the females do not begin the process until dawn, lending credence to some fishers' early-morning success with the dun form. However, the predictable fishing occurs when the adult winged spinners fall after mating, spreading their wings flat on the water in death. Then the trout will lie close to the surface in the feeding lanes, or circle the still pools gulping the spentwings on their rounds. Because the trout take station just under the surface where their cone of vision is very narrow, and perhaps because the easy feed preempts their native caution, it is not necessary to throw a long line. Get upstream from a pod of trout and drift your fly down to them. If you can distinguish one trout from another, place your fly on its nose. Put slack into the leader by stopping the rod before line and leader are fully laid out. If a disturbance appears somewhere close to your drifting fly, lift the rod—gently does it. You may have a fish. On the other hand, you may not. Don't feel bad if you get skunked at first. We all have; still do. Trico fishing may be the ultimate art. If you can exorcise the white curse, you can do anything.

Lightweight rods and floating lines are required. Your leaders should taper to .005, or to .004 if you can handle the finer diameter. A #20 fly is usually okay, but some experts go smaller—those with eagle eyesight.

There are other tiny mayflies, some of which appear early mornings, but the tricos are immediately identifiable by their exceedingly long tails.

Some anglers believe that the mating fall begins when the morning air temperature reaches 68 degrees. We are inclined to agree, having tested the theory on numerous occasions. Which means that the spinner fall may occur very early or as late as 9 or 10 AM. Ah, joy, when the tricos spread their wings at a gentlemanly hour.

FISHING THE WHITE WINGS

In this part of the world the white-winged Pass Lake is on everyone's short list of mandatory flies. Many call it a superfly.

For more than a century the fanwing Royal Coachman has been the ace in the hole for pounding up trout when nothing else will bring them to the surface. Its less gaudy predecessor, the plain old wet Coachman, with a wing of white duck quill segments, still brings trout to net on days when the Gold-Ribbed Hare's Ear and Pheasant Tail nymphs do not interest bottom feeders. The parachutes, with white post upstanding, a modern development, are frequently the choice for late-evening fishing over suspicious brown trout.

The White Wulff replicates the *Ephoron* mayfly and other pale summer-evening hatches of the north central states. It is also cast over browns feeding on *Hexagenia* under dark of moon. The Brown Bivisible is an all-purpose, all-hours attractor—heavy hackled for fast water, sparse for slow water.

Few insects have white wings: Dun, blue dun, gray, and tan are more common. Yet the flash of white on an artificial fly is often necessary to induce a strike.

Most experienced fly-fishers assign size of fly or presentation to first place on the list of factors that produce success. There is no doubt that size is important, but every angler will agree that the proper placement of the fly is key to success in heavily fished waters.

The white wing, cocked and dry, or wet and visible some distance down, permits precise placement and control of the drift. It allows the angler to find the narrowest of feeding lanes or to drop the fly exactly at the edge of a bank cover. The white wing is a flag or marker that rides the curling tongues and currents, signaling to the caster to go right go left, mend the cast, puddle the leader to permit a free float.

If the trout are not rising to the occasion on your river, coax them to strike with the measured and controlled drift of a white wing in or over their subterranean hiding places.

UPSTREAM OR DOWNSTREAM

Lone-wolf trout fishers seek the solitary reaches of uncrowded streams where they can practice their art unobserved. They guard their secrets jealously and deflect questions about their rivers and their "superflies" with elliptical replies. Most trout fishers, however, travel in partnership.

Trout streams divide neatly into two parts for partners—upstream and downstream. Either direction is okay, but the techniques of fishing the fly in each differ.

Trout face into the current, upstream, to see food coming down to them and to extract oxygen from water flowing over their gills. Therefore, when you're fishing downstream you must wade slowly and carefully so as not to send threads or clouds of silt ahead of you to spook the trout.

The trick when fishing down with a wet fly or a nymph is to allow only enough slack in the leader to allow the fly to drift at current speed without drag, bouncing the bottom where the trout lie hidden. Floating line will be seized by the current, will curve or belly downstream, and will pull the fly to the surface. Throw short casts, keep the rod tip high, and keep as much line off the surface as possible. Leader tippets should be long and fine. Many anglers weight their sinking flies. Unweighted or lightly weighted flies will wiggle or tumble naturally. Some of us string a brass bead ahead of the fly when absolutely necessary.

When a trout takes a subsurface fly, the angler's strike should be slow, to allow the trout to take the fly and turn back to its lair. If the strike is instantaneous, too often the hook will be yanked out of the fish's mouth. Most of us strike too hard and too fast. We should use the slip-strike. When the trout hits, let a little line slip through your fingers as you lift the rod. The slip-strike is especially useful on streams where the trout run large. To counter the tendency to strike too fast, some famous early authors coined the phrase, "Now I will strike my trout." We can never wait so long.

Downstream with a dry fly is a different proposition. To permit a free float, you need to put more slack into the drift. Work an S-curve into the line and leader by waggling the rod side to side toward the end of the cast. Or "puddle" the cast by pulling back at the end of the cast so that the leader falls bunched up. While the line and leader are straightening, the fly floats freely—as would a living insect. You can also reach out when the line is straight to add a foot or more to the float.

Going upstream, wet fly or dry, requires a different manipulation of the line. Because line, leader, and fly are drifting back toward you, you must take up slack by stripping. Slide the line in a loop or cradle formed by the forefinger of your rod hand and pull line with the reel hand, usually in increments of a foot or so at a time. The intent is to take up the slack without moving the fly unnaturally.

With an upstream sinking fly, the strike must be just about as fast as you can react. Many upstream nymph and wet-fly fishers use strike indicators. (See "Double Your Chances.") They all serve the same purpose: They twitch when a trout takes the bait and signal you to strike back at once. If you opt not to use a strike indicator, you will have to watch the end of your line intently, because the take is often subtle.

With a dry fly fished upstream there's no need for an indicator: The surface disturbance when a trout takes is evidence enough.

HOW TO CATCH A BIG BROWN TROUT

Let us get the definition of a big brown trout of the way first. A large, stream trout is one longer than 15 inches. Curiously, there are many more big browns reported caught, eyeballed for length, and released by catch-and-release anglers than are counted by Department of Natural Resources crews in electro-fishing surveys. It's all too true that fighting browns appear larger than life. A 16-inch brown from Trout Run Creek on an August evening actually measured a respectable and honest 13 inches. Anglers who keep their fish are assumed to be more exact with their measurements, but sometimes we wonder. We have named some anglers "two-plusers" because they eyeball all their fish as being 2 inches longer than they really are. There is also a pod of "four-plusers."

Big browns do not come easily. Putting aside the dubious claims of a special intelligence acquired by trout that have been previously caught and released, browns become large by happenstance. When smaller, they wandered into particular niches in a stream that afforded superior cover from predators—man, herons, eagles, otters.

Big browns lurk in the deepest and darkest holes. They hide under tangles of deadfall or underneath root wads. They laze out the daylight hours under bank covers or current deflectors that have been installed by the DNR.

While we were watching a DNR crew install lunker structures on the Rush River of Wisconsin, the first had barely been placed and covered with rock when a 16-inch brown (eyeballed) swam out of nowhere to take possession of that newly created niche.

Large browns feed during the darkest hours. This is not an invariable rule, of course. There are no absolutes in trout fishing. One afternoon Bob Linsenman, author, guide, and friend, observed a humongous brown sipping olives on the lower Kinnickinnic of Wisconsin. But that trophy disdained his artificial. When you find a big brown, it won't bite. Life is hard, brother.

Recently Jim sat for more than an hour in the "Devil's Seat" (a spot where you may sit at ease, boots in the water, and cast over a pool) on Trout Run, watching and waiting for one of several outsized inhabitants to feed at the surface. Finally one rose to something small. Jim cast over the lie with a #16 Elk Hair Caddis. A beaver hove into view, swimming downstream. She saw Jim, banged her paddle, and dove. The brown sank into the weeds, not to rise again anytime soon. The hard treatment—again.

A recent study is instructive. Bill Thorn, a researcher for the Minnesota DNR, studied 511 pools on 21 streams of southeastern Minnesota. He concluded that pools with three different cover types—undercut banks, deep pools (more than 2 feet in depth), large boulders, root wads, and submerged trees—were most likely to hold big trout. Pools with at least three types of cover were up to 47 times more likely to hold a large brown trout than were pools with only one cover type.

We recall a day of electro-fishing on the Willow River of Wisconsin with Scot Stewart, then the area fish manager. Working our way upstream, we were dismayed at the paucity of brown trout in this classic stretch, which consisted of a succession of pools and riffles. Finally we came to a deep pool with an undercut on the left, a huge root wad, and a tangle of underwater branches. There we turned belly-up three brown trout, the largest at 21 inches and the smallest at 15. Proof positive that the Minnesota researcher had gotten it right—four elements, if you count the branch tangle, which we do.

There is a lovely, fragile stream in western Wisconsin that produces delegations of brilliant baby brook trout, plus an occasional mother or grandfather in the 10- to 12-inch class. While Bill was coaxing brookies out of hiding upstream, Jim was approaching a classsic pool. Aha! Size, depth, a riffle, and a lip into the pool, Jim thought. It should hold a couple of large trout. Not so. The pool was clean—no boulders, no root wads, no undercuts. Zilch. A tip of the hat to Bill Thorn, again.

Many years ago, in our salad days, we watched fly-fishers at evening wading downstream with three big wet flies on a stout leader, taking oversized browns from the Namekagon. That's a lost technique in these days of tiny flies and light tackle, but you might think about it.

The best way to catch a big brown is to fish the streams that have produced delegations of lunkers in the past. They aren't spring creeks—there must be depth and volume and forage fish to fatten trout. Be willing to plumb the big pools or deep runs with Black Nose Dace, Woolly Buggers, Muddlers, crayfish, and such. Go from late afternoon into dark; or go in early morning, well before you see "the whites of their eyes." Sit and wait in the Devil's Seat. A short prayer will do no harm.

LITTLE CREEKS; BIG REWARDS

All of us should have a nice little spring creek (that's pronounced "crick" hereabouts, by the way) in our back pockets when the rivers are too busy, too warm, or blown out.

For instance: Opening day of the special early trout season was busy on some of the major rivers in west central Wisconsin where I like to fish. When my friend Jeff decided it was too crowded on a famous river stretch, he tried to relocate downstream. To Jeff's amazement, the competitive guy below him *ran* downstream (putting out a wake) while holding out his rod to make sure he covered the run. Jeff said, "Forget it, I'm not going to outrun this guy." We pulled up stakes and headed to one of our little spring creeks and finished the day by catching several brook trout.

I just plain love little creeks. Fishing new water turns me on. I fish trout all season, even during the dog days of late summer. Cold spring creeks have it all: They are exciting and educational. These little jewels will heighten your senses. The fragrances are intoxicating, the wildlife is up close, and the fish strikes are startling. Small streams usually offer smaller trout, but the trout are apt to be wild, easier to fool, and invariably beautiful. Except when I fish the western states, I seldom purposely pursue big trout, although I have caught my share here. A 12-inch brookie caught on home waters can make my day, or week.

One thing that is paramount in fishing small water is to slow down. We hear it everyday from someone, it seems—even my instructor in beginning calligraphy class leaned over my shoulder and said, "You are doing fine, but slow down."

Small-stream trout are usually more forgiving of a poor presentation than a clumsy approach. I try hard not to put out a wake, and I cast to 45- to 90-degree angles. Casting straight upstream will "line" the fish. Short casts to right and left work well, but when a fish strikes at such close quarters, it can startle you into missing the hook-up. Of course, drab clothing that blends with the flora is a must. Stalking along the stream with a low profile is a necessity.

Experience has taught me that when possible, getting in the water has its advantages. Walking the banks is tough where there is brush and the fish can see you. Open meadows are easier, but stay low. If you get in the water, blend in with the banks and approach supercarefully. You'll be amazed at how close you can get to trout. A good percentage of small streams look too gunky to enter, but quite often they will be solid in the center where the main current runs.

Most of these waters are underfished and often hold high densities of fish–albeit smaller ones. The hatches are usually similar to those on the big rivers. It is wise to use roll casts, sidearm casts, and slingshot casts. Most of all, patience pays off.

On smaller creeks I often use classic "searcher" patterns, such as Royal Coachman, Coachman streamers, Adamses, Mickey Finns, Muddlers, Parmachene Belles, and Professors. If you lack confidence fishing terrestrials, small creeks can be a quick fix. Little-creek brookies and browns are less sophisticated than their big-river cousins. Once in a while you will hook into a big honker, so hold on; it will get hectic. Big trout are in there; to hide they need only a spot under a log or an undercut the size of a large shoe box.

Creeks are deceiving: A lot of them are so clear they look to be only 3 or 4 inches deep, and fishless–but chances are you're walking by good water. Many anglers fish only the major rivers and major hatches, causing crowding. By doing it that way they miss "the big journey," learning by trial and error, dealing with the variables–solving the riddles.

Upper Midwest DNRs from Michigan to the Dakotas are paying more attention to small streams. Local conservation and sportspeople's clubs, and organizations like Trout Unlimited, have engaged in habitat improvement on small creeks. Pick up a TU state council newsletter from one of these states and you will see listed dozens of projects on streams you've never heard of.

Of course, I could start naming creeks–there are thousands of them to fish wherever you live–but as I said, the fun is in finding them.

The Tackle

Occasionally in this work we must venture where angels fear to tread. So it is with our tackle recommendations. The choice of tackle is personal, depending on experience, sentiment, prejudice, availability, and, not least, the ability to pay. Reasonable fly-fishers will disagree over which fly rod is superior for use on our midwestern trout streams. Anglers, exhausted at the end of a fruitful or fruitless day, will still find time to gather around their pickup trucks to argue the merits of their respective equipment. Even Bill and Jim differ over matters of less than substance.

Therefore, you won't find any dogmatic statements in this section on tackle. Well, perhaps a few.

Before the Second World War fly-fishers for trout were limited in their choices of tackle. Rods were made of bamboo—most often long, heavy, and slow. Leaders were laboriously hand-tied from short sections of gut, which required preliminary soaking and popped easily, most often, according to myth, on the run of a world-class trout. Silk lines were a misery to keep afloat. Artificial flies were large and gaudy. Creels were both clumsy and capacious, designed to carry home limits of fat trout.

All that changed after the war, thank goodness. Now the varieties of tackle are seemingly endless and often confusing. The trout are smaller on average, but wilier than ever. And most anglers no longer carry creels.

One thing has not changed: The fly rod is still the most important piece of equipment, and merits careful selection. Here is where Jim and Bill part company briefly. Humphrey's choice for anywhere in the country is an 8$\frac{1}{2}$-foot-long graphite 5-weight rod with a fast action, from any reputable manufacturer or rod maker. A fast-action rod may require a higher degree of coordination, but the resulting ease of casting is worth the practice. A 7$\frac{1}{2}$-foot 3-weight rod has enough firepower for many of our Wisconsin and Minnesota creeks. Graphite rods range in price from a low of $70 to a high of $500, and much of the difference may be cosmetic. You can even assemble your own under the skilled direction of fly-shop experts at considerable savings. Still, there is something magical about the look and feel of bamboo that has more to do with tradition than with practicality. So if you can afford one, go for it.

Bill Shogren prefers longer rods. His favorite is a 9-foot 3-weight. Bill says the length is handy later in the season, particularly when he is wading a narrow stream with steep banks and high weeds at the margins. The 3-weight is perfect for many spring creeks, which demand a delicate presentation. The 3 also has enough umph when a weighted nymph or streamer is called for.

Most fly-fishers choose two-piece rods because they are cheaper than three- or four-piece travel rods, but some of us have good things to say about the multipiece rods. They are easier to transport on aircraft, for one. It's our opinion that there is no diminution of action due to the extra ferrules.

A single-action fly reel is the first choice of most fly-fishers. There are many good reels, from modest to outrageous in price, that will store a full line with a generous measure of backing. Here's another instance where Bill and Jim diverge. Bill prefers Scientific Anglers reels, Systems I and II. Jim's favorite is the #1494 Pflueger/Shakespeare Medalist, which will store all the line and backing anyone will need and handle the powerful surge of a 2-foot trout as easily as the tentative tug of a tiddler.

The fly line must be matched to the rod. That is, a 5-weight rod requires a #5 line. Although double-taper lines are often recommended by fly shops, your first line could be a weight-forward floating line in one of the fluorescent colors. High-visibility lines will help you observe and control the placement and drift of the fly.

The leader will be 9 feet of monofilament, tapered from .019 inch at the butt to .007 (4X) at the point. For dainty flies, you may add 18 inches to 3 feet of tippet, .006 (5X) or .005 (6X). Some commercial brands are consistently a millimeter thicker than the diameter given on the spool, so you may decide to invest in an inexpensive micrometer or monofilament gauge. Tippets are tied to the leader with a surgeon's knot, aka double surgeon's knot. We still aren't convinced that braided or furled leaders are all that wonderful, but you can prove us wrong.

The choice of fly to tie with a clinch knot to the end of your tippet is a subject of endless speculation and worthy of a book. In fact, there are several shelves of books. Here, we refer you to our section on the Terrific Twenty. You can take it from there; and no doubt you will.

You may not need all of them, but surely you will desire other accoutrements of the modern angler.

Hip boots are cooler than chest-high waders during the heat of summer. They are easy to walk in and allow you to wade deep enough on 60 to 70 percent of your trips. Hippers with plain old lug soles are cheap enough to discard after a couple or three seasons.

Dedicated trout fishers also own chest-high waders, invariably with felt soles, because the felts grip better on slimy rocks. Felts, however, are never as safe as lugs on ice—a fact to which we can attest following a series of pratfalls on the snowbanks and ice shelves of the Whitewater during the special winter season.

Now the selection of wading gear becomes more complicated. Most modern fly-fishers opt for stocking-foot waders, worn with a stout, felt-bottomed wading shoe over. A common practice is to wear heavy socks inside waders, socks over the waders, and some kind of gravel guard over the top of the boot. Neoprene waders are preferred during the winter, but are generally uncomfortable under summer skies. Breathable waders are the latest development to separate anglers from their money. So far, ours have been worth the cost.

All boots and waders leak eventually, so ease of patching may be an important consideration in your selection of a particular material. If you invent an all-purpose glop or tape that works every time on all manner of surfaces, you will have made your fortune.

Last on this fascinating subject: Try on boots and waders before you buy. Different manufacturers use varying combinations of foot size and leg length, a critical consideration with chest-highs. If the waders are too short in the crotch, you won't be comfortable after a couple of hours of wading;

if they're too long, the accordion pleats around your knees will abrade the material. Always allow for a pair of heavy socks over your regular socks.

A dark green or camo vest with no reflecting hardware on the front, and not too many pockets, is another necessity for the complete angler. Pockets have a tendency to fill up, and the vest becomes a millstone. You'll need a ripple-foam fly box, polarized glasses or clip-ons, a snippers for clipping tippets, a forceps for removing hooks taken deeply by trout, and the recommended staff for tricky wading.

You may want a small net and a flat creel with which to capture and carry home an infrequent meal of small, fresh trout. As you develop experience, you will naturally acquire miscellaneous accessories of the modish angler. They might include a thermometer, specimen bottles and an aquarium net for plucking insects from the film, a magnifying glass, a butterfly net to swoop the adult insects from the air, and other esoteric items. A packet of pH strips is useful for measuring the acidity or alkalinity of water. They can be found in some pet shops; otherwise, electronic testers are available.

There is an immense range of gizmos and gadgets on which you can waste money, but some useful things will be found around the house. A dressmaker's ball-headed pin is useful for cleaning the eyes of flies before you tie them on. Stick the pin in the foam of your fly box.

And so here comes The Compleat Angler, fly-casting upstream, all spangled and flashing with the jewels of his art.

We close without comment on the hat he is wearing!

1│WISCONSIN

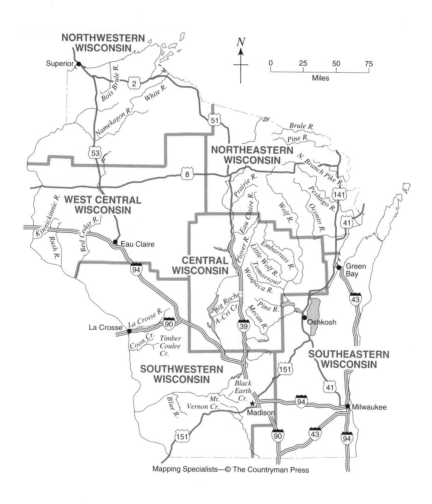

NORTHWESTERN
WISCONSIN

Superior

Bois Brule R.

White R.

Namekagon R.

NORTHEASTERN
WISCONSIN

Brule R.

Pine R.

N. Branch Pike R.

WEST CENTRAL
WISCONSIN

Kinnickinnic R.

Rush R.

Red Cedar R.

Eau Claire

Prairie R.

Eau Claire R.

Wolf R.

Peshtigo R.

Oconto R.

CENTRAL
WISCONSIN

Plover R.

Little Wolf R.

Embarrass R.

Tomorrow/
Waupaca R.

Green
Bay

Big Roche-
A-Cri Cr.

Pine R.

Mecan R.

Oshkosh

La Crosse

La Crosse R.

Coon Cr.

Timber
Coulee
Cr.

SOUTHWESTERN
WISCONSIN

Blue R.

Mt.
Vernon Cr.

Black
Earth
Cr.

Madison

SOUTHEASTERN
WISCONSIN

Milwaukee

N

0   25   50   75
Miles

Mapping Specialists—© The Countryman Press

3 | Southwestern Wisconsin: Spring Creeks in Hidden Valleys

The winding roads bear such evocative names as Hidden Valley, Hoot Hollow, Dry Dog, Zero Hero, Romance Lookout, Far Nuff, Never Sweat, Rattlesnake, and Morning Star. There are Old Mill Roads and countless River Roads—Blue River and Green River among them. In truth, there is a rainbow of colors in the old names.

You'll find Timber Coulee and Spring Coulee and other coulees—"coulee" being a French Canadian word for "ravine." There are ethnic remembrances of the earliest settlers of this hill country: Indian Creek, Irish Ridge, Russian Coulee, Dutch Hill, Swiss Valley, German Flats, British Hollow, and Bryn Gyrwen, a hill named by some long-dead Welsh miner to remind himself of home. There are mountains, too: Tabor, Ida, Zion, Sterling, Vernon, and, of course, Hope.

Among the earliest settlements, Hard Scrabble, Fairplay, Nip-and-Tuck, Shirt-Tail, Shake-rag, Hoff Noggle, Trespass, and Tail-hole have disappeared. Only a handful, such as New Diggings, Lead Mine, Plugtown, Avalanche, and Cataract, remain to remind us of the direct and hard-edged speech of the immigrants. In later, more respectable times, the names were softened and changed to commemorate dead heroes and live governors, or voracious land speculators.

Come late August, winding down from the highlands into the hollows and bottoms, past limestone towers and through bee-loud glades, paralleling fields of corn the color of weathered brass, you'll turn a corner and see at streamside, even now, a woman gathering the huge green leaves of tobacco in tanned and muscular arms. It is picture-book country, with dusty gravel roads and narrow, sinuous blacktops, and long vistas of meandering spring creeks with browsing, drowsing cattle on their emerald banks.

This is the Driftless Area of Wisconsin, which was left untouched by the glaciers, some 15,000 square miles of onetime prairie and oak openings, carved by the rains of time into hills and "mountains," eroded into valleys, hollows, coulees, glens, dingles, and dells, and drained by hundreds of named spring creeks and warm-water rivers. It is a huge, rough right triangle of land, more than 100 miles on each leg, wedged between the Mississippi River and the Illinois border. The bellied hypotenuse is Interstate 90, connecting Beloit, Wisconsin, on the Illinois border with La Crosse on the Mississippi.

Some links of hills are called the Blue Mounds because at the end of day they are just that—blue mounds rippling against a washed sky. There are also names like Castle Rock and Pike's Peak to differentiate one crenellated tower from a distant, limestone spire. There's Wildcat Ridge, named in the 1820s for those sly beasts that roamed the hills when the settlers came up the Mississippi from St. Louis and points east. The homesteaders came in stern-wheelers, side-wheelers, and wagons from Milwaukee, to burn the oaks and plant corn. Welsh and Cornish miners came to dig lead out of vertical shafts and to burrow winter homes into the sides of cliffs.

Wisconsin is known as the Badger State. Folklore has it that it was named for those first soft-rock miners, and that is as good a story as any, although the shy and dangerous badger still mines his hidey-holes in the quiet valleys.

This gigantic triangle, part of which is appropriately named the Hidden Valleys for commercial and tourist purposes, includes portions of 14 counties. A wandering fisher will find trout in all of them, even in Rock County, which is only a couple of hours by car from Chicago.

Twelve counties are of special interest to the footloose fly-fisher. They contain 413 trout streams and more than 1,500 miles of brook trout, browns, and rainbows. That's almost enough for several lifetimes of exploration.

For 15 years, 8 of the 12 counties opened for trout fishing on January 1, rather than on the first Saturday in May. It was a cherished experience for us to travel to southwestern Wisconsin to fly-fish for trout, often under blue skies, sometimes in snow or sleet, as early as the second week in January.

At first 10 counties were open for the special winter season. Then that was reduced to eight, because of extraordinary pressure on several first-class streams near La Crosse. During much of this period fish managers believed that the winter season had no deleterious effect on the stock of trout. More recently the evidence has come to suggest that trout are vulnerable to fishing pressure when they stack up in the pools during periods of low water. It is true that on some winter trips we found the brown trout congregating in clear pools, but that didn't seem to us to make them any easier to coax out with an artificial fly. Added pressure for closure came from a majority of anglers in the eight counties who attended spring county conservation meetings, and from the state council of Trout Unlimited. As of 1995 that wonderful experiment ended.

Then, after additional research and extensive debate, the DNR introduced a statewide early season for catch-and-release with barbless hooks: from March 1 to the first Saturday in May. That lasted through 2000. In 2001 the Natural Resources Board authorized a first Saturday in March opener on most streams west of US 51 or south of WI 23, and to include a few streams outside the boundaries. This early season ends a few days short of the regular opener to allow anglers to get a little rest. As before, C&R with barbless hooks is the rule.

Whatever changes in regulations become law in future years, we respect the careful deliberations of the researchers. It is the goal of the Wisconsin Department of Natural Resources to maintain and enhance the opportunity to enjoy quality trout fishing for legions of fishers.

With so many productive spring creeks from which to choose, it's impossible to guide you on a stream-by-stream tour, so we'll examine 28 streams that are suitable for fly-fishing over educated stream trout. All are classic, spring-fed hard-water streams. Many are exceedingly fertile and produce multiple hatches of aquatic insects. Don't be put off by terms like "creek" or "river." Some creeks are larger than some rivers, and some rivers are quite modest.

Eight Streams of the Southwest Corner

We will review first our favorite streams in Grant and Iowa Counties in the southwest corner of Wisconsin. They were among the eight counties that opened early through 1994, so our profiles include a few interesting anecdotes that describe winter fly-fishing. You will find these short stories useful on other streams that may be opened for an early season in the future.

We'd label six of these eight streams as first-class. One is marginal; another is small, with only a few pools. Castle Rock Creek has huge pools that will cause any true-blue fly-fisher to salivate. Seven streams include sections placed under special regulations, Category 5.

CROOKED CREEK
DeLorme 33

Crooked Creek in Grant County, south of the Wisconsin River, is Category 5 from WI 133 to the headwaters, a distance of 5.4 miles. Its browns are wild— that is, naturally reproducing. About 3 miles south of Boscobel on US 61 you will find Town Hall Road. You should be able to see the double-arched bridge way off to the west from US 61. There's a DNR stile at the bridge and a superb pool. We always stop at the bridge to tease the brown trout. Or maybe they're teasing us.

We've usually found trout midging under or in the shadows of the bridge. Maintain a low profile and approach from downstream.

Which reminds me of an incident. I parked the car, climbed the stile, and walked down the east bank, hunched over to keep out of sight of the feeding browns. Ah! I thought. What a way to start a day in early March. Clear skies, temperature in the 50s, no competition from other anglers, and the browns taking midges at the surface.

Fifty yards or so downstream I crossed the riffle and began a stealthy approach along the west bank. When I was close to casting range I dropped to my knees and began to inch forward, painfully.

Just then two young guys stopped their car on the bridge, got out, leaned over to look, waved to me in friendly fashion, pulled their car off the bridge, hopped the stile, and began to flail the water.

So much for the beginning of a great day. There is such a thing as courtesy to other anglers who have already staked a claim to a promising bit of water, but I guess the kids didn't know any better.

There are a couple of small pools downstream that you must fish on your knees, but generally the stream is narrow and deep, with water plants at the edges. Upstream to the next bridge on US 61 is pasture. It's not posted against trespass, but you'll want to ask permission at the white house. Aaron Gabriel, a writer from Chicago, reported wonderful fishing through the pasture for both browns and rainbows.

We can't leave Crooked Creek and Boscobel without leaving you with a bit of history. The old hotel in Boscobel is the birthplace of the Gideons, the folks who supply Bibles to hotel and motel rooms worldwide. It seems that one night in September 1898, John Nicholson and Sam Hill, traveling salesmen, met in the lounge. Discovering, after a conversation that lasted into the wee hours, that they had similar religious convictions, they founded the Gideons. It's a fair guess that they weren't trout fishermen or they'd have been out on the streams.

Boscobel is a quiet town, with comfortable facilities for travelers. The Hotel Boscobel is now home to the Boscobel Heritage Museum and Library and is part of a historic downtown featuring many beautiful stone buildings. On a night in late March 2000 when the University of Wisconsin defended its way into the Final Four, the hotel saloon was bedlam. The prime rib dinner afterward was delicious, and deliciously quiet.

THE BIG GREEN RIVER
DeLorme 32 & 33

From the heights of Mount Ida (at the junction of US 18 and County Road K), west of Fennimore, you can look down through green pastures, past forested slopes, and into the valley of the Big Green. To the east, only min-

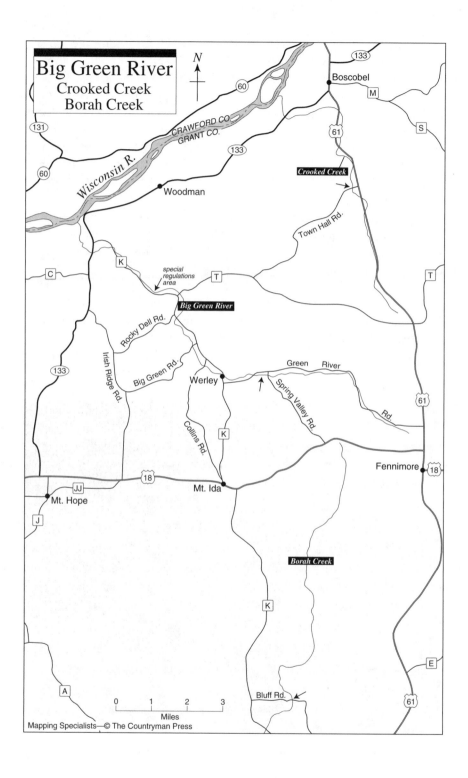

Big Green River
Crooked Creek
Borah Creek

N

131

60

133

Boscobel

M

S

Wisconsin R.

CRAWFORD CO.
GRANT CO.

60

133

61

Crooked Creek

Woodman

Town Hall Rd.

C

K

special
regulations
area

T

T

T

Big Green River

Rocky Dell Rd.

133

Irish Ridge Rd.

Big Green Rd.

Green   River

Werley

Spring Valley Rd.

Rd.

61

Collins Rd.

K

K

Fennimore

18

18

Mt. Ida

JJ

Mt. Hope

Borah Creek

J

A

K

E

61

| 0 | 1 | 2 | 3 |

Miles

Bluff Rd.

Mapping Specialists—© The Countryman Press

utes away, lie the broad meadows of Castle Rock Creek and the narrow, twisting glen of the Blue River.

The Big Green, upstream from WI 133 near Woodman, has 11 miles of water, a section of which is Category 5; the remainder is Category 3, planted with brown trout. Snaking through pastureland, sometimes with one edge against a wooded limestone ridge, it is narrow, averaging 12 feet in width. A few expert early-season nymph fishers will take 30 or 40 fish in a morning. They work excruciatingly slowly upstream through the open land, casting a #14 or #16 Hare's Ear Nymph, a Green Caddis Larva, or a dry Blue-Winged Olive.

One March 25 on the upper Green, with the air temperature at 35 degrees and the water at 48 degrees, while I was throwing figure-8s into a powerful breeze (and sometimes 9s and maybe even 10s), the browns began to rise at noon for lunch to a goodly hatch of miserable, struggling *Baetis*. I took just enough trout to satisfy my ego before deciding that life was too short to suffer so for the Art of Fly-Fishing. My emerger had a dark olive-brown body with a ball of gray rabbit dubbing on top. A purist might have preferred to drop a #18 Blue-Winged Olive on the nose.

Take Spring Valley Road into the valley from just opposite the Fenmore Hills Motel and Supper Club (our usual headquarters) on US 18, 2 miles west

Loren Carver on the Big Green River

of Fennimore. Between the two bridges on the Green it's low-profile fly-casting with a 4- or 5-weight rod, .005 (6X) tippet, and tiny flies in the early weeks. A visitor can also find the headwaters of the Green on Green River Road, 1 mile north of Fennimore, west of US 61, or on County Road K from Mount Ida to Werley.

Downstream toward Werley the river widens, the pools deepen, and in places the brush closes in. A large spring enters from the hillside at County Road T and Dutch Hill Road. About 3 miles of the Big Green from County Road T to WI 133 is restricted to artificials only and catch-and-release, Category 5. It's probable that the significant increase there in larger trout is the result of these special regulations. At least one local angler, Roger Kerr, thinks so. He reported the best trout fishing of his life one recent June in that Category 5 section.

Fly-fishing the special-regulations water can produce unexpected results. It's the most beautiful water through pasture upstream from Werley, where the DNR has installed lunker structures. Farther downstream Bill spooked one fish that looked to be about 14 inches. Then he caught a legitimate 20-inch rainbow, on a Hare's Ear beadhead with a little bit of split shot. It was a real reel screamer. Jim couldn't believe it! Evidently our friends from the DNR plant more than browns in the Big Green. A few more browns deigned to look at our offerings after some labor, but none approached that first trophy, which, by the way, was carefully released.

In mid-March 2000 five of us gathered on the Big Green at the DNR easement on Rocky Dell Road. It was a typical Wisconsin March day—a day for layered clothing and a short leader to punch through the 40-mile-per-hour wind gusts. The anglers were enthusiastic; the trout not so. Humphrey got his jollies by watching an inquisitive cow sidle up to Loren Carver while Loren was trying to lay a nymph against the edge of a structure; Loren then whispered at length to that cow, probably instructing the animal on streamside etiquette and protocol. Our champion, Peter Morse, took at least one trout everywhere we stopped on the Green, the Blue, and Castle Rock, although the blue-winged olives never raised their pretty heads. Even the early black stoneflies failed to show.

Bill once summed up our experience this way: "This Big Green is a wonderful river! There are so many places for big trout to hide. That's what this river must be about—good-sized trout, not necessarily about numbers of trout. I don't know anything quite as nice as this. All pasture, a lot of deep runs, 15 to 25 yards wide in many areas. It's just got to have some amazingly big brown trout in it. You couldn't find an easier stream in the whole wide world to fish. Everything's open: It's really neat."

BORAH CREEK

DeLorme 25

Bill Shogren enjoyed a pleasant evening after a fine meal at a supper club in Fennimore. Plying the waters with a Pass Lake streamer one June night produced five browns in the 9- to 10-inch range. The water quality is not prime but it does support planted browns and a few holdover large ones. Take County Road K south from Mount Ida, then head about 1 mile east on Bluff Road to a Category 5 special-regulations section.

Permission is required in the stretch along Borah Road through a series of pools and riffles in pasture.

CASTLE ROCK CREEK

DeLorme 33

Castle Rock Creek begins as a trickle from a ravine on the east edge of Fennimore in Grant County and winds some 22 miles northeast to its junction with the Blue River. In times past that ravine was used as an occasional dump, so we've always had some doubt as to the water quality of the upper reaches.

About 6 miles downstream from Fennimore, along County Road Q, find Church Road and turn southeast to the bridge, the beginning of approximately 6.5 miles of designated trout water, and the head of about 1.5 miles of Category 5, "fish for fun" water, artificials only. The remainder of the mileage is Category 4. There may be some trout upstream of Church Road, but the real action will be downstream as far as Witek Road. Access to the designated trout water is excellent because much of the mileage is under DNR easement.

Castle Rock Creek, also labeled Fennimore Fork on the trout regulations map, offers a different configuration from most other southwestern Wisconsin streams. Upstream of the first bridge on County Road Q, east of Church Road, it's a broad pasture stream with huge, slow pools alternating with riprapped corners and a few graveled runs. There's a short section of paving on the northwest side of the first County Road Q bridge, which provides off-road parking. Downstream to the second bridge it's somewhat narrower and heavily riprapped, with a variety of habitat more typical of the other streams in the area. It's possible to park at the second bridge down and, for a small fee, fish through a private campground. As I recall, the last time we fished the campground we paid our fees to the folks at Kohout Farm.

Quick to rise during a rainstorm and slow to fall, the creek is always

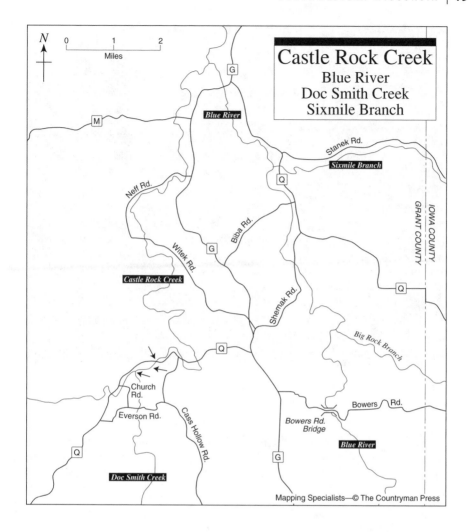

slightly milky due to runoff from pasture and field and percolation through limestone. Summertime water temperatures are not likely to exceed 70 degrees. Because natural reproduction is poor and the stream is popular with anglers from Illinois and other distant places, all three species of trout are planted.

One expert advises that he's had consistent and quite fabulous success with a Royal Coachman bucktail. A Pass Lake, or any similar white-winged caddis pattern in #14, will do equally well if the trout are not rising to an identifiable hatch.

The gigantic pools upstream of the County Road Q bridge will have to be approached in an attitude of prayer—on your knees on the bank—not

JIM HUMPHREY

Dick Frantes on Castle Rock Creek, southwest Wisconsin

because you implore the intervention of divine beneficence, but because you will be visible against the sky to wary trout that have already tested the metal of a hook. Stay back on a long line and a fine leader. Float your fly close to the jumbled riprap. Late in the year you'll find mats of blooming watercress and the massed tiny pads of lesser duckweed at the margins. Drop your fly there; the trout will lie in shadow and rush to meet your fly, if they like the look of it.

Prior to 1995 a DNR survey revealed 200 fish 16 to 18 inches long, and hundreds in the 10- to 14-inch class, all in the catch-and-release section. There were also a few giant browns to 24 inches near the outlet of the big spring, which pumps 3,000 gallons a minute into Castle Rock. Not so long ago Bob Mitchell, former owner of Bob Mitchell's Fly Shop in Lake Elmo, Minnesota, released a 27-inch rainbow—brood stock from a hatchery, no doubt.

To fatten these superior trout, the creek contains substantial populations of scuds, leeches, and a few species of the smaller stoneflies. That thin hatch of early-April small black stoneflies is probably *Capnia vernalis,* known to the fraternity as the early black, but stoneflies are not common to these spring creeks, and the early black will have gone airborne by May.

You might think that so popular a stream would be under constant pressure. Yet we have been there in the early season in midweek and again during the dog days of August, and have encountered no other fishermen. May and June weekends will see a surfeit of anglers.

On an August evening under a gloomy sky, on the fourth cast against the bank of the first run downstream from the County Road Q bridge, a 14-inch brown rose to take a Cap Buettner Stonefly Muddler. The brown was a veritable football in shape, deeply colored, and determined to fight. Not one other fisherman was there to witness that titanic struggle.

But we particularly enjoy the early weeks on Castle Rock when the barometer is rising into the green range of "good fishing." The sun is shining. Visibility under washed blue skies is forever. Go fishing! our inner urges yell. And so our recommendation to you, dear reader: Go and enjoy the great pools of Castle Rock at least once in your life.

And we have gone with a gang of five, as recently as March 2000, but with indifferent results. It's our experience that the spring blue-winged olives do not take wing when the wind is gusting to 40 miles an hour. Nymphal forms were not productive either. The winter 2000 edition of *Wisconsin Trout,* the quarterly newspaper of the Wisconsin Council of TU, reported that nonpoint-source pollution had seriously affected the number and size of midsized trout, although the lunkers were still there. The Castle Rock Watershed Working Group, however—a consortium of landowners, environmentalists, government officials, and anglers—has begun rehabilitation. Hooray!

DOC SMITH CREEK
DeLorme 33

This 4-mile feeder shows some pretty water above its junction with Castle Rock in the pastures, but the water quality is marginal due to runoff from grazing land and high summer water temperatures. Only the lower 1.8 miles are considered trout water. We've had modest returns from the first quarter mile above the junction with Castle Rock.

THE BLUE RIVER
DeLorme 33

The Blue River at the Bowers Road bridge east of County Road G twists north to the Wisconsin River through a forested valley. Go east from Castle Rock to County Road G, then south to the first road running east. That's Bowers Road, where there is a DNR parking lot and a stile. Alas, a friendly dog who usually showed up, tail wagging, to share our sandwiches companionably, is gone. He was a good chap.

Between Bowers and Biba Roads, the downstream end of the designated trout water, a fisher may enjoy the solitude of primitive Wisconsin through 6 pretty miles. Upstream toward Montfort there's a stretch of Category 5 water; the remainder is Category 4.

Late one March Dick Hanousek of the Twin Cities took 13 good browns from the upstream Blue with *Baetis* emergers in a four-hour period. As he said, "Not bad for openers." These tiny blue-winged olives will be around in May and June, and on through the season.

On another March day Bill fly-fished upstream from Bowers Road, where he caught a couple of brownies and a rainbow on nymphs. "It's a beautiful day, in the 40s, I'd say. Overcast most of the time. I ran into a guy who fishes below that bridge. He goes in there quite often. He came out with three browns today; he thought they were rainbows. He was fishing pieces of chub. A 22-incher, a 20-incher, and a 14-incher, and they were shaped like footballs. Obviously, these fish must make a pretty good living in the winter months in these big, deep holes. He said there were many deep holes and good fish, and that he had missed a couple of bigger ones. Can you imagine it? That 22-incher had to be 6, 7 pounds!" This may be one reason why the early season was eliminated for a number of years. Only parts of some streams were protected by catch-and-release rules during that special winter season, so bait fishers could plumb the pools outside the limits.

In the summer of 2000 the Harry and Laura Nohr Chapter of Trout Unlimited purchased a 240-acre parcel on the Blue River at the Bowers bridge for eventual purchase by the Wisconsin DNR. About 1 mile of river will be open permanently to anglers.

THE SIXMILE BRANCH
DeLorme 33

Before you leave the Blue River, try the Sixmile Branch, Category 3. Go north on County Road Q to Stanek Road, east on Stanek to Pine Tree Road, then southeast to the Sixmile. All three species of trout are planted; you may find some of them in the pools.

The Big Green, Castle Rock, and the Blue are a trio of fly-fishing streams as good as you'll find anywhere in the Midwest, but that doesn't mean that your experience will be like shooting fish in a barrel. It's estimated that the Castle Rock trout have been caught an average of four times a season, and those suspicious trout on the Big Green and the Blue have been worked over by experts. And yet they are there, awaiting the drift of your Trico or the kick of a black cricket under the orange-freckled blossoms of jewelweed at streamside. Or maybe you should use a chub tail. We're just kidding!

This part of the world is amazing in many ways. "The supper clubs are alive and well. We got a steak sandwich for $5.95, and the place was absolutely packed; everybody was there. Everybody's friendly; it's so relaxed; it's really neat."

Facilities for the preceding seven streams are at Fennimore, Boscobel, and at the Fenmore Hills Motel and Supper Club 2 miles west of Fennimore on US 18. For a memorable dinner, enjoy The Silent Woman in downtown Fennimore. Obtain the free Welcome to Hidden Valleys, *a visitors guide to nine southwestern Wisconsin counties, for useful information. Most motels have it.*

OTTER CREEK
DeLorme 26 & 34

Travel east from the Fennimore Hills via US 18 toward Dodgeville to Otter Creek in Iowa County, our eighth stream. Take County Road Q north from the highway, about 2 miles west of Dodgeville. Stop at the bridge on County Road Q and take a look at one sweet run just downstream of the bridge. We've enjoyed tagging these browns with an Adams or a #16 Elk Hair Caddis.

The approximately 8 miles of Otter, from its headwaters down to County Road II, is a wide meadow stream planted with brooks and browns. Between County Road Q and the County Road II crossing downstream, a matter of 2 miles, it is Category 5; upstream from County Road Q it is Category 4.

DNR metal stiles, not always prominently placed, afford access along County Road II. Those tall, narrow ladders, which are also used throughout the Southwest, have been known to tip. Just ask us! Be careful going over.

Otter produces excellent hatches of caddisflies. The Dark Green Raggedy Caddis or Green Bodied Hare's Ear will do well as underwater searching patterns. Dry caddis patterns will be small in spring–#14 and #16. In the later months you'll find occasional hatches of larger caddis. At the downstream end near the County Road II bridge you'll find a narrower stream with bending grass at the margins. This is for hopper time, July and August. We have had some wonderful early fly-fishing days on Otter with an Elk Hair Caddis under bright blue skies, and later with a hopper or a small dry Muddler fished at the surface.

Facilities at Dodgeville. Mineral Point, about 10 miles to the southwest

A summer day on Otter Creek at the County Road Q bridge

of Dodgeville, is a historic lead-mining town. You may want to spend some time at Pendarvis, a collection of stone houses. Superior cuisine and tourist facilities there.

Five Streams of the Madison Area

TROUT CREEK

DeLorme 34 & 35

Follow County Road T north and west out of Barneveld from US 18 and US 151 to Trout Creek in Iowa County. This stream is approximately 35 miles west of Madison. All 8 miles of Trout Creek are Category 5 and include the three species of trout.

An expert of our acquaintance, Joe Balestrieri, always felt that Trout Creek was better than Grandma's apple pie and Wisconsin cheddar cheese, even though the creek runs narrowly through brush. Joe uses light rods and knotless, fine leaders for delicacy, and a sneaky slow presentation from a kneeling position. Fish downstream with a Gold-Ribbed Hare's Ear on a swimming nymph hook, or with Pheasant Tail nymphs and soft-hackle wet flies tied after the Sylvester Nemes method. Midge dries are necessary, #22 and smaller. Scud and sowbug imitations, plus ants, hoppers, and beetles, are useful during the hot months. It was here that Joe B. watched a trout nosing into eelgrass and shaking its head to dislodge snails, which the brown then proceeded to gobble up. The snails were about the size of a BB.

Recommended drys are small Light Cahills, Blue-Winged Olives #18 and #20, and Sulphur Duns #16 and #18. The many species of caddisflies are represented by the Small Black, Spotted Sedge, and Dark Blue Sedge. The above list reads like a prescription for any of the spring creeks of the Hidden Valleys.

Trout Creek has long been a blue-ribbon stream, but at this writing we can't rate it quite so highly; the flow appears to have slowed and the water has darkened. Although Joe is not optimistic, by the time you read this report, Trout Creek may have been restored to glory.

Facilities at Barneveld or at Spring Green on the Wisconsin River, close to Frank Lloyd Wright's Taliesin, the American Players Theater, and Tower Hill State Park.

BLACK EARTH CREEK

DeLorme 35

Since our first edition in 1995 Black Earth Creek, in Dane County west of Madison, has been the subject of many commentaries, including a compre-

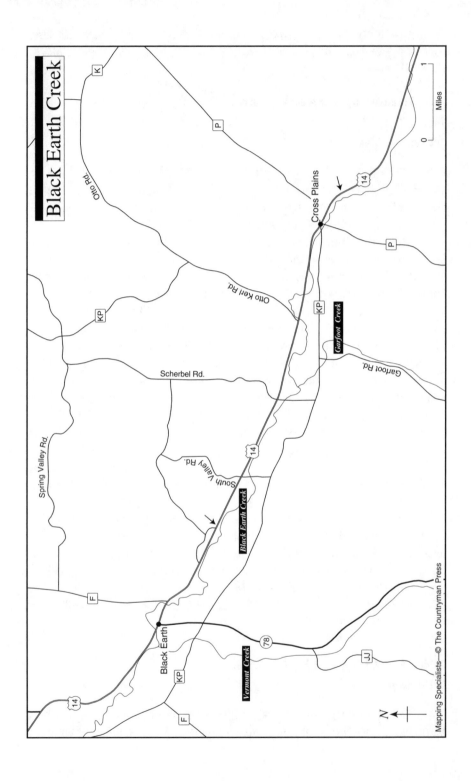

Black Earth Creek

hensive profile in *Exploring Wisconsin Trout Streams* by Steve Born et al. (University of Wisconsin Press, 1997). *Wisconsin Trout,* newspaper of Wisconsin Trout Unlimited, *Wisconsin Natural Resources* magazine, and *Midwest Fly Fishing* have all embellished the story. All reports agree that this is still a fine brown trout stream and that many organizations and citizens are struggling to save it. All admit that population growth and suburban expansion threaten its future. We still like it but are now devoting more attention to the smaller streams to the west, some of which we will describe in this second edition.

Black Earth is popular with anglers near and far, but it is not always shoulder-to-shoulder fishing. Avoid the weekends if you can; fish into the evening and even later if you don't mind playing tag with bats. Bill Shogren, together with Bill Haugen and Dave Fass of Minnesota TU, enjoyed super fishing over the Hex hatch as early as June 13 one year. Other anglers arise early for an hour or two of peace. Still others fish the dog days of July and August with grasshoppers.

The creek begins as a trickle along US 14 west of Middleton and gathers water at Festbe Spring east of Cross Plains. A section of it east of the village of Black Earth, from South Valley Road to Park Street, is rated Category 5, artificial lures only, with complicated bag and size limits. Read the regulations.

The creek, which contains 1,600 browns per mile according to a recent electro-fishing survey, has undergone extensive rehabilitation by the Wisconsin DNR with the aid of local chapters of TU. The banks have been reshaped and riprapped, lunker structures installed, and cattle restricted by 5,000 feet of fencing. To which the wild brown trout have responded with thanks.

In addition to the Hex, notable early emergences are the little black caddis and the Hendrickson mayfly. Caddis are common throughout the season. Scuds, sowbugs, leeches, and the usual variety of terrestrials are trout fare during the appropriate time periods. There is a DNR parking lot at Cross Plains and access at four or five bridges.

The Black Earth is a showcase stream that is worth preserving; but it won't be easy.

Superior facilities for everything at Madison, and modest accommodations at Cross Plains and Black Earth.

MOUNT VERNON CREEK
DeLorme 27

Mount Vernon Creek in Dane County, southwest of Madison, is popular with fly-fishers from Illinois as well as from Madison and the surrounding area.

Two miles between WI 92 and County Road U are classified Category 5; artificials only, a daily bag limit of three, only one of them a brown—which must be at least 20 inches!

This beautiful stream has been tended and manicured as a showpiece by the DNR. Cattle have been excluded by fencing, and easements are marked. Joe Balestrieri of Milwaukee, who prizes this stream, stalks the hatches from upstream of the village of Mount Vernon to the public parking area downstream. He makes his approach from County Road G in town. On one May 28 Joe and his brother Jim encountered an emergence of sulphurs. They caught and released browns to 14 inches on sulphur drys and a nondescript brown nymph. Joe, who is a rod builder and a developing collector, admits to using three different rods on Mount Vernon, sometimes all three on the same day: a long rod for the late-season "elephant grasss" and a short rod for the sneak through brush. Medium for the in-between, we suppose.

On a bright April day during the special early season, Bill Shogren spent two hours testing his skills on the creek. Around 1 PM a light tan caddis hatch appeared. The hatch was sparse, but the husky browns were in earnest. Most often this creek is clear and the trout cautious. Bill characterizes Mount Vernon as demanding, and if you do well here, he says, you can do well anywhere.

Proceed with caution and patience; apply your experience if you intend to finesse any of the three species of naturally reproducing trout. Because it attracts anglers from great distances, it is a stream to visit during a weekday after the May and early-June rush. Toward the middle of June the Hex may be on the evening wing. Carry two flashlights, locate a pool, and wait for the long, wiggling lift of the supermayfly of the Midwest. For the night release of big brown trout, barbless hooks are de rigueur. You will need a catch-and-release net.

All facilities at Madison, Mount Horeb, and Verona. Advice available at Lunde's Fly Fishing Chalet in Mount Horeb, WI 53572, on WI 92. See thousands of types and brands of mustard at the Mustard Museum in Mount Horeb!

GORDON CREEK
DeLorme 27

Gordon Creek in Dane and Iowa Counties just west of Mount Vernon is a little-known jewel. Take WI 78 south out of Daleyville to County Road A and follow it southwesterly to the bridge in the upper half of the Category 5 mileage, which extends downstream for half a mile south of WI 39 and upstream to Brue Road. If we can estimate the stream wiggles, that is approximately a reach of 5 miles restricted to artificials and total catch-and-release.

Not long ago at all, Shogren's pal Steve Payne fished down from the bridge with fair luck (skill?) through the pasture, but when he hit the wooded area, look out! His beadhead Woolly Bugger snaked out several 16-plus-inch browns from the deep holes under fallen trees and brush piles. Steve advises dropping that Bugger above the hole and letting it sink into the difficult spots. Start stripping and "hold on; they hit with a vengeance." Stealing along the banks is not easy, so negotiate those sweet spots from above and use a variety of casts.

You will find other small and productive streams in an almost perfect circle with Steve's pocket as the hub and Mount Vernon on the circumference. Humphrey remembers a secret, guided trip to a stream with an Irish name. Was it Dougherty or Brennan, not far from Madison, Wisconsin? The fishing was pretty good. You could profitably invest a few days in the area, away from the more popular attractions of Black Earth or Mount Vernon Creeks. Joe Balestrieri has promised to tell us about Blue Mounds Creek, very soon.

ROWAN CREEK
DeLorme 36

Rowan Creek, about 35 miles north of Madison in Columbia County, is intersected by Interstate 90/94 some 4 miles west of Poynette. The freeway exit to Poynette is County Road CS. Upstream of US 51 at Poynette there is a section of Category 5 water through more than a mile of DNR lands; the remainder of its 8 miles is Category 3. More than half a mile of it through cattails and bulrushes was purchased by The Nature Conservancy and transferred to the DNR.

Access to the downstream section is by trail from a DNR parking lot on County Road J, which is immediately east of I-90/94. Go north on County Road J from County Road CS about 1 mile to parking. There is a second parking lot on County Road CS about half a mile east of County Road J. Closer to Poynette on County Road CS there's a park from which you should be able to foot it to the creek. In town you'll find more DNR parking on Main Street on the upstream side of the bridge; downstream is a picnic ground and ball field. Just east of US 51 on Tomlinson Road find East Road, going south, which will take you into the open DNR lands. At still another DNR parking lot, on Loveland Road east of Poynette, the stream is narrow, dark, and deep, alternating through hay meadows and brush. There you'll find a FEDERAL AID IN FISH RESTORATION PROJECT sign commemorating the work of the Southern Chapter of Trout Unlimited, the Columbia County Sportsman's League, the Columbia County Conservation Fund, and the Trout Stamp Fund. You'll also find a spring under a grass mat that will permit you to bounce on it as if it were a trampoline.

Rowan Creek is popular with anglers from a wide radius, so there's no guarantee that you will have the stream to yourself. Best to go on a bad day when other anglers are put off by overcast or rain. We've had it all to ourselves in March in miserable conditions, but we caught trout on the usual small stuff—Brassies, Pheasant Tails, Adamses, and Griffith's Gnats. Our friend Jason Carpenter, from Missouri, on our recommendation stopped on his way north to fish Rowan Creek in September. But he reported that the river was so soggy at the margins that he could hardly get close to it.

Facilities at Poynette.

Twelve Streams North of the Wisconsin River and West of Interstate 90

RICHLAND CREEK

DeLorme 33

Richland Creek in Crawford County is just across the river from Crooked Creek at Boscobel. It parallels US 61 just north of WI 60 and the Wisconsin River. It's a small creek, a bit more than 8 miles in length, and planted with brook and brown trout. If you stay overnight at Boscobel, you could send one of your partners to Richland to fish the evening through the pastureland. Marietta Valley Road is a loop road off US 61 that takes you west of the stream just north of WI 60. From Marietta you can follow Spring Valley Road upstream.

Facilities at Boscobel.

BEAR CREEK

DeLorme 34

Bear Creek, in Richland and Sauk Counties, includes approximately 11 miles of water suitable for trout. It rises in the scenic Bear Valley near the village of Sandusky on WI 130 and falls south to the Wisconsin River at Lone Rock, the city accursed with the coldest state temperatures on many winter days. Lone Rock is but a skip and a jump from Spring Green and Frank Lloyd Wright's Taliesin, the American Players Theater (mostly Shakespeare), the justly famous House on the Rock, and, by no means least, the magnificent Wisconsin River waterway. If on some lovely summer day the family prefers to enjoy the fantastical delights of the House on the Rock while you choose to hunt trout, begin at County Road B on WI 130 north of Lone Rock, if only for a glance at the river here. Over the years the creek has been straightened and bermed to hasten the runoff, but gradually it is reclaiming its traditional track. If there are trout this far down, this is the place in grasshopper time. The grass on the berms and at the margins will be high. Stay back and use your long rod.

Upstream there is access at the Marble Quarry Road bridge in the village of Bear Valley. Farther north there's a Public Hunting and Fishing Ground at County Road N, the lower end of a couple of miles of special-regulations water. The creek here is narrow and promising downstream through an overgrown field; up is brushy. Beyond the County Road N bridge the creek moves away from the road to the foot of cliffs. No doubt there are accessible pockets—which you will have to find for yourself. Not to raise your hopes, it's Humphrey's opinion that this stream is marginal due to runoff. The valley is as scenic as any traveler might ask, but the stream has the air of being abandoned. However, he has been wrong before; and August may see the stream come alive. Perhaps we will organize a visit to the American Players and Bear Creek next August?

WILLOW CREEK
DeLorme 34

The estimated 16 miles of Willow Creek above Ithaca Dam on WI 58 in Richland County contain planted brook trout and naturally reproducing browns. In a reversal of the usual configuration, the lower 12 miles are superior to the upper 4. Our preference is to fish upstream from Wheat Hollow Road on WI 58, where there is a Public Hunting and Fishing Ground. The creek here is partly open and of a satisfactory width for fly-fishers to practice the art. Jim likes this section for esthetic reasons. Upstream, at Smyth Hollow Road and another PH&FG, it's clear and moderately swift. Recommended. At the village of Loyd and above, the stream is smaller than we like and somewhat degraded through pasture. Our last trip to the Willow was a bust because of high and murky water, but we've got it on our little list. The valley of the Willow is just about as pretty as it gets in southwestern Wisconsin. No doubt the village of Avoca on the Wisconsin River was named for that Irish village immortalized in a sentimental and nostalgic song sung by John McCormack.

THE PINE RIVER COMPLEX
DeLorme 33 & 34

The Pine River, Category 3, some 14 miles of water above the village of Buck Creek on WI 80 in northeastern Richland County, includes a complex of seven streams within its watershed. We like the main stem of the Pine around Hub City. It is bigger water than many of the streams of southwestern Wisconsin and absolutely beautiful, winding through fields of hay and corn and around limestone castles. We haven't yet spent enough time on it to prepare a definitive report on all the feeders, but it's certainly one that demands further attention. A number of feeders and a section of the West Branch of the Pine are Category 5, a sure sign of interest by the DNR, and therefore worthy of exploration. Access is easy at numerous bridges in that tangled country.

Facilities at Richland Center.

CAMP CREEK
DeLorme 33 & 41

Curt Dary, an aquatic entomologist and dedicated fly-fisher whose superior wisdom and skill we bow to, states categorically that Camp Creek, east of Viola in northwest Richland County on WI 56, is one of the 20 best streams in Wisconsin—high praise indeed. Its 5.5 miles of natural brook trout and browns are rated Category 5, an indication that the DNR accords the stream special status. Access is at the County Roads G and MM bridges or by a short stroll between cornfields from the neat little park on WI 56, 2 miles east of Viola. Another enthusiast swears that his fat #10 Carpenter Ant will inveigle trout consistently.

Our experience on Camp Creek has not been all that wonderful, perhaps because we haven't fished it consistently. And that points up a moral that we will draw quite often in these pages: You may find a section of stream that is everything to you that the Good Lord might allow, while Humphrey or Shogren can't "lay up a dime" there. So we don't claim, can't claim, that our streams are the best that you will discover in Wisconsin and Minnesota. Our streams are good ones, but you'll find better if you just poke around on your own.

Facilities at Viola.

THE WEST FORK OF THE KICKAPOO RIVER
DeLorme 41

Much has been written about the West Fork of the Kickapoo in Vernon County, east of the cities of Viroqua and Westby. Trout Unlimited's *Guide to America's 100 Best Trout Streams* gives this restored southwestern trout stream high marks.

As was true of so many of our trout waters, the West Fork was degraded due to irresponsible farming practices and lack of stewardship. Now, decades later, this water has been rescued because of the efforts of the Wisconsin DNR, volunteer sportsmen's clubs, and local landowners. Kudos go to Roger Widner Jr. of Avalanche, who spearheaded much of the stream improvement. The Blackhawk Chapter (Janesville, WI) of TU committed itself to restore the fishery at the urging of Dave Vetrano of the DNR. County conservationists, the U.S. Agriculture Stabilization and Conservation Services, and the University of Wisconsin have all participated in restoring this stream to blue ribbon trout status.

The more than 12 miles of the West Fork contain huge numbers of brown trout. Stocking programs are utilized, and good carryover results in many big fish. Because the water quality is improving, natural reproduction is within our grasp. Indigenous brook trout are reestablishing themselves in the upper reaches and in the feeder creeks.

Major hatches of Hendricksons, sulphurs, light cahills, blue-winged olives, and caddis are prolific and predictable. During May and June blue-winged olive hatches bring up so many rising trout that the pools are boiling.

There is a 9-mile catch-and-release section from County Road 82 upstream to the village of Bloomingdale. Sixteen- to 18-inch trout are not uncommon.

The West Branch is a major trout river. The entire watershed, and that of the Coon Valley complex, is incredibly beautiful. There are fine B&Bs, motels, and supper clubs. Coon Valley to the north is noted for its spring coulee creeks—some of the best in the world. You will have much to choose from; and not many fishers have fished them all.

The West Fork has been celebrated as one of TU's 100 best, has been lauded in *Midwest Fly Fishing* magazine and in *Wisconsin Trout,* a publication of Wisconsin TU; and explored comprehensively in *Exploring Wisconsin Trout Streams* by Steve Born et al. (University of Wisconsin Press, 1997). The Fall 2000 issue of *Trout* published by TU's national organization provided a comprehensive history of the entire watershed of the Kickapoo. So, we will not attempt to gild the lily.

SUGAR CREEK

DeLorme 32

Sugar Creek is a gem of quality. It will be found upstream of Ferryville on the Mississippi in the northwest corner of Crawford County. It is a long way north of Prairie du Chien (plain of the dogs) and a long way south of La Crosse. It is less than 20 miles from Viroqua and about the same from Viola, both towns loci for other fly-fishing adventures.

This 9.5-mile stream parallels County Road C, which points northeasterly out of town. The first mile or so beyond town limits is of somewhat lesser quality; the upper 7 miles contain planted brook and natural browns. It is likely that the planted brook trout have reproduced satisfactorily in recent years, as they are wont to do in other accommodating habitat. Sugar is small and clear, with good numbers of both species well distributed all the way to the Bible camp upriver. Check out Sugar for more access points, and discover new haunts.

THE SOUTH FORK OF THE BAD AXE RIVER
DeLorme 40

Of the two forks of the Bad Axe River, we prefer the South Fork, which empties into the Mississippi River near Genoa in Vernon County. An older DNR manual lists the South Fork as 16 miles of marginal water planted with brown trout. It's likely that subsequent habitat work has succeeded, because the river has produced large brown trout in recent times. There is an improved area downstream from the village of Purdy on County Road N. Take WI 56 east out of Genoa to County Road N, to the Bad Axe Lutheran Church, which is about all that remains of Purdy. You can also reach it by going west on WI 56 from Viroqua.

The improved section through meadowland is easy to fish and is consequently hit pretty hard. If you can obtain access (not always easy) to some wooded stretches that see fewer anglers, you may run into some trout "as long as your arm."

There are deep holes where the reel screamers lurk. Early morning and evening with streamers would be the ticket.

Bad Axe may be a romantic name for a river, but the last battle of the Black Hawk War in 1832 was anything but romantic when 300 Native Americans were killed at the confluence with the Mississippi.

TIMBER COULEE CREEK
DeLorme 40

Timber Coulee Creek is one of a complex of streams that come together to create Coon Creek at the village of Coon Valley in northwestern Vernon County. We consider Timber Coulee the premier brown trout stream of the group, which includes Spring Coulee, Rullands Coulee, Coulee, and Bohemian Valley Creeks. Trout Unlimited lists it as one of the 100 best trout streams in the States. Approximately 4 miles from County Road P upstream to Olstad Road is Category 5: artificials only and one trout of 14 inches or longer.

Fly-fishing the edge of the riprap on Timber Coulee Creek

This classic open stream is perfect for painting the surface with a small dry fly, and often the browns will come from under the structures and seize that dragless float. At other times anglers will search with a Prince Nymph.

Timber Coulee has been tended and improved by the Wisconsin DNR for more than 20 years, and before that by volunteers who were encouraged by the previous work of the U.S. Soil Conservation Service and the Civilian Conservation Corps. Brown trout were last stocked in 1986. One electro-fishing survey produced a few 20-inch browns, but a subsequent survey did not. Probably they had moved downstream into deeper water. Rainbow trout are stocked in Coon Creek and in Bohemian Valley. Brook trout are scarce in this collection of waters.

Access is easy at a number of small DNR lots where the stream may be so attractive that your hands shake while you try to tie on a fly; but we recommend exploring away from the lots in places where the trout haven't yet been spooked. This spring we found such a place where the river riffled into a deep corner pool, then straightened into a run past a scrim of trees. Fine

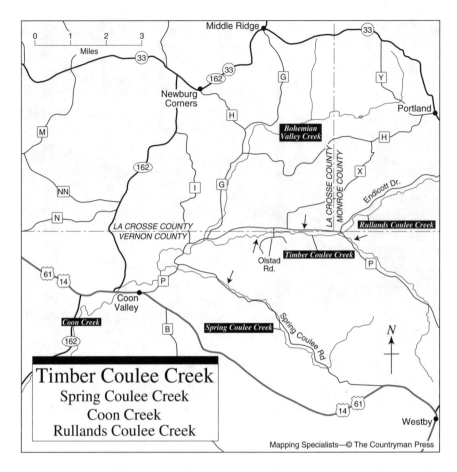

Timber Coulee Creek
Spring Coulee Creek
Coon Creek
Rullands Coulee Creek

Mapping Specialists—© The Countryman Press

trout were rising to invisible somethings, not those ubiquitous blue-winged olives. Nor to Griffith's Gnats, nor to Prince Nymphs. Nevertheless, it was a glorious day to be alive on one of the prettiest streams in creation. Upstream from Olstad Road there is roadside access, and then a bridge crossing, and suddenly you break out into the open and see—a surprise towering into the sky—the stilts and swoop of the Snowflake Ski Club jump, incongruous in this remote valley, even anachronistic. It is one of the vanishing jumps that take us back to sunny winter boyhood days, when bright banners on gleaming poles snapped in the wind and daring young men, like Bill, soared in the sky.

Dining and overnight accommodations in Coon Valley. Guide services from Rockin' K Farms in Coon Valley, WI 54623. Give yourself an additional treat by dining at DiSciascio's superior Italian restaurant in Coon Valley.

JIM HUMPHREY

Electro-fishing on Timber Coulee

RULLANDS COULEE CREEK

DeLorme 40

Rullands Coulee, 4.5 miles long, a small feeder to Timber Coulee mostly in Monroe County, is about 1.5 miles east of Olstad Road on County Road P. It holds naturally reproducing brooks and browns, and was recommended by Dorothy Schramm, one of the best fly-fishers and casting instructors around. But it is difficult to tear ourselves away from Timber Coulee.

SPRING COULEE CREEK

DeLorme 40

Spring Coulee is another excellent trout stream to explore if you can bring yourself to abandon Timber Coulee. Access is at the bridge on County Road P east of the village of Coon Valley, where the stream is quite narrow. Or proceed up Spring Coulee Road on the east side of the stream to roadside parking in the meadows.

COON CREEK
DeLorme 40

Coon Creek is an open, lazy creek 8 miles long, formed by the junction of Timber Coulee, Spring Coulee, and Bohemian Valley Creeks. Some maps label Bohemian Valley Creek by its old name, Coon Creek. Coon Creek is planted with brown trout. Although we'd rate it as a third-class stream down from the village of Coon Valley, improvements have been made in the village section. When the Wisconsin Department of Transportation decided to replace the bridge on US 14 and US 61, DNR fish managers Dave Vetrano and Ken Wright seized the opportunity to create a handicapped-accessible fishing area. There is now a park, an 850-foot trail with 10 paved fishing spots, and a section of rehabilitated stream, complete with 20 in-stream structures, riprapped banks, and a Hewitt ramp, which is an artificial plunge pool. Many agencies of government and conservation organizations contributed to the effort, including Trout Unlimited.

Bohemian Valley Creek is recommended by fly-fishers of our acquaintance, but we can't vouch for it on our own.

Facilities at Coon Creek on US 14 and US 61, and at Westby.

Two streams north of Interstate 90, west of Interstate 94, and south of US 10

THE LA CROSSE RIVER
DeLorme 41 & 50

The La Crosse River, near Sparta on I-90 in Monroe County, comes highly recommended. It offers more than 10 miles of deep wading from Angelo Pond (northeast of Sparta on WI 21) up into the Fort McCoy Military Reservation. It contains native brook trout, planted browns, and planted rainbows. Water quality is reckoned not so good in the 2 miles between Perch Lake at Sparta and Angelo Pond upstream. In June it is possible to fish over evening hatches of the brown drake, *Ephemera simulans,* a central and northern Wisconsin superhatch, and on dark July nights the giant *Hexagenia* for trophy browns. If you meet fly-fishers arriving early evenings on the river to establish rights to a pool, and they speak of the "shad hatch" or "shadflies," they mean the Hex.

Easy access is at the end of a dirt road off of WI 21, a bit northeast of Angelo Pond, or at the Byron Avenue bridge farther northeast; or from the west through DNR hunting and fishing lands.

For the approximately 4 miles or more that lie inside Fort McCoy, a special permit from the army is required. It is obtainable at fort headquarters on

WI 21. The army and Trout Unlimited have completed several stream improvement projects inside the fort.

All facilities at Sparta or at Tomah on I-94.

THE NORTH FORK OF THE BUFFALO RIVER
DeLorme 61

The North Fork of the Buffalo begins in some tiny streams east of Interstate 94 in Jackson County and parallels US 10 on the north. The upper 13 miles produce natural brook and brown trout. The lower 11 miles between Osseo and Strum in Trempealeau County receive plantings of all three species of trout. The upper mileage is accessible at bridges and from the Buffalo River State Trail, which also parallels highway 10.

Humphrey has stopped a dozen times on the upper river but has not yet found elbow room for dropping a fly. The wormers may do very well there in the pockets. At County Road G, 5 miles east of Osseo, it begins to look interesting; at County Road R on the way to Augusta there are DNR easements upstream and down. Some open streamside, some brush. Fishable, but sandy bottom. One will try the margins over dark bands of silt, or the corners where it deepens. Jim wouldn't spend much time here, on the general principle that there's a more promising spot downstream under the 94 bridge. Yes, you see it here first. A few yards north of US 10 on R, take Alvestad Road west to a bridge. You might want to try your skill where the trout will surely lie at the margins until dark. Next, Alvestad Road joins County NN; go west young man to the DNR lot a hop, skip, and a jump east of I-94. Here, the river is deep, still not wide, but fishable where the banks have been heavily riprapped. Jim finds it amusing, but not easy, to fish under the freeway. It is surprising how many Wisconsin streams are bridged by I-94.

Through Osseo the stream is degraded by backyard barbecues and greenswards to the river's edge. On the western edge of town, you may park in the wayside on the north side of US 10, cross the highway, and check the river for access and signs of rising trout. From here on to Strum, where the trout water ends above a lake, the Buffalo is wide, slow-moving over sand and silt. Between the wayside and Strum there's access along Highway 10, from the Buffalo River Trail, where it now lies on the south side of the river, and at DNR entries on bridges at County Roads 000, Tracy Valley, and Peterson.

Although we cannot recommend the Buffalo River without reservations, we know that you will sometime discover this long line of the Buffalo on one of your maps and wonder if it is worth exploring. It is, but not much more. Naturally, someone will tell us of its virtues and of the fabulous browns taken at dawn in the slow waters between Osseo and Strum. Hmmm; perhaps next time we should try that.

There, you have more than 30 spring creeks and rivers from which to choose. They constitute only a sample of smooth creeks and riffling rivers. You will discover better ones, we know. As you can't tell a book from its cover, you can't survey a stream by a glance from a single bridge. Crowded by brush and slow at the first bridge, at the next it may open into a garden of delight.

We enjoy all of the pastoral streams of southwestern Wisconsin. We remember an August afternoon, with the sun casting long shadows on the upper valley of the Big Green, and a lone angler, a latter-day Robin Hood in Sherwood green, throwing a cocky dry in a lazy loop and delicate drop to dimpling trout. In the distant background, a chalk-white farmhouse, a crimson barn, a steel-gray tower of silo, all framed by the purpling hills of Earth. In the foreground, black and white Holsteins laze in the shadow of a rusty bridge.

We recall, instantly, an evening on Castle Rock under a lowering sky, so near it seemed that one could touch the bellied clouds. A Stonefly Muddler, yellow under with a blue wing, dropped within an inch of the duckweed: a short, slack drift, then a wiggle. Then that explosive bulge in the surface that shouts, Trout on! The netting of the brown, the lift of net, water drops like diamonds streaming. And the last act, the gentle release of a fine fish to freedom. Your bright trout is there, in Castle Rock, the Big Green, Mount Vernon, or in one of the more than 400 spring creeks deep within the Hidden Valleys.

4 | Central Wisconsin: The Ice Age Streams

This collection of streams lies on the northeastern border of the Driftless Area, a huge and unique area covering parts of several states, which was bypassed by the glaciers that once covered all of Canada, the northeastern United States, and the central states south to what is now St. Louis. To identify and commemorate this phenomenon, the state of Wisconsin has defined and is acquiring rights-of-way for the Ice Age Trail, which roughly follows the glacial edge. Inside the Driftless Area of central Wisconsin, the streams carry a burden of sand and gravel that is outwash from the edge of the glacier. Within the former limits of the Wisconsin Drift of the Labrador Ice Sheet, the streams flow over a bed of gravel strewn with boulders that were rolled south by the terminal thrust of the glaciers. Some of our profiled streams meander over outwash sand and gravel, with silt at the margins where the trout lie in shadow; some streams reveal stretches of sand alternating with pitches around boulders. A few of them, such as the Little Wolf, rush downhill sporting and sparkling among the rocks and over ledges to the mighty Wolf River.

Going north from Westfield in northwestern Marquette County, the traveling fly-fisher will find a succession of productive streams: Lawrence, Caves, Tagatz, Chaffee, and Wedde Creeks, the Mecan River, Lunch Creek, the White River, Willow Creek, the Pine River, the Tomorrow/Waupaca, the several branches of the Little Wolf River, and the Lower Plover, plus many others of lesser reputation.

Waupaca County alone encompasses 40 trout streams that total 200 miles. Most of them support natural brook and brown trout. A handful, including the Crystal and Waupaca, are planted with rainbows.

We can't describe all of the many streams in the 11-county area, but we want you to know that many have been improved by the DNR with help from volunteer organizations through stretches owned by or under lease to the Wisconsin DNR. The Milwaukee Map Service map of southeastern Wisconsin indicates the DNR lands in overprinted blocks of green. A word to the wise, then: If you arrive at one of the streams not profiled, begin your exploration in the green lands, where the stream is usually small but improved, and generally productive of brook trout; then work downstream into the heavier water, which is the domain of larger brown trout.

LAWRENCE CREEK
DeLorme 43

Lawrence Creek in Marquette County, a popular stream, has been studied and improved under the direction of Robert L. Hunt, formerly of the Wisconsin Department of Natural Resources, for more than 30 years. Many of the in-stream structures first tested on Lawrence have since been used elsewhere. You'll never have it all to yourself during the trout season, but every devout fly-fisher should see it once, upstream of Lawrence Lake on Eagle Avenue about 3 miles west of Westfield, as an example of what can be done to improve habitat. There are about 4 miles of Category 2 water for naturally reproducing brook trout through those tailored waters above Lawrence Lake in Marquette County, including a bit in Adams County. There are two main access points: one on Eagle, 0.6 mile west of 2nd Drive, and a second on 1st Avenue. From the DNR lot on Eagle, this trail is broad to a footbridge and evidence of recent installation of brush mats.

This sweet creek is a place for light rods, fine leaders, small flies, and a stealthy approach from downstream. Avoid the weekends, if you can. Fish evenings or under overcast.

In recent years 6 or 7 miles below the lake and dam have been added to the list of designated trout waters, Category 3. Two springs issue at the site of the abandoned Dahlke brewery downstream of the dam.

Facilities for travelers at Westfield on US 51.

CHAFFEE AND WEDDE CREEKS
DeLorme 44 & 53

In the first edition of this book we had to pass these two streams with only a side glance due to the press of other work; but we did not forget them. In the spring of 2000 John Vollrath of Stevens Point took us to see a new 3-mile section of the 1,000-mile Ice Age Trail that follows Chaffee Creek. It is truly a place of beauty and a joy forever. Go with us.

Three and a half miles south of Colonna on US 51 take the off-ramp into a wayside. On the north edge of the parking area find a zigzag through a fence to the Ice Age Trail; it follows a ridgeline through a golden tallgrass meadow, then steps down through a scrim of trees to a footbridge over the creek. This is about the prettiest picnic spot you are likely to find, when the creek is tinkling over stones and the sun is laying patterns through the trees. Share it with your significant other. You may even spook a small brook trout in the corners. At the north edge of the bridge a spring burbles through sand like a thick sauce cooking on a stove, or like the paint pots at Yellowstone. Then follow the trail under the highway, or retreat and locate the continuation of the trail on the other side of the highway at the dead end of Dakota Avenue. (Find this in the upper left corner of DeLorme 44.)

From the Dakota dead end, a lane goes north to the creek. Here the creek winds through oak and pine barrens, so the going is fairly easy and exceedingly photogenic. Youngsters from the Rawhide Boys Ranch worked for two days in the rain to open the 3 miles. Downstream and east of County Road B you will be in the Chaffee Creek State Fishery Area, and as the stream strengthens it just gets better to our eyes until it attains perfection on County Road Z, just west of County Road Y. Here the stream meanders so tightly that it almost coils in on itself. It is deep, narrow, and cold, with many old structures. Fish it prayerfully, on the knees, preferably at the end of day or under cloud. A fine show of caddisflies was laying eggs between 10 AM and 2 PM on April 22, and a few elusive brookies were picking them off. Chaffee Creek, the upper 3 miles in Waushara County and 10 in Marquette, is a tributary of the Mecan, and Wedde Creek is a tributary of Chaffee. Wedde pleased us less, but no doubt some anglers will view it differently.

And that leaves Caves and Tagazt and Lunch Creeks, et al., for another day; or for you to find and cherish.

THE MECAN RIVER
DeLorme 44 & 53

Tread carefully the sandy track of the Mecan in lower Waushara County and upper Marquette—you may hook up with something that you can't handle on a fly rod or anything else. In May 1994 anglers or canoeists reported seeing a hippopotamus in the Mecan River. Crazy! said DNR personnel, but they had to investigate, eventually, to find a dead hippo being winched out of the river at the business end of a pickup.

It seems that the camel let the hippo out of his corral at a game farm, and the hippo hightailed it for the water to frolic. Every time the owner of the game farm tried to lasso the hippo, the happy beast swam downriver. Finally the owner shot it and winched it out.

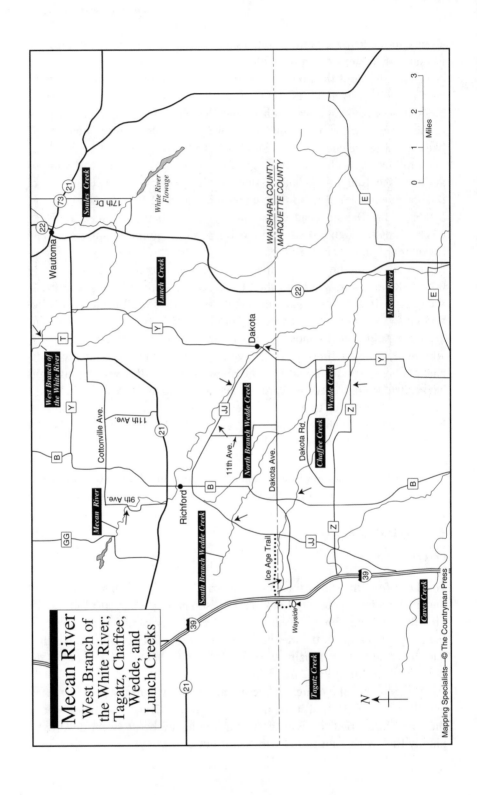

Mecan River
West Branch of the White River; Tagatz, Chaffee, Wedde, and Lunch Creeks

Soules Creek

White River Flowage

17th Dr.

Wautoma

Lunch Creek

West Branch of the White River

Mecan River

Cottonville Ave.

11th Ave.

9th Ave.

Richford

Dakota

North Branch Wedde Creek

11th Ave.

Dakota Ave.

Dakota Rd.

Wedde Creek

Chaffee Creek

South Branch Wedde Creek

Ice Age Trail

Wayside

Tagatz Creek

Caves Creek

Mecan River

WAUSHARA COUNTY
MARQUETTE COUNTY

N

Miles
0 1 2 3

Mapping Specialists—© The Countryman Press

JOYCE HUMPHREY

Jim Humphrey nymphs upstream on the Mecan River at the JJ access. Is there a hippo lurking under the bank cover?

The Mecan is a sand stream some 17 miles long, from Mecan Springs (6,700 gallons per minute) downstream to WI 22, one of those rivers that received outwash from the glacier. It has been improved with wing dams and other structures at a number of locations. There is easy access on DNR lands along County Road JJ upstream from the village of Dakota, at the bridge on 11th Avenue, and up from Richford at 9th Avenue in the state fishery area. Or you can check the outlet of the springs at County Road GG. In 1998 the Perrier water company asked to pump and bottle water from Mecan Springs. The company was denied but is now looking elsewhere in the area. All for something that a thirsty person can get out of a faucet!

Approximately 12 miles at the upper end are rated Category 3; the lower 5 miles are Category 5. All three species of trout are reported to be naturally reproducing, although we wouldn't stake our lives on the likelihood of catching a native rainbow.

The Mecan is reputed to produce a hatch of *Hexagenia* on late-June and early-July nights.

Facilities for travelers at Wautoma.

THE WEST BRANCH OF THE WHITE RIVER
DeLorme 53

The West Branch of the White River, west of Wautoma in Waushara County, is favored by fly-fishers for many miles around. Although not much more than 5 miles long above its junction with the White River proper, and not wide, it has been rated first-class by the DNR. Our favorite access is at County Road T, 3 miles west of Wautoma, where there is a DNR parking area. A second recommended entry is on the main White River, at the bridge on 17th Drive and Cottonville Lane, 3 miles south of Wautoma. You can fish upstream to the junction of the two streams through some very enticing water. There is DNR parking just above the bridge off 17th Drive. Downstream is the head of the flowage, which will be difficult wading for more than a short distance, but we recall one August evening when a very large trout gulped a very large something at the surface only a few yards below the bridge. That one refused our several oversized mayfly artificials; nevertheless, it was a heart-pounding experience, and we have that brown marked for a return engagement. The nighttime Hex appears on the river, usually toward the end of June and early July.

The West Branch, Category 2, open May 6 through September 30, contains the three species of wild trout; the main stem has natural browns and rainbows.

Complete facilities for travelers at Wautoma.

WILLOW CREEK
DeLorme 53

Willow Creek in Waushara County is one of those anomalies that we have mentioned elsewhere. Although called a creek, it is larger than many rivers. About 10 miles of water, from the origin just east of WI 22, 2 miles south of Wild Rose, to the bridge on Blackhawk Road south and east of Mount Morris, are granted a first-class rating. The next 10 miles down to the Auroraville millpond are somewhat less productive, but all of Willow Creek contains native brooks and natural browns. Brook trout will dominate the upper half, where it is rated Category 2; the lower half, Category 3, will cough up some decent browns. There is a state fishery area in each section, but we prefer the open stream at the bridge where County Roads S and Z intersect 2 miles north of WI 21, particularly during grasshopper time. There is also easy access upstream to DNR parking on the east side of the creek along 24th Road, where the water runs slow and smooth. The mud banks signal the possibility of a Hex hatch.

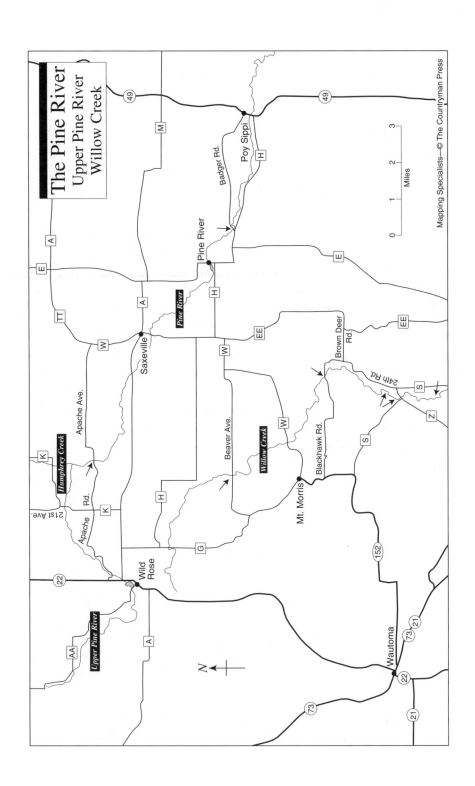

The Pine River
Upper Pine River
Willow Creek

Mapping Specialists—© The Countryman Press

Miles
0 1 2 3

N

However, you may choose to begin upstream in the green DNR lands marked on the Milwaukee Map Service map, at 21st Drive or Badger Court. Another entry is at the bridge on Beaver Avenue.

Facilities at Wild Rose, Wautoma, and Redgranite.

THE PINE RIVER
DeLorme 53

Wild Rose has long been a staging point for fly-fishers. You can fish Willow Creek and the Pine River and its several feeders, including Humphrey Creek (no relation).

The Pine River begins as the Upper Pine west of Wild Rose in Waushara County; drifts through town, where it becomes the Pine River; loops north through DNR lands, where it picks up volume from three cold feeders; then meanders southeast through Saxeville to Poy Sippi. Its approximately 20 miles contain wild native brook and naturally reproducing brown trout. The best fly-fishing will be found from the north loop on County Road K in DNR lands and on down to Saxeville. You can also reach the DNR lands from Apache Road. It was in this section that a 27-inch brown was creeled recently.

We've fished the Pine as far down as County Highway H and 28th Court, but with indifferent success at that end. The bed there is thick sand with little in-stream cover. If there's any action, it will occur on an early-season evening, or possibly in the late season with terrestrials.

From Wild Rose down, the stream is rated Category 3, with a daily bag limit of three trout of 9 inches or longer.

The three reference maps we've used to define the Pine disagree as to the names of the feeder creeks. We judge the DeLorme map to be the most accurate.

Facilities at Wild Rose.

The Streams of Waupaca and Stevens Point

East of the city of Waupaca in Waupaca County you will note three small streams that join the Tomorrow/Waupaca close to the city. Emmons Creek is notable for a fall run of spawning brown trout from the Waupaca Chain O'Lakes. Trout to 7 pounds have been taken in September. Alas, on our last visit to Emmons we had difficulty finding open stretches of stream on which to ply our art. Emmons Creek has its primary source in Fountain Lake, which has all the appearance of a remote spring pond, but the lake is not listed as a trout lake. The creek, beginning below a small dam, has the look of prime brook trout habitat, though it's shallow and brushy at the head. There is a public lot a bit more than 2 miles east on Emmons Creek Road, but there again the fly-fishing is spotty. Roadside access is also available on Rustic Road 24, where we met a pair of anglers coming out from the downstream reach, which did appear to be wadeable. They volunteered that this was brown trout water; the brook trout were farther upstream. They also admitted to not having much of a day, although we didn't get a peek into their creels. At last report the state of Wisconsin owned 1,050 acres along the creek.

RADLEY CREEK

DeLorme 53

Radley Creek (and its tributary, Murry Creek) is another story—a grand one, we think. Although a fisher could begin at Suhs Road, 1 mile east of West Dayton Road, we like to begin on WI 22, below the junction of Radley and Murry. Here there is an off-road lot and a likely trail upstream through abandoned fields. Then, if you want to try downstream, go south on WI 22

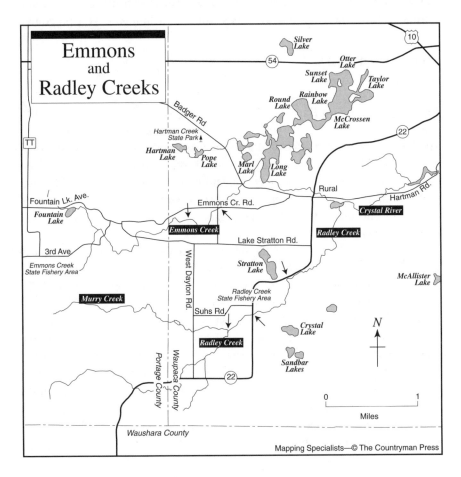

a hop, step, and a jump, then east on Radley Road to the second access auto lane (bypass the first access and lot, which is for hunters). The 0.3-mile trail going north to the river from Radley Road ends at a turnaround where the river margins are soggy and the wading through brush may be tricky, but productive.

If you are not an explorer, go quickly north and east on WI 22 to the Radley Creek Fishery Area and parking lot. This long section is about as welcoming as a Wisconsin trout stream gets. Downstream there are old structures and deep holes that hold large trout; upstream through an old field is wading water through a mix of riffles and runs. As you wade upstream, the highway rises away from the river and the slope is thick with old white pines. There is a walk-in east from Stratton Lake Road where the brush closes in once more.

The Crystal River is a canoeists' paradise that runs through the village of Rural, with its graceful and elegant 19th-century homes, most of them on the National Register of Historic Places, a tea shoppe, a bed & breakfast, and a village store where Sunday visitors savor old-fashioned ice cream cones.

THE TOMORROW/WAUPACA RIVER
DeLorme 53 & 65

Many years ago Vern Hacker, a former fish manager for the Wisconsin DNR, told Humphrey that the Tomorrow/Waupaca River could be the premier trout stream in the state if Nelsonville Dam was removed. In 1984 the DNR bought the dam and removed several of the planks, but the sill that remained impeded full flow and complete drainage of the greasy old pond. In 1988 the removal was completed and the river began to heal. As we note elsewhere and often, these low-head dams create ponds that become heat sumps in summer.

Subsequently, because of the potential for the Tomorrow to become a blue-ribbon trout stream, the river has been under intense management and rehabilitation by the DNR with help from the Frank Hornberg Chapter of TU, which is centered at Stevens Point, together with other chapters. One aspect of the management is the careful, almost exquisite, application of categories and regulations. We could reprise the rules in detail here, but they well may change as the managers and biologists gain insight into the changing functions of the river. Currently, two separate categories apply to several sections, and segments of the river are not open for the early season. In short, for this stream you must read the regulations listed under both Portage and Waupaca Counties. Regulations on many trout streams will change over time, resulting in an improved experience for you.

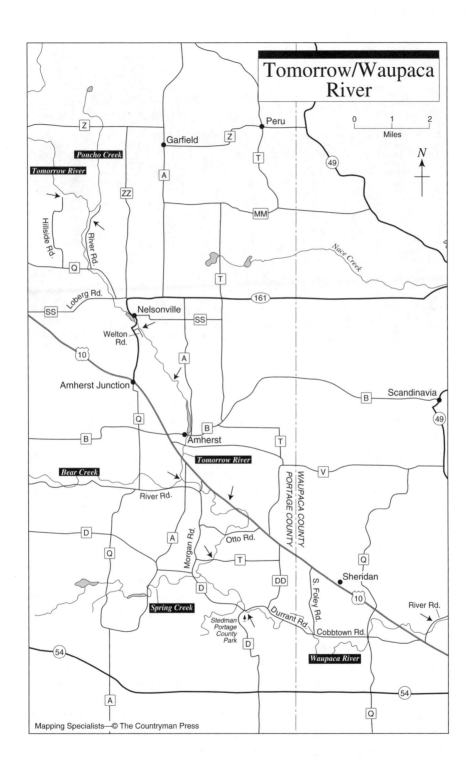

Tomorrow/Waupaca River

JIM HUMPHREY

Rehab work on the Tomorrow River

The river rises north and east of Stevens Point in Portage County. At County Road OO it is much too small and brushy to fish; the first recommended entry is on River Road on the east side of the river upstream from County Road Q. The Richard A. Hemp State Fishery Area is about 1 mile north of County Road Q. We have had remarkable success there catching and releasing bright little native brook trout, with an occasional brown to whet the appetite. Only a few yards north of the fishery parking lot you'll find a short trail that ends at an abandoned farm bridge. Upstream is narrow and deep; you'll have to fish from the banks, which have been brushed back in recent years. This is not easy fishing; you will find downstream somewhat easier, where wading is possible in spots. Cast to the edges with artificials only for your limit of one 10-inch brook trout or one 14-inch brown. Not enough for breakfast, but you practice catch-and-release in any case.

Access is also possible from the west side at Echo Road. Take Hillside Road for a mile north of County Road Q, then head east on Echo to a corner. The old trail is now fenced there, so you may have to walk half a mile or so to the river. It was easy and open there on our last trip.

Next down from the Richard Hemp area is the Clementson Road bridge, with easier wading down through shallower water over a gravel bottom. From here down to First Stream in Nelsonville the category is 4, and this section is open for the early season. About the second week of June we found a satisfactory hatch of sulphurs at the bridge. Next comes the County Road Q bridge—posted upstream and posted on the west side downstream, but wadeable from the east bank. There are deadfalls and sweepers that can be negotiated by experienced fly-fishers through this picturesque stretch.

We have taken brook and brown trout upstream from the Loberg Road bridge through some beautiful wading water over gravel.

Rising Star Mill at Nelsonville downstream is now a community art center with the river flowing placidly through a parklike setting. The drained land above the mill is private, but you should be able to fish the stream between the high-water marks without trespass. Of course, the best procedure is to politely ask the landowner for permission to walk the bank.

Immediately south of Nelsonville on County Road SS you should find Welton Road, a dead end running east to the river. First there's an auto trail to a DNR and TU work site. At the curve there is a second lot large enough for several cars. If the ground is soft, check the access. An honorable fly-fisher who shall remain nameless grounded his four-wheel drive in the corner lot and had to be rescued by a friendly farmer with a tractor. This section has been improved with many days of hard hand and back labor. Brain labor, too! Riprap and brush bundles have been installed to narrow and speed the currents, and to provide habitat for young trout and aquatic insects. On my last trip I did not float a fly: I spent all my time admiring the works of our TU friends and the DNR. Significant sections of the river from Nelsonville downstream to Waupaca are under special regulations that are too elaborate to summarize here.

Wandering south along US 10, we particularly like that lovely, wadeable stretch downstream from the County Road A bridge, south of Amherst and on the west side of US 10. Then, between River Road on the west of US 10 and Buchholz Road east of US 10, if you look closely, you'll see a short Keener Road. The pool and riffle downstream hold some very large brown trout, if you're skilled enough to tease them out. You may have to go deep with a sinking line or even a section of lead core in front of a stub tippet. Downstream from County Road A there is a variety of venues where on a darkling late-June or early-July evening you may encounter the Hex lumbering off the pool. At the turn to August you may find the white fly, *Ephoron,* patrolling the surface.

We have parked on the west shoulder farther south on 10, just north of the former Wayside, where giant black and giant brown stoneflies inhabit the riffles prior to a June 1 crawl to emerge on the shore. Farther south on US 10, take Otto Road west to the bridge; the stream is narrow but open over a cobble bottom. Then go west to Morgan, south on Morgan, and double back east on County Road K. Here, in all its new glory at County Road K bridge, is the center of a 4,000-foot section that has been extensively and intensively rehabbed under the direction of Al Neibur, DNR regional fisheries biologist. Members of four TU chapters participated in the installation of boulders, lunker structures, half-logs, root stumps, and fencing to restrain cattle. It is really a remarkable project that ought to inspire other fisherpersons to go and do likewise.

Humphrey always pauses at Stedman County Park on County Road D (at its intersection with County Road DD) to admire the view or to take lunch, but the bottom is boulder strewn and wading is difficult. Go south on Durrant Road from County Road DD to the first bridge. On one fine summer evening he met three fishermen who volunteered that the upstream path on the right side led to some good holes for large brown trout. He noted, though, that they went downstream to fish. However, Jim returned the next day and surprised several colorful browns upstream of the bridge in tiptoe water, which means that you must wear chest-high waders and search over a sand bottom for holding water at the margins, in the riffles, or within deadfall.

Durrant ends at its intersection of Cobbtown Road and Foley Road. Half a mile north of the intersection on Foley you'll find parking for access to the new 1,000-mile-long Ice Age Trail. For Humphrey, this is a newfound treasure where he hikes into history to practice an ageless art.

The hunt for trout downstream is a dubious proposition, for the river widens, deepens, and warms. There are large brown trout there, but you will have to work hard for them at fewer access points. There are differences of opinion among anglers. Some believe that the lower river is satisfactory for their search for trout; some have expressed derogatory opinions of the lower river. The Tomorrow/Waupaca is not yet as good as Vern Hacker hoped it would become, but it is improved, and improving. Now, if we could only get rid of the Amherst flowage, another shallow pond and heat sump in the village of Amherst. The dam also prevents the migration of young trout from upstream into larger waters down. But the dam removal is resisted by local residents who like to look out over still waters of an evening.

If you study your maps you will see Bear Creek and Spring Creek, which join the Tomorrow in Portage County between Amherst and Stedman Park. We've done the exploration and have found no fly-fishing places, although wading anglers may fish the shallows of Adams Lake at the head of Bear Creek. There is a public landing west of County Road K. Tubers might fare better.

All facilities for travelers at Waupaca or at Stevens Point.

PETERSON CREEK
DeLorme 53

Peterson Creek, a small Category 2 stream, rises in west central Waupaca County. It is included here because it is typical of many of the smaller brook trout streams in central Wisconsin that have been improved by a local chapter of TU. Find it about 7 miles east of Amherst (Portage County) on County Road V where it intersects with Gurholt Road. About half a mile north take Gilman Road to a gravel road to a Public Hunting and Fishing Ground. Upstream is negotiable for a way for anglers who prefer the short rod and fine leaders for small wild trout. A second landing is on Jensen Road just south of County Road V and east of Gurholt Road. The Frank Hornberg Chapter has worked there on 750 feet of stream, installing wing dams, brush bundles, and matting, resulting in increased spawning and a concentration of useful aquatic insects.

Facilities at Amherst.

THE SOUTH BRANCH OF THE LITTLE WOLF RIVER
DeLorme 53

Peterson Creek feeds into Sand Creek and thence into the South Branch of the Little Wolf River near the junction of WI 49 and County Road V just south of the village of Scandinavia in Waupaca County. The approximately 13 miles of the South Branch, Category 3, from Iola on the north, through Scandinavia, over WI 49 to the termination of the designated trout water at West Waupaca Road, contain wild brown trout, and according to local advice you may run into some bass.

Acceptable access points aren't frequent in sections of the stream best suited for fly-fishing, so we suggest the second bridge south on Elm Valley Road, below the junction with Blueberry Road, which comes in from the north. The bridge is approximately 6 miles north of Waupaca. Go downstream on the right-hand side through abandoned pasture. We'd fish it here, moving cautiously, with a slack cast. It's the kind of place we thoroughly enjoy early morning, early or late evening, or under overcast skies or in a light rain. If thunder booms in the sky, exchange your graphite rod for bamboo to ward off the lightning, but don't get your hopes up. Our experience is that thunder puts down the trout.

The third bridge south promises action upstream and down. Both directions are fairly open. Upstream you'll see the buttresses of an abandoned bridge. The narrows around old bridges are always productive. A few large trees lean over the downstream section—place your terrestrials in under the trees.

Facilities at Waupaca and Iola.

FLUME CREEK
DeLorme 65

Flume Creek in Portage and Waupaca Counties, a tributary of the Little Wolf River, is a first-class stream that supports natural reproduction of brook and brown trout throughout its 18 miles. It has a Category 3 rating. It rises above Rosholt north of WI 66, but the section we enjoy is that around the bridges of Lund Road and Ness Road, both east of WI 49 and a tad south of County Road C. Upstream of Ness the stream is open and knee-deep over sand and silt. A more adventurous fly-fisher may prefer deep and difficult wading up from Lund in a rocky stream where some holes are over her head. Bill nailed the brookies there on a Pass Lake.

At Northland, a cluster of three or four buildings on WI 49 west of Lund, you'll find a small park, a picnic table, an old iron footbridge, and 1,800 feet of meadow stream through what was once a millpond above a 100-year-old mill. In 1987 the dam was removed down to the sill, which still held back a 3-foot head. In 1990 the sill was taken out and the stream began to cut a channel through the silt. In an early electro-fishing survey only 100 trout were counted in the old bed. In 1996 a DNR crew began extensive rehabilitation. Boulders were placed, wedge dams and bank covers installed. It's possible that the DNR may clear a path through the easement, but on our last trip it was necessary to get into the stream and wade up over sand and fine gravel. We will return to that charming reach, but not on a hot, bright day. One of our advisers suggests that spring fishing is better than summer; and isn't that often the way of it? Downstream the river closes in through brush over gravel, sand, and rocks toward Lund and Ness crossings.

Facilities at Iola, an interesting town where many specialist magazines are printed.

THE LITTLE WOLF RIVER
DeLorme 65

The Little Wolf River is a heart's delight for a fly-fisher who looks for that typical western-style freestone stream. For most of its length of some 24 miles, from southeastern Marathon County through the northeast corner of Portage County to Big Falls in Waupaca County, it rattles around rocks and riffles over gravel. By no means is it the most productive stream in central

Wisconsin, but certainly it is one of the most beautiful. At the upper end it contains wild brown trout; at the lower, natural brooks and planted browns. For most of its length it is Category 4. A segment in Waupaca County is under special regulations.

We begin our fly-fishing on Wigwam Road about a quarter mile east of WI 49, in extreme northeastern Portage County, where Wigwam makes a sharp right-hand bend. A sign there takes you to parking for three or four cars; then follow the foot trail less than an eighth of a mile to the river. It may be only 20 feet wide and it will test your wading and fly-casting skills, but you must revel in the sight and sound of a tinkling freestone stream.

There is an indication of another Wisconsin Public Hunting and Fishing Ground at the east end of Wigwam Road, but we can't recommend it. An old tote road or trail curves from the turnaround to the river, but the land is posted and we never recommend trespass. Bypassing the posted trail is virtually impossible.

Return to WI 49; go south to County Road C, then east, then north on Ness Road—we've been here before in our profile of Flume Creek—to the Little Wolf River Fishery Area at a corner where Ness Road strikes north again. Perhaps three cars can squeeze into the lot. A short walk takes you to the river where it runs sweet and golden over gravel. There is one deep pool on the right, with a promising root wad, then downstream is a long, variegated run. The river here isn't much wider than it was upstream, but it was another visual delight on our day, with the sun slanting through the trees, the water shimmering, and, downstream through a tunnel of trees, the promise of trout taking our dry flies.

Back in the car again, go north on Ness to Little Wolf River Road. Traveling east, find the next access at Wrolstad Road, a south spur off meandering Little Wolf River Road. And this is worth another digression. Several years ago there was a short canoe carry from the east spur at the end of Wrolstad Road. On our last visit, a trailer house with a cropped lawn had obliterated the canoe trail. Consternation! That is a magnificent stretch of water, wide and wadeable among the boulders. Fortunately, now you can take the west spur to DNR parking at the turnaround and, on the south side of the road, a sign announcing PUBLIC ACCESS. The access is so new that there is no well-defined trail. Make your own trail for less than 100 yards to some fine fly-fishing water. Good luck to you, or good skill, as the case may be. Our hearts fell when we saw that the canoe trail had disappeared, but we feel better now. We assume that a 10-year easement had run out, but our friends from the DNR have arranged for another.

Our last stop takes us to another DNR parking lot, at the junction of County Roads C and J. An easy trail follows the Little Wolf on the north bank to the slab rocks and rapids above. We've fished over this complex bottom on numerous occasions, as have many of our friends. We've picked up respectable brown trout, but on a recent June day Jason Carpenter, a friend and fly-fishing guide from Missouri, reported the catch and release of a dozen brook trout taken during daylight.

Forget about it downstream of the bridge. It is narrow, very deep, and ends in a gorge and rapids that are best reserved for kayakers and expert canoeists.

The Little Wolf River, sometimes called the North Branch of the Little Wolf—but by any name a rose is a rose—is not an easy stream to fish. It is a miniature Wolf River, with some easy wading over gravel, but also more difficult stretches that will tax the ingenuity of any fly-fisher. It is a stream to which we return in the hope that eventually all of its secrets will be revealed. And isn't that the essence of trout fishing?

Facilities for travelers at Iola and Stevens Point.

THE LOWER PLOVER RIVER
DeLorme 65 & 77

We might call the Lower Plover one of our "sleepers." It is not celebrated in the literature of trout streams of the Midwest, nor do any of our friends whisper of its magic in our ears. You will find a profile of the Upper Plover in chapter 5 ("Northeastern Wisconsin"). The division between the Upper and Lower Plover is arbitrary. The Upper, celebrated by Bill Shogren, can be reached from Antigo on the north or from Wausau on the west; the Lower, of a size and configuration Humphrey prefers, is only half an hour's drive from Stevens Point.

This is a long river of some 26 miles, and in the lower reaches, a wide one. It rises in Langlade County and flows through the upper two-thirds of Marathon County to the village of Bevent on WI 153, the lower end of the designated trout water. Trout are also planted at Stevens Point between Jordan Park and US 10.

We'll travel the route upstream from the bridge on Bevent Drive, 1.5 miles west of County Road Y and south of WI 153. This is outside the designated trout water, and you will wonder why. Here the river is more than 100 feet wide, and there are deadheads, islands, sandbars, and rocks. And on our last visit, caddis were swarming and what appeared to be trout were rising for as far upstream as we could see. (They may have been chubs.) At the bridge three young men were picking huge crayfish in the shallows. We have had some spectacular fishing in the heavier, warmer waters of Wisconsin with a crayfish imitation. Your imitation should not exceed $1\frac{1}{2}$ inches in length: For some strange reason the larger versions will not attract

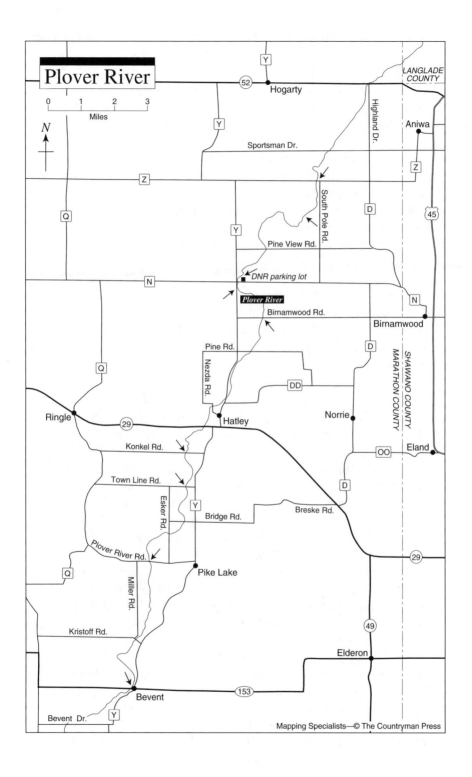

Plover River

0   1   2   3
Miles

N

Langlade County

Aniwa

Hogarty

52

Y

Y

Sportsman Dr.

Highland Dr.

Z

Z

45

Q

D

South Pole Rd.

Y

Pine View Rd.

N

DNR parking lot

Plover River

N

Birnamwood Rd.

Birnamwood

Pine Rd.

D

Nezda Rd.

DD

Q

Shawano County
Marathon County

Ringle

29

Hatley

Norrie

Eland

OO

Konkel Rd.

Town Line Rd.

Esker Rd.

Y

Bridge Rd.

Breske Rd.

D

Plover River Rd.

Q

Pike Lake

Miller Rd.

29

Kristoff Rd.

49

Elderon

Bevent

153

Bevent Dr.

Y

Mapping Specialists—© The Countryman Press

large brown trout. Perhaps the defensive mechanisms of 4-inch crayfish are too formidable.

Upstream in the village of Bevent there is parking on the northwest side of the bridge. The river is rocky and wadeable, with a good riffle downstream making for a fine fly-fishing reach. It will be more difficult wading up.

Next up is the Kristoff Road bridge, with gravel, cobble, and boulders downstream, rocks and deadfall up. On our last visit, during the second week of June, a spinner flight of sulphurs hung over the bridge. The males rose high overhead, then spread their wings and dove straight down into the mass. Birds came out of the tops of trees to pick off the mayflies. The brown trout, no doubt, were waiting impatiently for the spinners to fall at dark. But we had to continue our survey, alas! The Plover is rumored to produce hatches of brown drakes in late June and early July, and tricos around July 1. The *Hexagenia* come alive on sultry late-June and early-July nights in the upper river.

At Plover River Road the trout were feeding greedily upstream, possibly on a spinner fall. "Wow!" is the exclamation that slipped out. "Look at them!" And not another fisherman in sight.

This is spectacular fly-fishing water. It's 60 feet wide, smooth water with overhanging brush along the banks upstream, and perfect wading around boulders down.

Scratch the Esker Road bridge; there is wire across the stream.

At Bridge Road you'll find pretty water over bedrock. Downstream is your best bet, through channels, around islands, and into the pockets.

The Town Line Road bridge area is open, rocky, nice, but deep and tough to wade.

At Konkel Road there's a Wisconsin Public Hunting and Fishing Ground. The easiest action will be downstream, where you will need waders, and you may have to loop out onto the west bank from time to time.

We recommend that you skip the several bridges in Hatley on WI 29, although we found brookies feeding right through town.

Next up is the Pine Road bridge east of County Road Y. On the southeast side of the bridge a residence shows a fine, sheared lawn to a riprapped edge. Utterly charming, but we don't like to fish through somebody's front yard. Upstream is another story. At least 50 trout were feeding around islands and among rocks through clear, cold water. The bottom rocks are smooth, requiring felt soles. Use light tackle, because these are mostly brook trout, but we did find one large trout feeding on the west bank in a side pocket—a brown, we discovered. In 1995 the DNR began rehab work around Birnamwood Road with the intent of improving both access and the fishery between WI 29 and County Road Z. With the aid of four TU chapters, 5,100 feet of stream were improved: channel narrowed, boulders placed, bank covers and half-logs installed.

And now we come to County Road N, about 15 miles east of Wausau. For some of you this may be paradise. Both wild brook trout and large native browns are the product of these immaculate waters. It is a location that Humphrey lost many years ago, and now has found again. You could conclude that this is the end of the Lower Plover and the beginning of the Upper Plover. No matter. It is absolutely magnificent.

There is a Wisconsin DNR Public Hunting and Fishing Ground with parking northeast of the County Road N bridge. The river is wadeable, although not easy, for a space downstream from Pine View Road, and from an auto trail north of Pine View going east from County Road Y; and another south of County Road Z on the west side of the river. Shogren played with the brookies there.

Those of you who cherish native brook trout, with a few browns thrown in for good measure, can proceed upstream into the quality water of the Upper Plover. Those who are after brown trout can work upstream from Bevent or downstream from County Road N. The brooks and browns are naturally reproducing; there may also be some planted rainbows.

Three categories apply here: The upper few miles are Category 2; a short section is posted for Category 5; and the remainder is Category 4.

You won't find a more varied river anywhere. You pays your money and you takes your choice.

Facilities at Stevens Point, Wausau, and Antigo.

THE DITCHES OF WISCONSIN RAPIDS
DeLorme 52

If you will examine your *Wisconsin Trout Fishing Regulations and Guide* for Portage and Wood Counties you will note a curious pattern of streams—a pattern not repeated elsewhere. South of Stevens Point and east of Wisconsin Rapids you'll find a series of parallel ditches running east to west, all Category 2–designated trout streams.

This peculiar arrangement piqued our curiosity, so we had to investigate. Long ago this outwash flatland may have been a prairie laced with sinuous streams and spotted with marsh. Possibly the flat was covered with dwarf oak and pine. The early maps we have studied do not tell us precisely.

In the early days of the 20th century, when every flatland was being drained for cropland, the streams were straightened and small diversion dams were added for irrigation. Aldo Leopold, author of the revered *Sand County Almanac*, called the period from 1910 to 1920 "the decade of the drainage dream." Since then the land has been intensively farmed through a succession of crops, with some range given over to cattle. Currently hay, corn, sod, mint, and potatoes are produced, although a very large area has been acquired by the state for prairie chicken habitat and booming grounds. Lately, cranberry producers have developed 4,200 acres on the site of the onetime Buena Vista and Leola Marshes, with 3,000 acres planned. Cranberry bogs do not contribute to healthy trout streams.

The majority of these ditches hold naturally reproducing brook trout; a lesser number contain planted brown trout. The lower ends of several of them were never ditched, or they have reverted to a more natural state, winding and brush lined. The best advice to trout fishers comes from a resident who fishes the ditches early and often. He says you should fish the ditches just below the diversion dams, but be there early in the morning or the trout will have been fished out by earlier risers. One knowledgeable lady angler recommended Ditch 6.

We have examined Five Mile, Seven Mile, and Ten Mile Creeks, the lower ends of several of the ditches, for short distances above their junctions with the Wisconsin River. There is fair habitat for both trout and fly-fishers, and even a Category 5 section on the last stretch of Ten Mile Creek, but in general we'd not grant any of them a high priority. Buena Vista Creek, downstream of Ditches 1 and 2, is planted to brown trout annually—600 of legal size per year is typical—but we suspect that they are snapped up by anglers from Wisconsin Rapids during the early weeks of the season.

In short, there are too many better streams in the area for you to waste your time on the ditches, but we knew that you'd be curious, as we were. Our duty demands that we sometimes tell you which streams to avoid.

Facilities at Wisconsin Rapids and Stevens Point.

BIG ROCHE-A-CRI CREEK
DeLorme 52

The Big Roche-A-Cri, a tributary of the Wisconsin River, rises near US 51 in western Waushara County and flows approximately 16 miles through northern Adams County. The nearest city of any size is Wisconsin Rapids to the north. The village of Friendship, near Little Roche-A-Cri, Fordham Creek, and Roche-A-Cri State Park, is south of the lower end of the creek on WI 13. This is all flat country, so you won't find much in the way of tumbling rapids and rippling riffles.

Fly-fishers, like everyone else, develop prejudices in favor of some streams and against others, often as a result of subtle effects rather than because of the numbers of trout taken. Our favorites include the Kinnickinnic, the Wolf, and the Namekagon of Wisconsin, and Trout Run and the

South Branch of the Whitewater in southeastern Minnesota, each for different reasons that are more emotional than physical.

The ambience is all, for some of us. Some like the wild and rough Wolf; other fishers become ecstatic when searching the pockets of a brook trout stream like Tiffany or the Upper Plover.

Big Roche-A-Cri, Categories 2 and 3, is a perfectly respectable stream, but we don't like it. The upper 6 miles above County Road W contain wild brook trout, and browns are planted down to Roche-A-Cri Lake. Why don't we like it? "Sullen" would be the adjective to apply if it were human. It's slow, narrow, deep, and murky, and drains some of the most unprepossessing flatlands ever seen. Downstream from County Road W it's also unduly posted against trespass, by folks whose small holdings are littered with the rusted hulks of cars and other assorted junk. There is a state fishery area west of US 51 in northwest Waushara County and a mile north of County Road O that might intrigue some of you.

Little Roche-A-Cri to the south has wild brook trout; Fordham Creek's 6 miles are reputed to hold wild brooks, browns, and rainbows. Wild rainbows are a rarity in interior streams, so Fordham is worth a look, although access is limited.

Facilities at Friendship, Wautoma, and Wisconsin Rapids.

THE LITTLE PLOVER RIVER
DeLorme 52 & 53

The Little Plover, which joins the Wisconsin River at Whiting, a suburb of Stevens Point, is a tiny Category 2 stream about 3 miles in length, containing naturally reproducing brook trout. It's sweet and petite from Kennedy Avenue downstream to a bit west of US 51. It runs through the Little Plover River Park at Hoover Avenue, the site of intensive rehabilitation by students from SPASH, Stevens Point Area Senior High. If you look closely in the park stretch, you'll find brush bundles to narrow the stream and speed the flow, and riprap of round stones covered with dirt and seed. It is an example of the work that can be accomplished by ordinary folks with educated guidance from the Wisconsin DNR fish managers.

If you have an opportunity to work on a stream under the direction of a DNR fish manager, seize it. It may be even more exhilarating than catching and releasing a trout.

5 | Northeastern Wisconsin: The Wilderness

Northeastern Wisconsin covers a vast area and contains a glorious variety of topography, flora, and stream profiles. It includes the gracious and well-named Prairie River on the west, the huge, wild, rocky, and dangerous Wolf above Langlade, and to the east the enormous tailwaters of the Peshtigo below Johnson Falls Reservoir near Crivitz. In the far northeast near the Michigan border you may search for brook trout in the inner reaches of the Pike, Pine, Popple, and Pemebonwon, rivers that twist through remote and tangled wilderness. The eastern Brule, which separates Wisconsin from the Upper Peninsula, is a big river and a photogenic masterpiece.

There is a stream for every taste or persuasion, from open meadow to secret silver rivulet at the end of a lonely trail through jackpine stands and blackberry brambles. You can't experience the spectrum of streams in this area in a day; even a week won't suffice. And we can't tell you all that we know in the pages allotted. Some streams and rivers we've fished intensively; others have received only cursory attention. We must leave it to you to discover some treasures of your own.

Jim Humphrey recalls his first look at the North Branch of the Pike: "It remains one of the clearest memories of my fishing life. I was standing at the top of Eighteen Foot Falls with my 8-foot, 9-weight bamboo bass rod in hand and some kind of attractor dangling from a stout leader. Upstream for as far as I could see, perhaps 100 yards, the glide was spackled with the rings of rising, feeding trout—and me a novice, or novitiate more properly, without the least idea how I could coax them to strike. I was smart enough to know when I was licked, so I went down to the foot of the falls and winkled out a brace of trout with a small streamer. That was 40 years ago, when I was enamored of bass and not yet hooked on fly-fishing for trout.

"I hope that I know a bit more about trout fishing now, and I know that the falls pounds down from the heights. I suspect that the trout will still confound even an expert."

We'll come back to the far northeast later on in this survey.

Seven Streams of the Antigo Area

Bill Shogren recommends that you establish your initial base at Antigo in Langlade County while we wade you through the first collection of streams at the southern end of the northeast section of Wisconsin. Bill, who likes the companionship of a few fly-fishing friends, says that you could send members of your party out in several directions for a variety of experiences, then share tall tales at the end of a day.

During the dog days of August this area of Wisconsin offers wonderful trout fishing. Daytimes, you can fish the fabulous Prairie River, the East and West Branches of the Eau Claire, and the Upper Plover. At night in early August the best game out of town is the white fly hatch on the Wolf or the Prairie. Big Hay Meadow Creek, a tributary of the Prairie, offers superb wade fishing all day long and into the evening. "Get your fishing buddies and head for Antigo, Wisconsin," Shogren advises. "There are ample accommodations at reasonable prices, and the variety of streams offers fishing for every type of trout fisher—the old, the young, experienced and inexperienced, all can catch trout."

THE PRAIRIE RIVER

DeLorme 76 & 77

GLEASON, THE TROUT FISHING CAPITAL OF THE WORLD. The sign is weathered, a relic of Babbitt boosterism perhaps, but on a June evening when the air is alive with the flutter of mayfly wings, when a great brown trout bangs at a #10 White Wulff and pops the leader on his second leap, we can believe, almost, that Gleason may be in the running for that exalted title.

The sign dates back 40 or 50 years, when the Prairie was a renowned stream. Then the deterioration began, perhaps from the warming of water due to the gradual silting in of Prairie Dell Pond, perhaps as a result of poor farming practices and other development along the river. Perhaps it was only that the big trout were pounded to death by experts casting three wet flies by night.

The Prairie River rises in wild, cutover, sand-and-bog country in northeastern Langlade County and lazes in a southwesterly direction through Lincoln County for more than 40 miles to join the Wisconsin River at Merrill. The Prairie is a big river, averaging 64 feet in width with a flow of 15 to 40 cubic feet per second, according to a Department of Natural Resources survey. It is comparable in width to the Bois Brule, Namekagon, Wolf, Peshtigo, and Tomorrow/Waupaca. The first 12 miles in Langlade County contain wild brook and brown trout, but access above the village of Parrish requires that you put one foot ahead of the other. The DeLorme map does show some

JOYCE HUMPHREY

Joyce Humphrey's picture of Jim on the Prairie River

unimproved roads or fire trails leading to the headwaters east from County Road Q north of Parrish, but we can't guarantee their utility.

At Parrish you can fish downstream from County Road H, where there is a DNR lot. From a corner where Pine Drive turns north, hike in to where the Ice Age Trail crosses the river. The river from Parrish down to US 51 at Merrill was described by "Dry Fly" Dick Frantes, Jim Humphrey's fishing partner for many years: "I was very favorably impressed by the absence of litter, the niceness of all the fishers we met, the high percentage of fly-fishers, the ease of fishing and accessibility, and all the convenient parking areas. Lots of hip-boot water; wide-open river." Access is indeed easy at many bridges and across public lands and easements. It is Category 4, except for a short section of Category 5.

Above the village of Dudley on WI 17, where the river has been improved with riprap and bank covers by the DNR with the help of Trout Unlimited, brook trout predominate. From Dudley down, brown trout come to hand more often.

You could begin your exploration at the County Road C bridge upstream from Merrill and about 25 miles west of Antigo if you wish to follow Bill's advice to center at Antigo. It's big, slow water at the County Road C bridge,

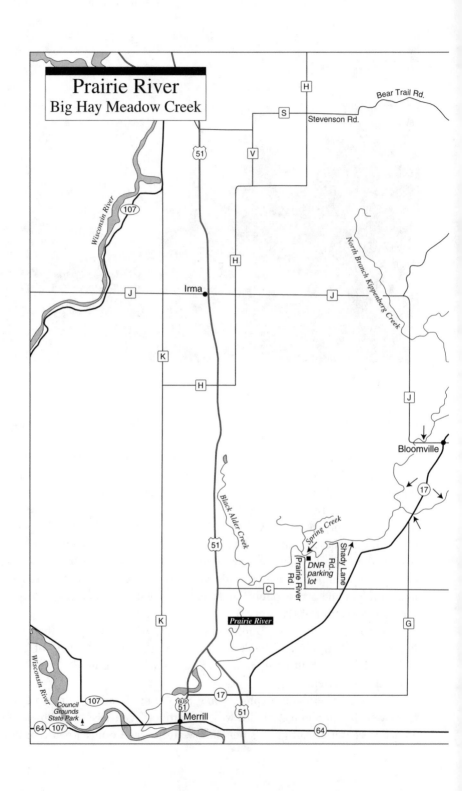

Prairie River
Big Hay Meadow Creek

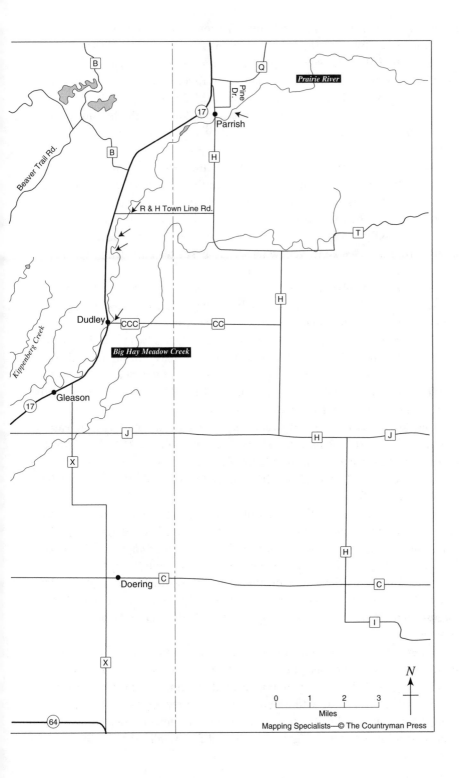

about 4 miles northeast of Merrill, and on opening day the roadside parking will be jammed for sure. On off days you may find a couple of parked cars. We know that there must be some very large browns in that section, but esthetically we prefer to begin at the Prairie River Road DNR lot, 2.5 miles east on County Road C, then north to the river. There you will find Yankee Rapids upstream and several superb long pools down. In the first long pool and beyond, if you are lucky and skillful, you may tie into an oversized brown.

We enjoy most those early-August evenings when the white fly (also known in the eastern United States as the trailer, because the male spinner sometimes trails his shuck like a skywriter's banner) patrols close over the river. Often the brown trout will leap clear in their attempt to snatch it.

The white fly is a spectral late-evening emergence that appears on many large northern Wisconsin rivers where there is silt for burrowing. The male flies bankside and molts within seconds, then returns to patrol a length of 20 feet, back and forth, inches above the water, waiting for the females to show. Because of the haste with which the male dun molts, some anglers have assumed that the molt takes place on the wing.

This *Ephoron leukon/album* is unique. The male has two tails; the female has three, but the middle tail is rudimentary and may not be noticed. The female does not molt from dun to spinner. The white fly is one of our largest mayflies, not far behind the brown drake or Hex. A diligent fly-fisher will want to hang around for the spinner fall after dark.

One August 11 the white fly appeared between 6:30 and 9 PM. I released a couple of modest browns and lost one huge brown on a #12 Blond Wulff. I didn't say this was easy fishing; large trout never come easily. On the big pools of the lower Prairie, if mayflies and caddis don't do their stuff, swim an artificial crayfish on the bottom.

Other hatches include the blue-winged olive, *Baetis* genus, season long; pale evening duns, not identified but probably one of the *Ephemerella;* the March brown, *Stenonema vicarium;* the brown drake, *Ephemera simulans,* June 1–18; the light Cahill, *Stenonema/Stenacron,* June 8–12; tricos, from July 8 to August 4, when the morning temperature reaches 68 degrees; the white-gloved howdy, *Isonychia,* from late July through the middle of August; and the blue dun, *Paraleptophlebia,* from the end of August through September.

Other notable trout foods are the giant brown, giant black, and golden stone stoneflies, as well as chubs, sculpins, and crayfish. Caddis appear all season long, but the most remarkable of that group is the black dancer, *Mystacides alafimbriata,* with antennae so long they appear to be tails. We spotted the amazing black dancers at Dudley on June 11, tied on a Black Caddis, and immediately caught and released five small brook trout.

The second entry east off County Road C is at the end of Shady Lane Road. It's broad and flat here. Downstream is the head of Yankee Rapids. On a recent excursion Shogren found the interstices among the boulders in Yankee Rapids filled with sand, which had drifted down as a result of the removal of Prairie Dells Dam. And that's a story worth some comment.

In a number of places in this book you'll find good reasons why dam removal is generally desirable on our midwestern streams. We won't repeat that information here, but we'll summarize the results of the removal of this particular dam. First off, the river temperature below the dam has fallen by an average of 7 degrees—remarkable. Tons of sand and silt have moved downstream—not good. But the DNR has constructed a sand trap downstream at Shady Lane Road. The trap is a rectangular trench lengthwise down the river. It may be 40 feet long and 4 feet deep, and must be dredged periodically. Thousands of tons of sand and silt have been removed from the Prairie Dells sand trap. In 1992 alone the trap was dredged four times; 1,500 tons of sand were removed at a cost of $2,400 each time. The cost was borne by local chapters of Trout Unlimited.

There are differences of opinion as to the result. One frequent angler told Bill that Yankee Rapids "has been fishing well this year." Bob Talasek, who ran the Wolf River Fly Shop in Langlade, said that the dam removal had hurt the lower Prairie, but that the upper river was fishing great.

Bill experienced strenuous wading around the boulders in Yankee Rapids, but found not much in the way of trout. A pod of trout was feeding on some small stuff, #22 midges, he thought, in a slick above a boulder, but he couldn't get them to take. Water temperature was 68 degrees. A few large yellow mayflies also appeared, but the trout ignored them. These could have been *Stenonema/Stenacron,* which always appear sporadically. It's our guess that the river below the sand trap will gradually flush out and that the fishing will improve. Max Johnson, former area fish manager for the DNR at Antigo, loves the Prairie. That is high praise indeed, because Mr. Johnson devoted more than 20 years to the study and improvement of his streams.

A few years ago Pat Hager, a skilled fly-fisher and student of aquatic insects, took Humphrey down below Prairie Dells Dam, before its removal, for the evening fishing. They didn't break any records but were impressed by the spectacular scenery in the gorge—the overhanging cliffs, the deep pools, the quiet, and the feeling of being distant from all the cares of civilization. If only the trout had cooperated! But, we reiterate, trout fishing is not only the catching and releasing of trout. Trout fishing is often a matter of place, and of timelessness. The dells will be found off a loop road near the junction of WI 17 and County Road G.

At Yanda Road, also called County Road J, there is a big eddy in the pool and a riffle below the bridge. Upstream of here, on an overcast Sunday morning in mid-August, Bill fished a 200-yard stretch full of trout splashing for tricos. "Geez, it's a blast," he said into his tape recorder. "It's about 8:30 AM; trout are everywhere, and this one might be a good one; it's a brookie, about 12 inches. See if I can get him to splash for you. Can you hear him?"

I heard the reel zip, but it was a brown. Bill reported that the trout preferred a poly-wing rather than a featherwing Trico, which makes one ask, Why? It's one of the unsolved mysteries of our game, thank goodness. If we could solve all the puzzles and conundrums of the sport, we'd soon tire of it.

There are some other upstream entry points that we recommend. Try upstream from the Gleason bridge, which Bill called "enchanting," and where he did connect with several brookies on a scud and a Royal Coachman streamer. We also favor the footbridge area in DNR land on the east side of WI 17, opposite the north end of Echo Lake Road, a loop road, as well as the stretch upstream from R&H Road, which is highly recommended by Royce Dam, a skilled fly-fisher and fly-tier from Wauwatosa.

Jim also enjoyed memorable brook trout fishing at Heineman Road and Prairie Drive, north of the junction of the Prairie and Big Hay Meadow Creek, but his favorite, rediscovered after many years, is among the old bridge pilings where the river S-curves on Prairie Drive, next up from Heineman. In recent years the quality of the trout habitat has been called into question, principally by Dr. W. W. Jones, who owns land along the stream. Other anglers have concurred in that assessment and have formed The Friends of the Prairie River, designed to bring to bear the several interests—landowners, anglers, and the DNR. Some habitat has been improved utilizing the funds from the Wildlife Habitat Incentive Program, a conservation provision within 1995 federal farm legislation.

BIG HAY MEADOW CREEK
DeLorme 76 & 77

Bill Shogren goes rhapsodic over his hours spent on Category 3 Hay Meadow in August. "It's really nice—gravel bottom, deep holes. My first fish was a 10-inch brown on a Black Beetle. You could keep going and going all day."

Bill's suggestion is that you pack a light lunch and wade Big Hay Meadow up from the county park on a short loop road that parallels WI 17. Take your sweet time. There is no canopy to contend with and you can wade for 3 or 4 miles under open skies. Or you could drop a pal here for an all-day experience.

BIG PINE CREEK

DeLorme 76 & 88

Big Pine Creek crosses County Road D north of Harrison 6 or 7 miles north-west of Parrish. It's a small, tight stream, recommended by an angler whom we met on the Prairie. We found some eager brookies willing to snatch at a foam beetle fly in the pasture. Above the pasture is heavy canopy and difficult casting. It could become a learning stream for a novice who's over-whelmed by the big-water Prairie.

Anglers on the Prairie River, Big Hay Meadow, and Big Pine Creek could also establish their base at Merrill, which has complete facilities. Lodging and dining are also available at the intersection of US 51 and WI 64.

THE WEST BRANCH OF THE EAU CLAIRE RIVER

DeLorme 77

You'll find this stream on WI 64 a few miles west of Antigo in Langlade County. Its 24 miles upstream of WI 64 contain planted brook and brown trout. We can't give you a definitive report on what has been a marginal trout stream, except to remark that it is long and pretty with many upstream access points. This may be one that you will want to explore; or better still, assign it to one of your partners!

THE EAST BRANCH OF THE EAU CLAIRE RIVER

DeLorme 77

At the risk of being accused of hyperbole, we could characterize this river as awesome. This beautiful river has been improved by the DNR and TU. It was narrowed, crib shelters or lunker structures were added, and boulders were placed midstream. Approximately 17 miles of water above WI 64 contain native brook trout and planted browns and rainbows. Much of it flows through agricultural land, but all the riparian margins are tree lined. You should be able to take brookies galore on attractor flies. Usually the trout are small. Larger brookies will respond to nymphs and more sophisticated imi-tations. Bring your waders: This one is cold and deep.

This is another stream that retired DNR area fish manager Max Johnson is proud of, and rightly so. It's a showpiece and an example of what can be done to improve a stream through dedication and the cooperation of public officials and volunteer groups. In recent years about 4 miles of the stream between River Road and Blue Bell Road have been given a Category 5, spe-cial-regulations designation—artificials only, a bag limit of two (with complications), and substantial length limits of 20 inches for browns and 14 inches for brook trout. Yes, 14 inches for brookies!

Many years ago when I was returning from a trip to the fabled Wolf I stopped in Antigo at a convenience store. I was wearing my Trout Unlimited cap. A gentleman came up, noted that I was a fellow member of the fraternity, and encouraged me to fish the East Branch of the Eau Claire. He was fulsome in his praise and proud of his home water. What convinced me was his near guarantee of 14-inch brook trout. The moral of this story is—always wear your TU cap.

Here is an interesting sidebar to the story. There is some evidence that the native brook trout of the East Branch have devolved a tolerance for higher summertime water temperatures. Experimentally, fertilized eggs from East Branch brook trout have been hatchery-raised, and the resulting wild trout have been planted in streams in the Antigo area.

There are at least seven access points up from WI 64, with parking at County Road I at the culverts and at Blue Bell Road.

THE UPPER PLOVER RIVER
DeLorme 65 & 77

About 10 miles south of Antigo on WI 52 in Marathon County you'll find the Upper Plover in heavily wooded and bog country. Much of the top 10 miles is owned by the DNR, but the best fishing is probably upstream of County Road Z, where the river has been meticulously improved. The brown trout are beautifully colored, and they jump like crazy. Both brook and brown trout are wild. Water temperature was 38 degrees on the occasion of our last trip. Wear waders here, too. You will find a profile of the Lower Plover and a map of both sections in chapter 4 ("Central Wisconsin").

Facilities at Antigo.

THE WOLF RIVER
DeLorme 77 & 78

In 1755, when Lieutenant Charles Michel de Langlade, in the service of France, summoned his Indian warriors to march against Braddock at Fort Duquesne (now Pittsburgh) in the first battle of the French and Indian War, the country of the Wolf was the very heart of darkness on the maps of British America.

There's an intriguing bit of history, partly speculative. Langlade led the Indian ambush against Braddock. Colonel George Washington, of the Virginia Militia, organized and saved the British retreat. Could Langlade have

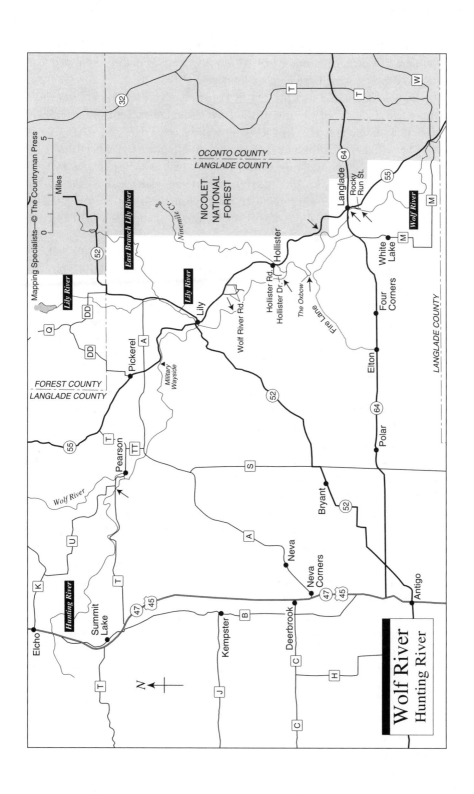

Mapping Specialists—© The Countryman Press

OCONTO COUNTY
LANGLADE COUNTY

NICOLET NATIONAL FOREST

Ninemile Cr.

East Branch Lily River

Lily River

Lily River

Wolf River

Langlade

Rocky Run St.

Hollister

White Lake

Four Corners

Elton

Fire Lane

The Oxbow

Hollister Rd.
Hollister Dr.

Wolf River Rd.

Lily

Pickerel

Military Wayside

FOREST COUNTY
LANGLADE COUNTY

LANGLADE COUNTY

Polar

Pearson

Wolf River

Bryant

Neva

Neva Corners

Antigo

Hunting River

Summit Lake

Elcho

Kempster

Deerbrook

N

Wolf River
Hunting River

taken a shot at Washington? In that battle Daniel Morgan, the "Wagoneer" and hero of Cowpens, drove wagons, and Benjamin Franklin scrounged supplies and wagons for Braddock's advance.

In 1763 Langlade was present at Pontiac's attack on Michilimackinac, where Langlade saved the life of the trader Alexander Henry in one of the more remarkable episodes in American history.

The village of Langlade and Langlade County are named for that redoubtable lieutenant, half French, half Ottawa, who fought against the British, later fought with the British as a partisan leader against the upstart Americans, and finally became a respected American citizen and the first white settler of Green Bay, Wisconsin. Fantastic! Langlade's history reads like an improbable novel.

In 1863 President Abraham Lincoln ordered the army to build a military road from Fort Howard on Green Bay, Wisconsin, to Copper Harbor on Lake Superior. It was still a dark and wild country then, when the engineers camped on the Wolf at what is now the Military Wayside on WI 55 north of the village of Lily. The road making was rough, through tamarack thickets and swamps, fording a hundred streams and uncounted beaver brooks, through tangles of birch, maple, and hemlock, and under the brooding vaults of white pines 5 feet in diameter and towering to 150 feet.

Black bears snuffled through the scattered glades for bushberries, eagles and ospreys caught spiral drafts in sweet blue skies, and river otters hunted speckled trout in crystal pools. Panthers and gray wolves howled threats on cool and misty nights.

It is wild and lonely even now along the banks of the white-water Wolf in Langlade County at evening's end when the canoeists and rafters have gone from the river and mayflies ring the water with their rises. The panthers have gone west, but wolves still ululate to distant mates. The river whispers menacingly around gigantic boulders, and blackness moves under the twisted, phantasmagoric cedars. From downstream you hear that rhythmic swish-swish of fluorescent line writing ephemeral words against the sky; you are reassured by the presence of your partner. Suddenly, there's that startling splash close to your drifting Brown Drake. You lift rod and strip line. Fish on! It's a Wolf River brown, shaking luminescence as he leaps. It is a wonderful night to be alive, matching the hatch on the fabled Wolf of Wisconsin.

A peripatetic fly-fisher may count his blessings that the Congress of the United States, the state of Wisconsin, and local political subdivisions, acting in rare concert, have preserved this historic and scenic river for the enjoyment of 21st-century anglers.

More than 60 miles of the upper Wolf, from the village of Pearson at the north end of Langlade County downstream to the southern border of

Jim on the Wolf River at Burnt Point

Menominee County, have been characterized by the Department of Natural Resources among those trout waters that "show good survival and carryover of adult trout, often producing some fish of better than average size but stocking sometimes is required to maintain a desirable sport fishery." Because water temperatures are not ideal for the reproduction of trout, some 30,000 brown trout are planted each year in the public waters with help from the Wolf River Chapter of TU and the Wolf River Conservation Club. The trout are scatter-planted from rafts over 26 miles in order to utilize the tremendous range of habitat.

Early in the season a fisherman is bound to pick up an occasional brook trout in public waters, but as the water warms, most of the specs will retreat to the cooler feeder creeks. Stunted smallmouth bass are found in gentler currents around the boulders. In the early 1990s Herb Buettner, of the Wild Wolf Inn, proposed and led an attempt to reintroduce naturally reproducing rainbows into the Wolf. By the fall of 1996 members of the Wolf River Chapter of TU reported the catch of rainbows to 16 inches. Wild strains of brown trout were also recorded. Even the catch of brook trout had improved. In 1996, 32,000 hatchery fingerling brown trout were added. In the first week of June 1996 Herb Buettner entertained his guests with a 15-minute tussle with a 19½-inch brown at the Wild Wolf Inn. In mid-June of 1997 Mike Hipps reported the catch of rainbows in the river around Buettner's, and a huge spinner fall of gray drakes at the Langlade bridge. This superb river can produce a smorgasbord of aquatic insects. On June 9 between 5 and 9 PM we encountered the small tan caddis, one of the *Ephemerella*, midges, a mating flight of the gray drake, an advance patrol of the brown drake, and a light Cahill of the *Stenonema* persuasion. On the 10th the river was running high and fierce; all we could do was to take close-up photographs of the resting brown drakes.

In Langlade County 34.5 miles of the Wolf are under the protection of the DNR, which pursues an aggressive program of acquisition and control. No further development of the shoreline is permitted. Property owners are not free to expand or materially alter their facilities. During the past 25 years 75 percent of the shoreline has been purchased by the state, at a cost in excess of $5 million.

Approximately 27 miles of the lower Wolf through the Menominee Indian Reservation (coterminous with Menominee County) have been designated by Congress a National Wild and Scenic River. Although that section is closed to outsiders by order of the Menominee Tribal Council, it is a valuable ecological resource. Its many miles of spring-fed streams are nurseries for trout that stray into public waters, and the DNR obtains some wild rainbow eggs from the council.

The Wolf is a pristine freestone river, more typical of a large western stream, averaging 150 feet in width and 3 or 4 feet in depth. Through 20 named rapids and rips, from Lily to the Menominee line, the river drops 430 feet. In the flats and runs between the rapids, around the islands, and in the channels between huge boulders there are miles of superb wading water and an immense number of lies for watchful and hungry trout. But entry points to the Wolf River are few. Walking in to the river and wading in solitude are part of the wilderness experience.

Beginning in the north, there is easy entry in DNR lands at Pearson on County Road T, then downstream at the County Road A bridge. The Military Wayside on WI 55 offers a superb variety of bottom types for wading fly-fishers. The river near WI 52 at Lily is a bit more placid. Next down is Wolf River Road, which makes a loop from WI 55 to a Soo Line Railroad crossing and a dead-end road to DNR parking on the river. This is one of our favorite locations, even though it is deep and difficult wading upstream, and not easy downstream either, through the rapids, but we've spent some wonderful hours here.

Going south, find the spur road that runs south from west-running Hollister Road off WI 55. Hollister at WI 55 is a single building on the northeast corner of WI 55 and Hollister Road. Due west, approximately 1.25 miles, is Burnt Point, giving a spectacular view of flat water spotted with boulders upstream and rapids down. Be sure to see Burnt Point, but we prefer to fish at the end of the spur road, where there is a canoe access. Look for the south-running blacktop a couple of hundred yards before you get to Burnt Point.

Six miles of the Wolf, from the Soo Line trestle below the Hollister spur to Dierck's Pond, are under special regulations for no-kill with artificials only. There are also restrictions on the remainder of the river; these may change by the time you read this. Unnoticed by many anglers, since 1996 the river has been open for a late season from October 1 through November 15. This too may change.

The flats above and below the Langlade bridge can be an evening delight, and have been for us on many occasions. Access is easy and varied in Langlade. You'll find a parking lot on the southwest corner at the bridge, additional convenient places on the east, and three entries along Rocky Rips Road. There is also access to the west side of the river north of WI 64 by unimproved roads and fire lanes. If you have a high-clearance car or truck or four-wheel drive, you may be able to reach the Oxbow from either Four Corners or Elton—both on WI 64 west of Langlade—via a combination of gravel road and fire lane. We have observed anglers anchoring their rafts at the head of the Oxbow and fishing down. We didn't see any fish caught, but then we didn't linger there long; we were eager to fish the evening flats around the Langlade bridge. You'll need a detailed map if you search for the Wolf through the backcountry. Ask for the "Wolf River, Wisconsin's Trout-land" map at local commercial establishments. It is also possible to reach the Oxbow by hiking down the railroad grade from Hollister landing.

From the village of Pearson upstream the Wolf is watered and warmed by Swamp Creek and outflow from the two Post Lakes. Up there the river is not congenial to trout, but at Pearson the spring-fed Hunting River brings cold water and adds more than 15 miles of trout habitat. Two branches of the Lily River add 13 miles. Ninemile Creek enters the Wolf at Hollister. Several short feeders contain wild brook trout. Excluding the streamlets, there are nearly 75 miles of trout water open to the public.

The Wolf is aptly named. In spring, surging through the rapids and runs, it is the White Wolf, hungry and cold, licking its chops, hoping for an errant fisherman to challenge the wild rips and slick boulders. In the low water of summer under a bright sky it seems more like a tabby cat, sleepy and purring, but for all that it's ready to slash with a claw if trifled with. Dress in belted waders and use a staff. If you intend to fish the hatches into dark, reconnoiter the bottom first by day.

On bright midsummer days, following a couple or three days of 80-degree ambient temperature, water temperature may reach the mid-70s. Cap

Examples of effective flies for fishing the Wolf River

Buettner, now deceased, a master fly-fisherman and active TUer, once said that a hot-weather fisherman had better learn to drift a Muddler or stream-er deep under the fast currents. A local expert fishes the pockets around boulders in fast water in July and August. Nights, though, are always cool in this north country. The river will also remain cool under cloudy skies—of which, you may be sure, there are many. A summertime fisherman might probe with a thermometer downstream from feeders in the shaded runs.

Another way to avoid warm water and sluggish trout is to take a long sies-ta at noon, then fish afternoons in the shadows of the cedars on the west bank.

Spring is a different story. One day in early May fine trout were feed-ing on Diptera at high noon in less than a foot of water right up against the bank in view of Buettner's Motel at Langlade, where we had been enjoying our midday R and R. Inducing those trout to accept a #18 Blue-Winged Olive, which matched the hatch, became a frustrating interruption.

Cap Buettner always said that the river is rich in aquatic life. Typical of Wisconsin rivers, it has minor hatches of *Baetis,* tiny blue-winged olives, throughout the season, tricos from late June, and a minor hatch of *Isony-chia,* the white-gloved howdy or mahogany dun, which appears between June 15 and July 15.

One late-May evening on the flats at Langlade I encountered simultaneously two different species of caddis, #16 and #12, one #22 microcaddis, two species of *Ephemerella* (Hendrickson and a pale evening dun), a single advance scout of the *Ephemera simulans* (brown drake), and two crane flies, one of which was identical in color to the pale evening dun. After frantically changing flies over those picky trout, I finally took four of them—two brilliant, prime browns and two recent plants, all on a #14 Hendrickson. Later, attempting to raise a large trout that hung out midstream and willing to experiment, I hooked and released two more on a #12 Ginger Bivisible. The next evening around 7 PM, a satisfactory hatch of *Baetis* appeared and the trout sipped on the blue-winged olives.

The river contains two species of the great black stonefly, *Pteronarcys;* the great brown stonefly, *Acroneuria,* which hatches around the first of June; the stonefly *Phasganophora,* known as the night creeper; and the large golden stone. Because various species of stoneflies hatch throughout the season, stonefly nymphs are always an excellent choice for bottom-bumping the runs by day and creeping the shallows toward evening. The Green Stonefly Muddler, Cap's creation, should be cast among the sweepers. We can't tell you how many times his Muddler has saved the day on other rivers. Weighted Muddlers and Matukas are good imitations of the three species of sculpins that hide among the pebbles. Chubs here grow to huge size. Even Izaak Walton would be pleased to feed a small wet fly to them in slack water. Big brown trout must relish them as well. Hoppers and ants are traditional summer fare.

Of major importance are five mayfly hatches, plus a sixth that Cap numbered on his personal list. Emergence dates may vary according to temperatures and hours of daylight, perhaps even lunar attraction and other factors known only to God. All are evening hatches.

Siphlonurus quebecensis, known locally as the grey drake, #10 and #12, emerges from May 28 to June 9, duration about three weeks. We think of this one as a dark chocolate quill, but perhaps it doesn't need another colloquial name. Cap Buettner designed an emerger for this hatch that we have used successfully on other rivers as a searching pattern.

Ephemera simulans, #10, the famous brown drake found on many Wisconsin rivers, also known as the March brown and chocolate dun, hatches from June 5 to June 15. One recent June 2 the duns appeared at dusk and the spinners mated at 2 PM the following day.

Stenonema vicarium is Buettner's sixth selection. Use a Gray Fox #10 or #12. Elsewhere it goes by as many as 10 names: dark Cahill, ginger quill, March brown, sand drake, and many more. June 5 to June 10 is the usual period.

Potamanthus, or cream fly, hatches from June 7 to July 1, though the species is in doubt. A Light Cahill #12 is almost a dead ringer for the cream fly. The nymph is sometimes called the golden bull.

Hexagenia atrocaudata, the green drake, #8, emerges from July 15 to August 25. It's known elsewhere as the big slate drake, great lead-winged drake, or, in most places, just Hex. This *Hexagenia,* which is a tube maker, is about a third smaller than the *H. limbata* found on many silty Wisconsin rivers, and it appears here a couple of weeks later.

Ephoron leukon, White Wulff #8 and #10, appears from August 1 to August 20. (See our description of the white fly hatch in the Prairie River profile.) Bob Talasek, of the Wolf River Fly Shop, described one hatch as "a blizzard on an evening in August." Cap Buettner called it a "superhatch."

On the evening of August 15 Bill Shogren found the white fly hatch in the fly-fishing section down from Hollister landing. "Jim, the hatch is on; it's about 8:15. The flies are coming up all over the place, they're towing their shucks. I've got a fish on right now." There sounds Bill's reel, and Bill panting with excitement. "Oh, what a nice fish! Got another one on, Jim. That first one was 16 inches. My God! Amazing to see the white flies coming upriver. A guy I met told me that last night he caught a 12, a 13, a 14, and two at 15 inches. Even allowing for him maybe being a plus-twoer, that's spectacular fishing. You've got to be set up to do your business. These hatches don't last long. It seems to me this lasted about 45 minutes."

Coming out after dark was another experience that Bill won't soon forget. "The joys of trout fishing late at night. The challenge is to find the path, then to stay on it. Jim," he called with a quaver in his voice, "I trust there are no weird creatures along this river. It's getting pretty spooky!"

If the surface of the Wolf is temporarily lifeless during your time on the river, fish blind through the riffles and runs with a Hare's Ear on the point and a Cap's Stonefly Muddler tied short on the butt to serve as both indicator and attractor. At evening switch to a large nymph on the point.

The Wolf between Lily and the iron bridge at County Road M is a popular summer weekend exercise for canoeists and kayakers. Those even-more-intrusive rubber rafts put in at the Hollister spur road and take out at Langlade or at County Road M.

It's a fact of life that fishermen must share the beneficence of nature with other enthusiasts. Fortunately there are a number of ways for fly-anglers to enjoy a share of unalloyed pleasure in wilderness surroundings. Visit during the week rather than on weekends. Search the trout lies upstream from Hollister, thereby avoiding all the rafts and many of the canoes and kayaks. Get on the river at early morning or at dusk. As a matter of personal observation, however, even a large and fastidious trout resumed feeding within 10 minutes after a raft went over his lie.

By local ordinance, raft trips may not begin before 8 AM and must end by 7 PM. Experienced Wolf River fishermen wade the lower river in the morning while the rafts are still upstream, then transfer their activities upriver in the afternoon. Other fishermen find runs and braids away from the main channel and pursue their sport in relative serenity. Or if you wish, join the throng, rent a raft, and fish at will between Hollister and County Road M. It's an experience that you may live to regret. If the water is high and hard, you risk a dunking; if the water is low, you'll surely hang up on some of the gigantic rocks.

Hollister to Langlade is a drift of four or five hours. Hollister to the County Road M bridge is an all-day float. Midweek under lowering skies or in a light rain can be untrammeled days on the Wolf.

Rafters and fishers have established a modus vivendi. Rafters prefer sunlight and heat of day; fly-fishers opt for overcast and cool of evening. When the rafters are fingering their frosty cocktail glasses in a supper club, the fly-fishers are hiking in to their secret places.

Local authorities and townsfolk are proud stewards of the river. Littering is subject to fine; bottles and cans are not allowed aboard watercraft. Twice each summer Boy Scouts traverse the river in rafts furnished by the Wild Wolf Inn to pick up flotsam and jetsam.

Dedicated trout fishermen everywhere have learned to accommodate themselves to circumstances. It is always too wet or too dry, or the river is too clear or too murky, or too hot or too cold, or thunder has put the trout down. There are too many fishermen or too few trout. It is a litany of pain that goes back to the days of Dame Juliana Berners and before. But a serious angler will always find trout in the Wolf River of Wisconsin. And even if not, the beauty and magic of this mighty river are compensation enough for the vagaries of weather and humankind.

We shall never see the river exactly as Langlade may have known it, nor as the beat-out army engineers saw it in 1863, but over time the few remaining cabins will disappear, the pines will reach for the sky, and our children will get a sense of a primal magnificence that once was. Aspen and willow will shade the margins and cool the water, eagles and ospreys will make their nests in skeleton cottonwoods, and otter kits will rest their forepaws on a fallen cedar to peer with childlike curiosity at strange, two-legged interlopers.

When the shadows come out of hiding and the twisted cedars bending assume the shapes of phantom French irregulars and Chippewa warriors, turn, turn resolutely into the gathering dusk and cast your big Brown Drake upon the molten pewter water. Listen for the reassuring hiss and swish of your partner's cast. Splash! Trout on!

The Wolf may be at risk. In 1986 Exxon Minerals Company proposed to construct and operate an underground zinc and copper mine and mill at

Joyce Humphrey on the Wolf at the Wolf Road access south of Lily

Crandon, Wisconsin. Some intercepted groundwater would be treated, then discharged into Swamp Creek, a tributary of the Wolf. Local environmentalists and trout fishermen opposed the plan, but state agencies appeared to be ready to approve. In 1987 Exxon put the construction on hold due to low world prices for the minerals. In 1994 the proposal was resurrected. And in the summer of the Year of Our Lord 2000 the Wolf was still at risk; only the name of the minerals company had changed. Exxon Minerals partnered early with Rio Algom of Canada to become Crandon Mining Company to become Nicolet Minerals Company. The discussion is somewhere in the courts, but we can't guarantee that the mine will not be approved. All for the sake of a few jobs and for the possible death of a river downstream.

About that military road: Ostensibly, the road was built to protect the frontier. From what? you may ask. From invasion by the South? From England entering the Civil War to support the Southern planters? Students of history suspect that the road was promoted by lumbering interests that wanted easy access to one of the largest virgin forests on the continent.

Facilities at Antigo, Buettner's Motel at Langlade, Herb Buettner's Wild Wolf Inn on the river (White Lake address), at Langlade and White Lake, plus American Plan and European Plan resorts in the area. There are two campgrounds in the Nicolet National Forest, 10 miles east of Langlade.

Mike's Service in Langlade provides both information and an excellent selection of flies.

THE HUNTING RIVER
DeLorme 77

Our old friend Eino Tutt of Wausau was a master at rolling big brown trout from northern rivers on a Hornberg. He was also a specialist at swimming a live minnow on the upper Namekagon above Cable, but that's another story. One of his favorite rivers was the 16-mile Hunting, a major tributary of the Wolf that joins it in DNR lands at Pearson.

A salute is due here to Frank Hornberg, Portage County game warden from 1920 to 1950 and creator of the fly that has captured the interest of thousands of big brown trout.

The river, which rises in Otter Lake near Elcho, averages 44 feet in width and is cooled by 11 tributaries and 17 springs above Summit Lake and along County Road T. It contains wild brook trout and planted browns, and has been extensively improved by the DNR. Our favorite location for early-morning, late-afternoon, and evening fly-fishing is the slow, broad water at the County Road T bridge, but you may prefer to begin your exploration at Pearson and at the roadside park west on County Road T, where the stream has been narrowed and deepened. Fish it at dusk with a Hornberg.

As of this writing, a long section of the Hunting River, from the mouth upstream to Fitzgerald Dam Road, is Category 5, artificials only, brown and rainbow trout 20 inches, brook trout 14, and a bag limit of two trout in total! That must tell you something about the quality of the river.

Facilities at Antigo, Langlade, and Crandon.

The Oconto River Watershed

The several branches of the Oconto River drain a huge watershed in Langlade and Oconto Counties and may be said to center at the intersection of WI 64 and WI 32 near Mountain. Water from the First, Second, and South Branches flows through the Menominee Indian Reservation, which is closed to visiting anglers, and flows out of the reservation as the South Branch near Suring. There are more than 75 miles of trout waters included in the four sections that we profile, not counting the feeders or streamlets. Most of the mileage lies within the boundaries of the Nicolet National Forest, which means that there is more public land and fewer roads. Even with a good map it isn't easy to find your way to the several branches of the Oconto, but we'll give it a shot.

THE SOUTH BRANCH OF THE OCONTO RIVER
DeLorme 78

If you are traveling east from Langlade and the Wolf River on WI 64, you will first cross the South Branch of the Oconto abut 3 miles east of Langlade. Here the river appears to be quite small, so we reserve a second profile for where it leaves the reservation as a far more desirable destination, far downstream near Suring. For practical fly-fishers, this upper section begins where Jones Creek joins, 6 or 7 miles upriver. Below Jones, Saul Springs adds more volume of cold water. From there down to WI 64 the wading is difficult over muck and silt. It is reported that canoes are useful in some of the wide spots. Below WI 64 the river widens and deepens and produces some large browns. You may also discover decent access around the County Road T bridge south of WI 64. For the record, an old one, this reach of the South Branch included 20 miles of good-quality water for natural brookies and both wild and planted browns.

Proceeding east, you will find the Second South Branch of the Oconto with about 8 miles of natural brook and brown trout. You may explore down from WI 64 along Mountain Lake Road.

Continuing east on WI 64, you at last reach the First South Branch about 12 miles east of Langlade and about 4 miles from Mountain. Ten miles of the branch downstream from WI 64 are considered first-class for native brook and planted brown trout. A 2-mile stretch upstream is probably a bit too warm due to inflow from a pair of lakes. At WI 64 the river has been improved with riprap and bank structures. Here is where we fish. There are two crossings downstream at County Road W and Bonita Road, neither of which have we fished in living memory, yet. We said that sorting these branches out wouldn't be easy; but the long and storied North Branch is easier to profile and locate.

THE NORTH BRANCH OF THE OCONTO RIVER
DeLorme 78 & 79

In her wonderful book *Favorite Flies and Their Histories* (1892; reprinted in 1988 by The Wellfleet Press, and rereleased by The Lyons Press in 2001), Mary Orvis Marbury quotes from a letter from an angler reporting his experience on the North Branch of the Oconto. We abstract a few lines from his more lengthy missive: "A party of four, the writer being one of the number, drove with teams from Shawano, last June, to the headwaters of the North Branch of the Oconto . . . Our catches could have been made enormous had we desired to kill the fish. The trout ranged from a quarter to two and a half

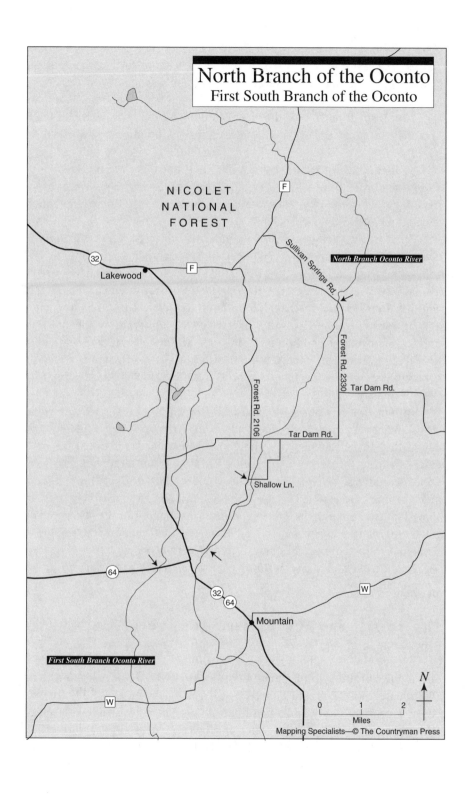

North Branch of the Oconto
First South Branch of the Oconto

NICOLET
NATIONAL
FOREST

North Branch Oconto River

Sullivan Springs Rd.

Lakewood

Forest Rd. 2330

Tar Dam Rd.

Forest Rd. 2106

Tar Dam Rd.

Shallow Ln.

Mountain

First South Branch Oconto River

Miles

Mapping Specialists—© The Countryman Press

N

pounds each, and were as fine a flavor as I ever took from New England waters. The last day before returning home, wishing to take some of the beauties to our friends, we arranged for a full day's fishing. The weather was fine, and the wind southwest. I never had such sport before. Though we spent but a small portion of the day fishing, our catch was, in round numbers, four hundred and sixteen; total weight, one hundred and thirty-three pounds."

No longer do we expect fishing like that, but there are times when 8- and 9-inch brook trout will rise eagerly to a Seth Green, Professor, or Montreal, favorites with Mary Orvis Marbury's correspondent, the redoubtable F. C. Shattuck of Neenah, Wisconsin.

The North Branch consists of 24 miles of first-class water, Category 2, above WI 32 at Mountain in Oconto County. It contains wild browns and wild brook trout. Rainbows may be planted in some years, depending on the availability from hatcheries. Off-road parking is at the bridge on WI 32, and additional entries are upstream along Loon Rapids Road, at Shallow Lane, and at Tar Dam Road. We also like it farther upstream at the Sullivan Springs Road bridge. Additional points are at Smyth Road and at County Road F. Between Loon Rapids and Sullivan Springs the Oconto is wide and generally smooth and deep, with a broken bottom. Waders are required for the evening fly-fishing.

Bill put in a few hours on the North Branch late in August. The water was slow moving, not deep, wide, and weedy. Brook trout were "game" that day as they rose to Adams drys and Coachman streamers between the weed patches and in the deeper impressions. They were not large, but they were gorgeous natives. We wonder what it would be like to float this water; so much of it is inaccessible because of bogs, fens, and swamps. There must be some fantastic Shangri-las where the big trout hang out, if only we could get there. Many anglers muse about hiring a small plane or helicopter to scope out the remote reaches and to find easier access.

Facilities at Mountain, north at Wabeno, or south at Suring, all on WI 32 in Oconto County.

THE SOUTH BRANCH OF THE OCONTO RIVER
DeLorme 79

Seven miles of the South Branch of the Oconto River, a few miles northwest of Suring on WI 32, from County Road AA downstream to WI 32, are Category 5, artificials only and a bag limit of one. There are also length limits. Because of the quality of the water and the ease of wading, the river has received attention from both the DNR and dedicated fly-fishers. Much of the

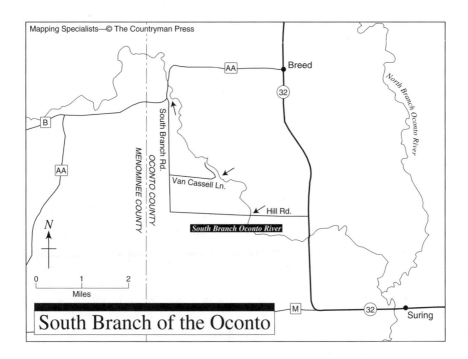

Mapping Specialists—© The Countryman Press

Breed

AA

32

B

AA

South Branch Rd.

OCONTO COUNTY
MENOMINEE COUNTY

North Branch Oconto River

Van Cassell Ln.

Hill Rd.

South Branch Oconto River

N

0   1   2
Miles

M   32   Suring

South Branch of the Oconto

stream is under easement, and several substantial blocks of acreage are owned by the state. We prefer to fish it from County Road AA down the west side along South Branch Road, finishing at a DNR parking lot and trail to a particularly charming stretch at the Hill Road bridge. The bridge is about 1.5 miles west of WI 32 if you are coming from the south. The Green Bay Chapter of TU completed a habitat improvement project in 2000.

Facilities at Suring and Mountain.

THE LOWER PESHTIGO RIVER

DeLorme 79

The Lower Peshtigo, west of Crivitz in Marinette County, with access from either County Road A or County Road W, has an unusual history. In 1955 Lyle Kingston, an engineer with the Wisconsin Public Service Corporation, and Virgil Muench, a conservationist and fly-fisher from Green Bay, convinced the corporation to grant an easement to the then Wisconsin Conservation Department (now DNR) on about 5 miles of the Lower Peshtigo between Johnson Falls and the foot of Spring Rapids. The purpose was to establish an open season restricted to fly-fishing. This was the first special-regulations stretch of river in the state. It still is special, rated Category 5.

The Peshtigo down here is huge and often dangerous due to fluctuating water levels from the operation of the dams upriver. We've been on the river at the head of Spring Rapids when the water rose a foot in a matter of minutes.

Because of the changing water levels, natural reproduction of trout is nil, but the experience of fly-fishing for stocked browns and rainbows can be exhilarating. This is a wild river through what appears to be primitive country, although it was logged and burned in the late 19th century. A respondent to a creel survey described his day this way: "This is a beautiful area with the grandeur of a western stream and a bonus of seeing various wildlife while working the river." And so it is for us.

Access from the east side is at Bizjak Lane off County Road A and at Medicine Brook via County Road A to Newton Lake Road, then to High Falls Road. We prefer, though, the west side entries from County Road W out of Crivitz to Kirby Lake Road, thence by 0.8 mile of single-lane sand road to the head of Spring Rapids, or upstream to Seymour Rapids from Kostreva Road. You will want the brochure and map "Your Guide to Public Service Recreation Land," available in the area or from the Wisconsin Public Service Corporation, 700 North Adams, Green Bay, WI 54301.

Because aquatic insect life is also disturbed by fluctuating water levels, we can't pinpoint any hatches. Better to fish the big river with Hornbergs, Muddlers, Woolly Buggers, and similar artificial baitfish. If trout are feeding on the surface, use a Brown Bivisible in fast water and a Spider on the slicks.

Facilities at Crivitz and in many of the resorts in the area around the impoundments. History buffs may want to visit the museum and graveyard at Peshtigo, Wisconsin, commemorating the catastrophic Peshtigo forest fire of October 8, 1871, which claimed 800 lives and ravaged more than 2,400 square miles of cutover country. This fire occurred on the same day as the Great Chicago Fire; both were driven by cyclonic winds.

THE NORTH BRANCH OF BEAVER CREEK
DeLorme 79

The 6 miles of the top of the North Branch of Beaver Creek are worth a visit to see this domicile of native browns and brooks. Go south from Crivitz on US 141 to the village of Beaver, then west on 14th Road, then north on 19th Road to the bridge. Fish upstream here between 19th Road and 25th Road. With the cooperation of the Green Bay Chapter of Trout Unlimited, the state has installed a platform for handicapped fishers in a wide, slow spot. Just to check the quality of the habitat, Bill was the first to pitch in a Hornberg and immediately took a lovely 12-inch brown, which he returned unharmed. We like to see accessible fishing paths and casting platforms installed around the state, because someday we'll all be old.

Facilities at Crivitz.

THE UPPER PESHTIGO RIVER
DeLorme 79, 90, & 91

The Upper Peshtigo is an enigma. Its long complex of branches and creeks comprises one of the major tributaries to Green Bay. It should be one of the biggest and best trout rivers, and it may be to those who know exactly where the trout congregate in colder water in summer. The problem is that the water is too cold in winter to support substantial natural reproduction of trout, presumably due to an excess of beaver dams on the many tributaries. But rivers are complex organisms. Warm summer water temperatures may stress the trout; the Peshtigo has many sections that are shallow and slow. Anchor ice in winter may scour aquatic life. Various types of pollutants can raise havoc. There may be other factors too subtle to be measured.

We have labeled this long complex of branches and feeders above the several impoundments the Upper Peshtigo, in order to distinguish it from the Lower Peshtigo below Johnson Falls.

The main Peshtigo River begins officially close to Argonne, in Forest County north of US 8, on WI 55 and WI 32, at the junction of the Middle and South Branches. The North Branch adds volume a few miles to the east, a mile or so north of County Road G. While the Middle and South Branches are fairly easy to access around Argonne, the North Branch rises in the bowels of the Nicolet National Forest, with very limited access. Bill says you may need a helicopter to get back in there.

The main river flows, often turbulently, for 40 or more miles in Forest County, then for 25 miles in Marinette County to Cauldron Falls Reservoir, the first of the Wisconsin Public Service Corporation impoundments. The tributaries are too numerous to tally, but many will provide first-class fishing for wild brook trout.

There's no way that we can give you a step-by-step tour of this magnificent river. Access points are many, although widely spaced through some of the most remote country imaginable, but we can direct you to five or six places that you won't want to miss.

First, we've had good fishing for brook trout along County Road O on the main Peshtigo northwest of Cavour. Or you might begin your long exploration at the campground at Big Joe Rapids on Kalata Road, a couple of miles north of Cavour on WI 139. (WI 139 leads north from US 8.) It was

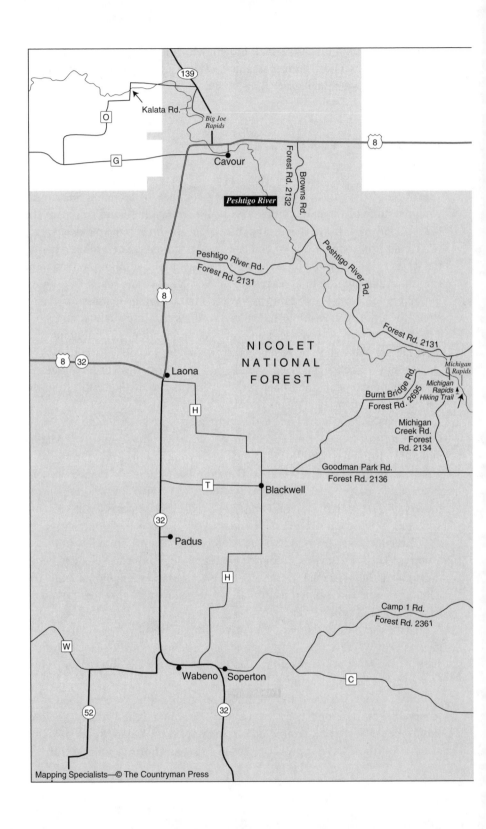

Mapping Specialists—© The Countryman Press

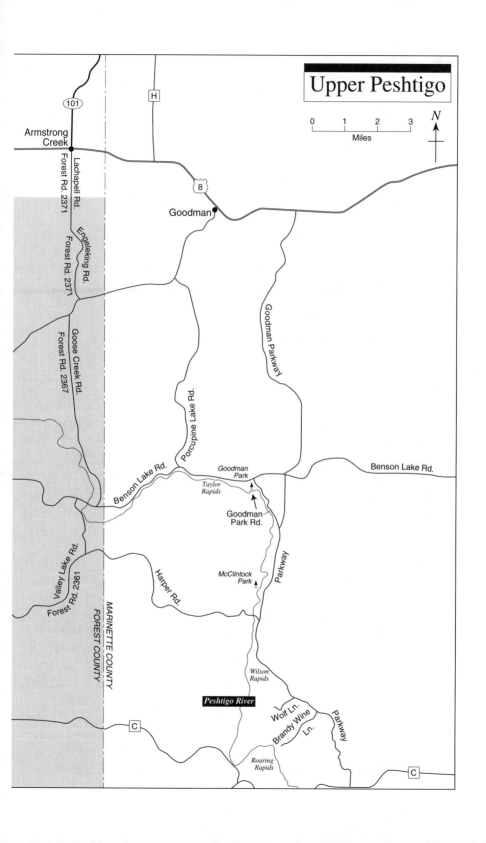

Upper Peshtigo

0 1 2 3
Miles

N

there on June 5 that we found a marvelous hatch of brown drakes hanging like berries from streamside brush. Upstream from WI 139 the river is Category 2; the remainder to Cauldron Falls Reservoir is Category 3.

Next, go downstream from Cavour to Michigan Rapids via Browns Road (Forest Road 2132) from US 8 east of Cavour, then south on the Peshtigo River Road (Forest Road 2131), then south to the Michigan Rapids Hiking Trail on Michigan Creek Road (Forest Road 2134). The hiking trail begins at the junction of Forest Roads 2134 and 2695 and loops for 2 miles along Michigan Rapids. The trail can also be reached from the west by Burnt Bridge Road (Forest Road 2695).

A fellow enthusiast, who fished the river for 33 years, mainly in July and August, reported fabulous success in the rapids. We won't repeat the numbers and sizes of trout he caught, because they boggle the mind. He also used some unorthodox tactics in that heavy water, but big-fish fly-anglers should be able to find the pockets. When he mentioned Coleman coolers filled with 16- and 20-inch browns extracted from the rapids and in the flat below, we had no reason to doubt, remembering similar catches on other rivers in northern Wisconsin. We doubt that anyone could duplicate his results now, but his advice is still valid. Fish the rapids and the tails but avoid the long, warm flats between.

Next down past many miles of river is Goodman Park, in Marinette County below Taylor Rapids, via Goodman Parkway. The parkway is listed as one of Wisconsin's Rustic Roads. You'll have to navigate by map to get from Michigan Rapids to Goodman Parkway. Visually, this immaculate park, with its island and Japanese bridge, is a trout fisher's paradise. On opening weekend it becomes a gathering of fly-fishing aficionados, but later in the season you may have it all to yourself.

Next downstream is McClintock Park, not quite so prepossessing but offering a mix of excellent habitat through and above the park. McClintock Falls is a series of rapids with bridges for exceptional views. Marinette County boasts 12 falls, all with easy access and most located in county parks. Anglers will find trout in the oxygenated water below the falls, and quite often in the glides above.

The Peshtigo is a popular summer canoe trail—fly-fishers will sob—but be cheered that most trips begin at County Road C below McClintock Park.

The Peshtigo should be one of the best, and may be again if the beaver dams are removed from the feeders, but for now you will have to search for trout in the oxygen-rich water through and below the many rapids and falls; fish early season or late, or cozen the river at nightfall and after.

Since 1996 the Peshtigo upstream of County Road C in Marinette County has opened on March 1 (now, the first Saturday), for barbless artificials and no-kill. It is also open from October 1 through November 30, with identical restrictions. Be advised that special regulations are subject to change any year.

Facilities for travelers at motels along US 8, and at the many motels and resorts around the impoundments.

THE NORTH BRANCH OF THE PIKE RIVER
DeLorme 91 & 99

As we promised in the introduction to this section, let us begin with the North Branch of the Pike River as representative of the streams and rivers of the far northeast. The several falls are in Marinette County, about 7 miles west of Pembine and a few miles south of US 8. Look for Lily Lake Road and the signs to Twelvefoot Falls County Park. The 25 miles of the North Branch are first-class waters for wild brook and brown trout. You'll always find trout in the turbulence below the falls, but that's no real test of a fly-fisher. Try the glides above the falls for that spackle of trout rising to midges or other small fare.

The North Branch of the Pike still runs free and clear from Railroad Pond just north of US 8 in Marinette County to the Menominee River. Above Amberg on US 141 it is Category 4; below Amberg it is Category 5. Approximately 29 miles of first-class water contain wild brook and brown trout. Our preferred section is still that which runs above and through Twelvefoot Falls County Park where you will find Twelve Foot and Eight Foot Falls. Eighteen Foot Falls is located about a mile north of the park. Access points upstream of the park are few, with some reachable only by long foot trails. Entries are closer together downstream, particularly along Pike River Road where there are two public entries by foot trail. A third entry is at the Semester School Road bridge. That is the way you ought to go for brown trout.

Facilities at Pembine and Amberg.

Other Rivers of the Northeast

We might treat the other branches of the Pike River, along with the Pemebonwon, Popple, and Pine Rivers, as a group because the fly-fishing conditions are so similar on each. The country through which they wind their way to the Menominee River is huge, dark, and tangled, access bridges are separated by miles of swamps and thickets of aspen and tamarack, and the rivers are not rich in aquatic life.

Access is generally easy in the upper reaches of the rivers in the Nicolet National Forest, probable at state and county road bridges, but probably not possible where a "Lane" ends at the river. Oddly, much of the land at the ends of these short lanes is posted against trespass. It is an unusual and disheartening experience to discover, in friendly Wisconsin, a narrow track through the deep woods that leads—you're sure of it—to a stretch of roaring rapids and leaping trout, only to find a primitive cabin and a warning to keep out. We suggest that you always cross-check between the DeLorme and Milwaukee Map Service maps before you go hiking off toward that distant waterfall or rapids.

These streams tend to warm during the summer months, and the trout become lethargic. During the dog days use a stream thermometer and test for the upwelling of in-stream springs.

THE PEMEBONWON RIVER
DeLorme 91 & 99

The South Branch of the Peme rises in Marinette County and cuts south of Pembine to join the huge Menominee River, the border between Wisconsin and the Upper Peninsula of Michigan. It embraces some 19 miles of first-class water and 8 of the second class, all of it producing wild brookies and planted browns.

Some years ago the Peme was the subject of a five-year research and management study designed to determine if removal of beaver dams would prevent habitat deterioration and declines in wild trout populations. Four hundred eighty-five dams were removed on the 10.5 miles of the North Branch and on 24 miles of tributaries. The results on the North Branch were disappointing, but the numbers of brook trout increased in the tributaries, which goes to prove that habitat improvement is both expensive and sometimes inconclusive.

The North Branch of the Peme includes about 23 miles of somewhat lower-quality water containing wild brook trout. Our suggestion is that you fish around Smalley Falls and in the 2 miles below Long Slide Falls. Take Morgan Road or Spike Horn Road east from US 141 about 5 miles north of Pembine for parking near Long Slide Falls in the county park. Hike upstream by maintained path to the smaller Smalley Falls.

Facilities at Pembine, Niagara, and Iron Mountain.

THE PINE RIVER
DeLorme 91

The long and complex Pine River reaches the Menominee River at Iron Mountain, Michigan, on US 2 and US 141. Although several of its feeders are first-class, the 31 miles above LaSalle Falls in Florence County are of marginal quality for trout. However, our friend from Missouri, Jason Carpenter, did extract a 20-inch brown from Snaketail Rapids on the upper Pine one recent early June near Tipler and close to the junction of WI 139 and WI 70. Although we would advise you to avoid the Pine River, we are often confounded by our friends.

Facilities at Iron Mountain.

THE BRULE RIVER
DeLorme 90, 91, & 99

This is the eastern Brule, not to be confused with the Bois Brule of northwestern Wisconsin. This great river begins at Brule Lake in Michigan and meanders for more than 50 miles to the Menominee River. The Brule is big and beautiful, and shows a variety of water types. Browns and brook trout are naturally reproducing. Access is not easy on the Wisconsin side because so much of it runs through the Nicolet National Forest, where the roads are few and far between. You can, however, fish with a Wisconsin license from the Michigan side. We had a blast near Nelma on WI 55 in August, where the river is wide with a slow, even flow. Along the banks under the alders, big browns can be taken during the doldrums of summer. During the day, slide your terrestrials under the sweepers; at night, feed the big browns a Muddler. More detailed information is found in *Trout Streams of Michigan,* by Bob Linsenman and Steve Nevala (Backcountry Guides, 2001).

The country of the northeast is deep and dark and wild. Some long sections of rivers have not seen the fall of an artificial fly since the beginning of time. The native brook trout are there in the fastness of the mysterious woods; the imported brown trout have gone native in many streams. You will find them if you slide on moccasins to the end of the trail, respect the habitat, and connect with the universe.

6 | West Central Wisconsin: A Green and Gentle Land

The streams and rivers of west central Wisconsin offer a pleasing variety, from the placid, intimate brook trout streams north of Eau Claire on the east to that fine trio of brown trout streams within striking distance of the Twin Cities on the west. The Kinnickinnic, which joins the border St. Croix above Prescott, is one of the best brown trout streams in the state. It is Janus-faced: Above River Falls it is narrow, cold, and wader-deep, with thick blue-black silt at the margins, and is frequently pinched by brush; below the city it is wide and open to easy fly-fishing in hip boots through a riffle and pool sequence for more than 8 miles. The Rush River is big-fish water, partly open, partly flanked by heavy undergrowth and limestone cliffs, with huge pools and long, frustrating flats. The most productive sections of the 40-mile-long Willow River lie in or close to the Willow River State Park at Hudson, offering solitude and serenity for early-morning and evening fly-fishers. McCann, Duncan, Tiffany, and others are productive small streams.

A School of Brook Trout Streams

"It's a bluebird day!" shouts Bill. Indeed, it is a rare clear day this late summer. Blame all of the rainy days this year on El Niño, that intermittent oceanic and atmospheric change off the coast of Peru. It is an example of the chaos effect—a change way down there means bank-full streams and saturated topsoil here, in northwestern Chippewa, northeastern Dunn, and southern Barron Counties.

But water, not too much, mind you, and never in torrents, please, gives our native brook trout wiggle room in these gems of streams. Water also encourages the mosquitoes to multiply, unfortunately. In another year it is La Niña that may bring drought, or otherwise give us fits.

MCCANN CREEK
DeLorme 73

"Fantastic!" yells Bill as he releases another water-bouncing brookie from the crystal waters of Category 2 McCann Creek upstream of the Old Mill Lane bridge, a few miles northeast of Bloomer off WI 40. There! We've pinpointed your first stop.

From here on, refer to your maps and don't lose your cool. Some bureaucrat, we suppose, at Madison, the state capital, is rationalizing the road signs in this part of Wisconsin. Or perhaps bureaucrats in the county seat are responsible. One theory assumes that 911 emergencies can be responded to quickly if a street number is known. At any rate the old, picturesque names, such as Corkscrew Road, which was aptly named, are being replaced with 1210th Avenue or 270th Street, or some such. Friends, we're losing our history under the guise of progress. We'd guess that a computer somewhere can locate 1210th Avenue on a grid easier than it can find Sheridan Road (270th Street). Probably Sheridan was named for the Civil War hero when a deer trail to a homestead was compacted into a wagon track that led to a coach road shortly after the War Between the States. Good-bye, General Phil Sheridan. We hardly remember you anyhow.

Steve Payne and Jeff Page, avid brook trout anglers

We'll use the old, descriptive names in the course of our itinerary out of respect for an area rich in history, with occasional brackets for the new street numbers where we have them.

Enough of the asides: Let us return to McCann. It's grasshopper time on the brook trout streams. A #12 Joe's Hopper is about right. Put on your waders—you'll need them on these narrow and deep little streams. Take your time, wade slowly up the middle, splatting your hopper fanlike from margin to margin on a .006 (5X) tippet. Don't send a bow wave ahead of you and be sure to absorb the beauty of this rolling country, with its prosperous farms, green forested ridges, and sumac bushes now touched with russet. Stalk those rising trout upstream from Old Mill to Morning Crest Lane and there sit and eat a sandwich. It's a bluebird day and all's right with the world. In September we also coaxed trout with a #18 Tan Caddis. On the 29th we fished through a spinner fall of the dark blue quill *(Paraleptophlebia debilis)*.

Bill waxes enthusiastic over these friendly streams. This is where you should bring your daughter to introduce her to the joys of fly-fishing, he says. Or a son. The streams are modest, not dangerous or intimidating. The problems presented to the neophyte are pretty forthright, not complex. The casts are short and the rods light and easy to handle. The hoppers float high and dry, and the take is topwater and aggressive. If not a daughter or son, introduce a friend to this art.

Bill allows that he saw hundreds of trout between Old Mill and Morning Crest, many of which he caught and released. They're not large, but gorgeous, and they come out shaking water as if they are scattering diamonds. What more could you ask?

You may fish downstream to WI 124, some 7 river miles, but below WI 64 the stream flattens and the trout habitat is less inviting. Below the WI 64 bridge we scared up at least a thousand mallards and a gaggle of geese, a sight to behold, but only one trout came to net. Although it is within the boundaries of a state fishery area, we weren't impressed with the stream in this stretch, but you might tread lightly there and uncover a variety of deeper pools and larger trout.

Complete facilities for travelers at Bloomer.

DUNCAN CREEK
DeLorme 72

Now drive west about 5 miles to Duncan Creek (Category 1 upstream of WI 64; Category 5 downstream to Lake Como Dam) to the bridge on County Road SS north of Bloomer near Horseshoe Road. There's a good run above the County Road SS bridge, then a neck, then a magnificent pool that will

Habitat improvement on Duncan Creek

warm the cockles of any fly-fisher's heart. Downstream is easy going through a mix of riffles and small pools.

Bill, who is not given to overstatement, says that this is even better than McCann. "It sure is a beautiful stream; I just fell in love with Duncan Creek."

There are just as many trout here as in McCann, but it seems to us that they run a bit heftier. We took them on a grasshopper and an Adams. Every time we dropped a fly into a likely spot—bingo! The Coachman streamer also worked well as an attractor.

"It's deep, clear water; temperature 56 degrees; cooperative fish. Sometimes they slash at the fly, sometimes up and out of the water and down on the fly; next time a sip. Some go crazy when they leap. Beautiful!"

There are three bridge crossings above County Road SS before you get into DNR land in the headwaters. These are all worth exploring. Bill also fished down from County Road SS almost to Lake Como at Bloomer through country open to fly-fishing. There are many more miles of designated trout water below Bloomer, all the way to Tilden. In 1998, 1,000 feet of crib shelters and riprap were installed in this area. The creek was narrowed, and the trout are responding to their new habitat. Larger brookies will result. At the end of a long-running controversy Bloomer decided to repair rather than remove its deteriorating dam. But the story will not necessarily end there: an engineering study might project a prohibitive cost.

Facilities at Bloomer.

SAND CREEK AND THE RED CEDAR RIVER
DeLorme 72

Next, go west from Duncan some 10 miles to the village of Sand Creek in Dunn County, about 2 miles north of WI 64 on County Road M. Centered at this charming little community, which reminds Bill of a Currier and Ives print or a Norman Rockwell *Post* cover, you'll find the end of 7.5 miles of beautifully rehabbed water containing wild brook and brown trout. Begin at Myron Park on County Road M in town, where you can wade upstream through a succession of riffles and pools, or drive east on County Road M to 1342nd Avenue, a dead end that curves around behind a repair garage and ends at a DNR parking area. From there on up in June we found brookies and browns cooperative, willing to attack a Coachman streamer, an Adams, or a Hornberg, all without prejudice. This stream is not as big as Duncan but it is a quality fishery. At 3 PM we counted a sporadic emergence of the March brown, *Stenonema vicarium*. March brown, indeed! You see what disinformation is distributed when we attach English names to American aquatic insects. The middle of May is about as early as you will find it in our parts; and gray fox would be a more precise description. There are excellent entry points upstream, perhaps even better than behind the garage.

We don't guarantee large trout, but Andy Lamberson did catch and release an 18-inch brown up here somewhere.

The Red Cedar River into which Sand Creek flows is a dream stream for canoeists. It is primarily a smallmouth stream, but a few large browns hang out at the mouths of the feeders where the inflow is cooler.

Facilities at Bloomer and at Chetek to the north.

UPPER PINE CREEK
DeLorme 72

Next, proceed northwest out of Sand Creek on County Road U, winding through the green hills of earth to Dallas in Barron County, where the three branches of Upper Pine Creek converge. You will have to ask permission close to Dallas, but upstream there is a Pine Creek Fishery Area along 5½, 4½, and 3½ Roads. Upper Pine Creek between Dallas and the Red Cedar River is not designated trout water, probably due to the warming effect of Dallas millpond. There are still 3,600 low-head dams in Wisconsin, many of them obstructing the free flow of what were, in historical times, trout streams.

Generally, on all Wisconsin and Minnesota trout streams you will find your best fishing where the DNRs have purchased blocks of land along the streams, or where they have leased easements. The blocks are shown in green on the Milwaukee Map Service maps and on the DeLorme by a leaping trout. Such stretches are likely to have been improved by bank stabilization, in-stream structures, and intermittent debrushing. But some streams will be cramped by brush and fallen snags, and beavers will have interrupted the flow.

In the spring and summer months on these brook trout streams, the trout will respond to Tiny Blue-Winged Olives, Adamses, ant and beetle patterns, and to colorful attractors. Trout that feed on those ubiquitous midges all season long will take a Griffith's Gnat most days. For underwater, try a Brassie. In September a grasshopper may be all that you need. There are other streams in the area that you may want to explore during your bluebird days in wonderful Wisconsin.

THE WILLOW RIVER
DeLorme 58 & 70

The Willow River wanders for 40 miles through the green hills of western Wisconsin in St. Croix County to join the St. Croix River at Hudson. Its prime trout waters lie about 4 road miles north of Interstate 94 near Hudson and only 25 miles east of the Twin Cities of St. Paul and Minneapolis and a seven-county metro area pushing toward 3 million inhabitants. Two Trout Unlimited chapters share interest in the Willow: the 1,300-member Twin Cities Chapter and the hands-on, hardworking members of the Kiap-TU-Wish Chapter centered at Hudson, Wisconsin. Although the lower Willow (and Willow Race) is one of the most popular trout streams in the state, it is seldom crowded, partly because there are so many fine streams in southeastern Minnesota and west central Wisconsin. A fly-fisher who is willing to walk in from Trout Brook Road, from the Burkhardt bridge, from the lot on 115th Avenue (River Road), or along Trout Brook Trail from the beach parking lot in Willow River State Park will usually find a section on which to while away a couple of hours without conflict.

Opening weekend and the last day of the season will find anglers stumbling over each other in friendly fashion, but when those wily brown trout and less-than-wily rainbow do not come easily to net, many casual fishermen return to one of more than 12,000 lakes for amusement.

Approximately 25 miles of the Willow, in several separate segments,

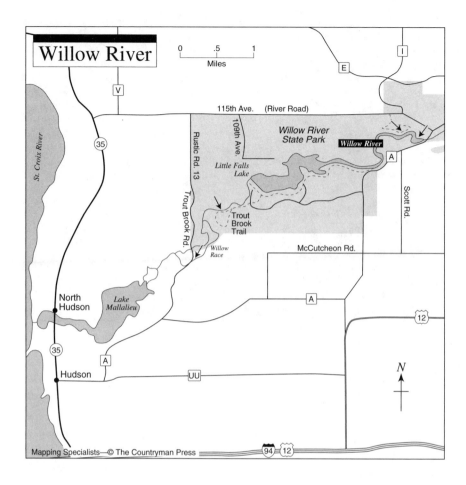

have been identified as respectable habitat for trout. More than 5 miles of the best waters are contained within the boundaries of the park, from the Burkhardt bridge at the junction of County Roads A and I to the twin bridges on Trout Brook Road on the outskirts of Hudson. Additional quality mileage, outside park boundaries, continues down from Trout Brook Road to Lake Mallalieu.

A daily activity fee is charged for entrance to the park at County Road A, another at the Burkhardt bridge on the same road, and a third west on 115th Avenue, aka River Road. A fourth fee-parking area has been added along County Road A between the park entrance and Burkhardt. From that lot you can walk down to the base of the old Willow Falls Dam, now removed. It is a tough hike back up the hill. We have not yet explored it fully, nor have we had reports of fine catches down there, although years ago the stretch below the dam was prime fast water.

Bill with a 15-inch brown on the Willow River

It was possible to fish without a fee upstream of the twin bridges on Trout Brook Road, but that has changed: however, you may fish downstream without charge. To find the bridges, take County Road A east from the north end of downtown Hudson (WI 35) to Trout Brook Road, also designated as Wisconsin Rustic Road R-13.

The Willow is known by three designations. The Willow is the long upper section from the headwaters in Cylon Marsh to the bifurcation in Willow River State Park, where the Willow splits to become the Willow Branch and the Willow Race. When they rejoin below Trout Brook Road and upstream from Lake Mallalieu, the river again becomes the Willow. Less than a mile downstream from Little Falls Lake and dam in the park, by foot along the Trout Brook Trail, you will find the bifurcation where the Race has been extensively improved with riprap and boulder retards. The Willow (and the Race branch) from Mounds Pond Dam upstream of Burkhardt and downstream to Lake Mallalieu are protected by Category 5 regulations: artificials only and a bag limit of one 16-inch trout.

Years ago we endured many dramatic moments with the brown trout between Little Falls Dam and the bifurcation, through a succession of long flats, pools, an island, a riffle, a long deadly flat, and then that intriguing cliff corner pool. More than one spectacular day is remembered there when the brown trout were like leopards leaping.

I remember one night down from the cliff pool, belly-deep in seeming silver, the last light fading, the bats side-slipping like fighters and the Hexagenia *clumsily lumbering aloft after a long float. Later, long later, Roger Fairbanks described how three nameless enthusiasts transferred by dark of moon a washtub of Hex nymphs from the Kinnickinnic to the Willow. Creative witchery, it was.*

In recent years the mile or so above the bifurcation has produced more bluegills than brown trout. This may be due to warm water flowing over the lip of the dam rather than flowing out of the lower level of a gate. However, other anglers may see it differently. One lady angler is reported to have been catching 18- to 20-inch browns below the dam on a Llama fished close to the bottom.

The mile-long Race, which is the better of the two parallel sections, possibly because of greater spring inflow, has undergone extensive research and rehabilitation during the past 25 years. The DNR, with the herculean hands-on help of Kiap-TU-Wish, has added riprap, bank structures, brush bundles, and half-logs. The Race, which averages 39 feet in width and 12 inches in depth, is perfect for wading fly-fishers. Years ago a 27-inch brown was taken from the Race on a spinner. More recently a 24½-inch brown was captured with an artificial fly. Twice. The second fisherman creeled the fish and was almost drummed out of the Twin Cities Chapter of Trout Unlimited.

The Willow Branch, a bit more than a mile in length, has always posed a problem. Although it is wide, with riffles and runs in sequence, it has never been as productive as the Race. Some anglers, nevertheless, prefer it for its relative solitude. You are less likely to encounter another angler. In one electro-fishing survey we didn't find many trout in this segment, but we did bring to surface a few very large browns from a couple of pools. Bob Reynolds, a master who has solved the problems of the Willow Branch and the challenges of the Rush River for large browns, puts his fly on the bottom of the pools even if that requires a short section of lead core. Jim was chagrined to watch Bob release hefty browns from a pool that Jim had just laboriously fished by more conventional methods.

The section of the river from the Burkhardt bridge at the junction of County Roads A and I down to Little Falls Lake in the park is newer trout water. In 1991 the state legislature appropriated funds to remove Willow Falls Dam at the head of Little Falls Lake. The dam was disintegrating and the pond was a silted heat sump. The following year the dam was breached, the pond drained, and more than a mile of new stream was riprapped. The river here has already developed character. It has carved its way down through 4 or 5 feet of silt and sand. Points and pockets and islands are forming. There are several picture-perfect riffles at the Burkhardt bridge where fly-fishers congregate to exchange anecdotes and prevarications;

you'll also find riffles and pools at the end of mowed trails from the 115th Avenue parking lot.

Steve Payne to Bill Shogren: "I'm pleased to report the Burkhardt stretch of the Willow is alive and well. On Monday I spent a few hours in the lower meadow section (just up from the canyon) and got into some nice fish. In one 50-yard run I caught two browns 16 or 17 inches and two rainbows about the same size. Also, the stockers the DNR released in March are now pushing the 12-inch mark and will only get bigger as the season progresses. By September there should be plenty of 13- and 14-inchers to be had, plus the larger trout that have migrated back into the area."

Before the application of Category 5 restrictions we had seen spin-fishers coming out with their limits of three rainbows to 15 inches. Larger browns have been caught and released, as Steve noted. Tim Faricy walked to the elbow upstream from the 115th Street lot and came out an hour later after having released two 16-inch rainbows. This is big and beautiful open water that you can explore all the way to the dells or canyon, as Steve has done. The foot of the old dam can be reached by going upstream along the Pioneer Trail from the park office, or much more easily from the new lot on County Road A north of the entrance.

None of the several sections of the Willow supports much in the way of natural reproduction. Each fall the Kiap-TU-Wish Chapter assists in the planting of 10,000 fingerling browns. Marty Engel, area DNR biologist and fish manager for a large area of western Wisconsin, notes that "there is no guarantee that a cold-water fishery will flourish above and below the dam site . . . The Willow has had a general warming in it overall. Loss of spring flow is a likely answer . . . from many sources, including human development in the area."

Anglers may also walk the banks or wade the lower river downstream from the twin bridges through newly acquired state property into wider and deeper water. Immediately below the Race bridge a demonstration rehabilitation has been completed. Riprap is extensive: Dozens of structures have been installed. The trout are hiding under cover, and they may not come out to waggle their fins at you. Lay a beadhead at the edge of the bank cover at the end of the day or under an overcast sky. Counting the two branches below Trout Brook Road, there may be as much as a mile of excellent habitat and a few 6-pound browns that cruise between the lake and the lower river. Many of our friends always choose the downstream reach to hunt for larger trout, while we often enter the park along the Race, and even beyond the bifurcation to old familiar scenes of glory.

In 1997, after a rigorous and occasionally rancorous argument, Mounds Pond Dam upstream from the Burkhardt bridge was removed and the 72-year-old pond drained. The river cut through several feet of muck, the exposed flats were planted with oats, and the river is developing character. While there is some cold-water seepage in the canyon area, there is no guarantee that trout will ever reproduce.

North of Burkhardt County Roads A and E join and run as one for 0.4 mile. Where County Road E separates to go east just before the bridge, there's a DNR lot at the end of a short spur. From the lot to the site of the old dam is about three-quarters of a mile worthy of testing with a streamer. In August 2000 this new section was planted to adult rainbows and browns and to brown trout fingerlings.

Your trout map also indicates sections of trout habitat upstream around Boardman on County Road A and around Deer Park on US 63. Many years ago a Deer Park tavern posted annually the fabulous catches of browns from the Willow. These upper sections are Category 2; the South Fork, which contains wild brook trout, is Category 4.

Other than the white fly at Burkhardt at the beginning of August, the dominant hatches on the Willow are caddisflies, midges, several species of *Baetis* (which may appear almost anytime), spinner falls of the fluorescent *Stenonema/Stenacron* seen most often above the bifurcation in June and July, and the trico, a reliable morning hatch from June 20 through September 26. Other anglers have reported sulphur hatches in June. An entomological survey noted the presence of four species of *Ephemerella*, as well as *Centroptilum,* a minuscule mayfly.

The Spider on a silken tippet settles more lightly than milkweed seed on this complex of currents below the island down the Trout Brook Trail. I blink my eyes, cameralike, to record the memory—the slant of sunlight through shimmering leaves, the liquid silver of water flowing, and the brassy flash of a brown trout under my ephemeral fly.

Facilities at Hudson and on Interstate 94, at River Falls to the south on WI 35, and at Stillwater, Minnesota, a historic river town on the St. Croix. The Rustic Hut is a supper club in Burkhardt; the J&R Ranch at I-94 and WI 12 is a superior steakhouse. There is a campground with more than 70 spaces in Willow River State Park.

THE KINNICKINNIC
DeLorme 58

Trout were sipping midges or minuscule mayfly emergers on the glide above the river ford, but the browns were indifferent to every artificial, no matter how artfully presented. Dusk crept from the willow thicket toward river's edge and a wraith of mist formed over the stream.

At 9:09 PM precisely, bats began to circle the run below the ford. The

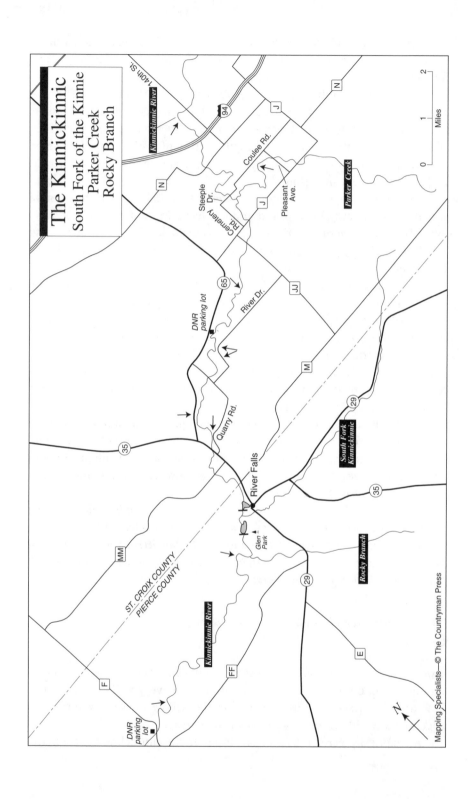

The Kinnickinnic
South Fork of the Kinnie
Parker Creek
Rocky Branch

140th St.

Kinnickinnic River

94

N

J

Coulee Rd.

Steeple Dr.

Cemetery Rd.

J

Pleasant Ave.

Parker Creek

N

65

River Dr.

JJ

DNR parking lot

M

Quarry Rd.

29

35

South Fork
Kinnickinnic

River Falls

Glen Park

35

MM

ST. CROIX COUNTY
PIERCE COUNTY

Rocky Branch

29

Kinnickinnic River

E

FF

F

DNR parking lot

N

0   1   2
Miles

Mapping Specialists—© The Countryman Press

river had become a sheet of pale watered silk. A scimitar of moon slashed the tops of pines. Some nocturnal beast padded through the woods, invisible. A great blue heron beat upstream on the hunt for rising trout, its wings like damp sheets flap-flapping.

Under the quarter light—moonlight and starlight and afterglow—exactly at 9:14 PM, the first Hex wig-wagged from the darkling stream. The emerging duns that followed were pale green, long green woolly worms with outrageous wings. They writhed in the film for 20 or 30 feet. When they rose, clumsily fluttering, they skipped again and again like an overloaded plane trying for liftoff. It was the beginning of that spectral hatch of the great night mayfly *Hexagenia limbata,* on the upper Kinnickinnic River of Wisconsin.

The first brown to take a #12 Blond Wulff was a slim 12 inches. The next half dozen, all in the 8- to 10-inch range, responded eagerly to a wiggling downstream float. Air temperature was a calm 75 degrees, water 60 degrees, typical of this superb spring creek.

By 9:35 PM the hatch was over in my 100 yards of river. Twenty minutes of fly-fishing for quality trout, and the river went dead. The Kinnickinnic is only 45 minutes east of the Twin Cities and its trout are finessed by experts, but I had encountered not one other fisherman.

I folded up and followed the edge of the potato field through powder-dry dust. The farmers needed rain. Fishing is like farming, it occurred to me, not for the first time. It is either too hot or too cold, too wet or too dry—or something. Maybe fishing promotes even more frustration. Sometimes on the Kinnie, the name given to it by its familiars, the air is so still and close that mosquitoes eat you alive and trout belly down in the weeds; or it's so windy that you can't control the cast. Or the water's so low and clear that you spook the trout, even beyond the reach of "far and fine." Or something. Ah well! Who ever said that life, or fishing, would be all pony rides on a May morning? A raucous night bird made me look back over my shoulder. Was it a salute or a touch of the raspberry?

Twenty miles of the Kinnickinnic River are superb trout water, from the spring holes above Interstate 94 in St. Croix County to County Highway F near the St. Croix River in Pierce County.

It is the premier trout stream of west central Wisconsin. Or rather, it is like two streams. For approximately 10 miles above the city of River Falls, the Kinnie is narrow, cold, deep, and clear, flowing over sand and gravel down the middle, with silt at the margins. It is a typical spring creek. Chest-high waders are necessary up there. Access is very easy: At least 17 access points—including a DNR parking lot on WI 65 and a recently constructed lot where River Drive turns a corner—and more than 75 percent of the streambank are either owned by or under easement to the Wisconsin DNR. Be advised that to keep visitors from having to chase all over the map, the spring holes are upstream of the bridge on 140th Street, which is about a mile north of I-94. Although the river appears on the maps above this point, it's gone underground during the past 30 years due to dewatering.

Very few forage fish are indigenous to the upper section; consequently, the trout do not grow to trophy size above River Falls. A 15-inch brown trout is rare. The upper river, including the mile or so through town, is Category 2: daily bag limit of five, minimum 7 inches for both brooks and browns. DNR fish managers have asked us kindly to return all brook trout.

In past years electro-shocking surveys have revealed astounding numbers of trout in the upper river—one year as many as 9,000 per mile at one survey station. Marty Engel says the numbers range from 5,000 to 8,000 per mile, and the biomass from 300 to 400 pounds per acre. In spring, before the waterweeds are up, the trout can see an angler coming from a mile away. Once the weeds are up, the trout will lie in the channels among the weeds. Pinpoint accuracy is necessary. Fly-fishers should wade upstream so as not to send a thread of silt ahead of them and put down the trout.

Below the last dam in Glen Park in River Falls, through the valley that some folks call "the gorge," the lower Kinnie is more like a freestone stream—rubble strewn, with dark pools at the bends, long, challenging flats, and a succession of riffles where small trout are plentiful and feed aggres-

Neil Dobbs on the Kinnickinnic

sively on midges all season long. Anglers can get by with hip boots in the lower 10 miles.

Large numbers of brown trout also inhabit the lower river, 2,000 to 4,000 per mile in a recent survey, through Category 5 water, special regulations: artificials only and a bag limit of one 16-inch trout. The entire river is of such quality that planting of trout was discontinued in 1974—and that last plant was only a token to satisfy put-and-take anglers.

Slightly warmer water below the dams has permitted development of several species of minnows, as well as leeches and some crayfish, through the gorge; consequently, the trout grow faster. An occasional trophy trout in excess of 16 inches will surprise a diligent angler who hikes into the remote reaches to fish in the shadows of the cliffs.

Downstream through tangled country, entry points are few and far between. Fishermen walk in from a pair of locations in the city—by easy trail from Glen Park to the foot of the dam (park at the tennis courts) or down the public trail from River Ridge Road. A third option is to work up from County Road F, some 8 river miles down the valley. If anglers are persuasive, they may make the acquaintance of some farmer who'll let them walk in on one of the long, steep trails between the city and County Road F. Several of the trails are dangerous, and coming out after dark is hazardous.

Many anglers thoroughly enjoy fishing right through town with access at the County Road MM bridge, at Heritage Park, and at a couple of bridges in town. We've never been enthusiastic about fishing within sound or sight of backyards and roadway traffic, but you might like to sample the Kinnie there.

Although we opened this profile with a romantic portrait of a night on the upper Kinnie with the fabled Hex, we're duty bound to report that the Hex is no longer a major emergence; the nights are still productive of fly-fishing intrigues, however. The disappearance of the *Hexagenia* may be the result of improved water quality—falling water temperatures, a reduction in siltation, a speeding of the flow due to the removal of brush and the installation of structures, or other factors beyond our ken. On the upper river the significant mayflies run to small sizes, generally #16 and #18. *Baetis* species are omnipresent. Anglers have reported sulphurs of the *Ephemerella* persuasion and yellow stoneflies, and scuds are everywhere. Without making too much of a point about it, probably the best way to fish the upper KK is upstream nymphing with a strike indicator. In any section where there is grass at the margins, hoppers in the hot months are the ticket.

The emergences on the lower river are more varied, and the mayfly forms arrive in larger hook sizes. March browns, *Stenonema vicarium*, appear sporadically between mid-May and mid-June. *Ephemerella invaria* and *E. rotunda* have been reported between May 25 and June 15. A persistent angler may run into slate drakes or white-gloved howdys, *Isonychia,* in July and again in August, but because the nymphs crawl to shore to emerge, the fly-fishing is at nightfall to spentwings and not to the duns.

Caddisflies appear in quantity on both sections, but most of the downwings are small. A #16 Elk Hair Caddis is recommended. A #20 Griffith's Gnat or Adams will replicate the prolific midges. Trico spinner falls occur most mornings toward the end of June, when the air temperature touches 68 degrees, and continue through season's end. Giant brown stoneflies emerge around June 1 on the lower river. On May 15 the helicoptering craneflies (yellow sallies) will rise.

On or about May 15 on the lower river, an angler may encounter the sporadic emergence of a #14 or #16 "blue-winged olive," which he might take for a mayfly. But this one is a crane fly, probably of the *Antocha* genus. It becomes an adult underwater and flies to the surface, where it rises like a helicopter, straight up, with its forelegs held upright like a spike. Although in the air the insect may appear to be a #16 or larger, due to its long legs and wings, underwater it's actually closer to a #18. These babies don't waste any time at the surface, so a soft-hackle is the ticket to success. The crane fly is common to many of our streams, but often missed by anglers who try to imitate it with a dry fly.

On May 25 at around 7:30 PM, John Schorn of the Twin Cities Chapter of TU found clouds of caddis in the air and some trout slashing at but not taking his caddis imitation. He captured a fly, discovered it was a crane, switched to a grayish #18 soft-hackle with yellow floss, and began to take trout.

Dr. Clarke Garry, of the University of Wisconsin at River Falls, has begun a multiyear study of the aquatic life of the two parts of the Kinnie. The result will be a welcome addition to a fly-fisher's bag of tricks. In a preliminary survey of the upper river, Dr. Garry did not find many Hex nymphs.

Two miles of water from County Road F to the St. Croix through the state park are very pretty. Some large trout are taken on Rapalas and bait, as are smallmouths and walleyes, but the hunt usually isn't worth the effort due to the lack of sufficient cover for trout. It's a lovely place for a summer picnic, though.

This is Shogren's and Humphrey's home stream. Jim numbers the Kinnie among his baker's dozen of the best trout streams anywhere.

Twenty miles of superb trout water await the fly-fisher who is willing to tread lightly the deep and narrow track of the upper river, matching the hatch with a tiny fly at the end of a spiderweb tippet, or one who is willing to walk into the lonely reaches of the lower river.

Those marvelous miles are the precious jewels of the fly-fisher's memory. We'll give two hours of our lives, anytime, to fish our separate 100

Jim at The Elbow on the Lower Kinnickinnic

yards of the Kinnickinnic on a sultry summer evening, with rising expectations when the bats begin to play.

In 1994 the Kinnickinnic River Land Trust was formed to protect the river and its watershed. The river was threatened by its proximity to the expanding metro area of the Twin Cities and by growth in Wisconsin's St. Croix County, one of the rising stars of exurban sprawl. The goals of the trust were to involve the community in conservation, protect the natural resource and scenic areas, improve water quality, and enhance wild trout populations. Nonprofit land trusts, countrywide, have developed unique methods by which to protect watersheds and other natural wonders from unbridled development. The accomplishments of the Kinnickinnic Land Trust are spectacular. Conservation easement donations have protected 2.5 miles on the river and 817 acres in the watershed. Kelly Creek, a tributary, and 46 acres around it were purchased and retained by the trust. The popular Swinging Gate half mile of trout water within a 53-acre parcel was purchased and resold to the DNR. And that is a story in itself. A small farm that included the Swinging Gate acreage was suddenly advertised for auction. Within days, a family active in the land trust bought the farm at auction and sold the river acreage to the trust; the trust in turn sold it to the state of Wisconsin. Without the trust, its members and contributors, and a very active executive director, access to one of the sweet stretches of the river would have been lost to us; possibly to be divided for a development of green lawns and NO TRESPASSING signs. The Kinnickinnic River Land Trust can be reached at P.O. Box 87, River Falls, WI 54022; phone 715-425-5738, fax 715-425-4479. The street address is 421 North Main Street, River Falls, in the Prairie Mill Building.

Three Tributaries of the Kinnickinnic

THE SOUTH FORK OF THE KINNIE
DeLorme 58

The South Fork of the Kinnie, a Category 2 stream, enters the Kinnie close to Glen Park after its trip through the university campus. The powers-that-be at the university and the city fathers and mothers of River Falls now recognize that any pristine river is a unique resource, esthetically and economically. We expect that the South Fork will improve as the various interests draw a bead on it. Access is at WI 35 going south out of town and at a couple of bridges close to WI 29 going east. Although the land along WI 29 is mostly level farmland, its flat and open nature would lend itself to easy rehabilitation with heavy equipment. Watch this space.

PARKER CREEK
DeLorme 58

Parker Creek represents another side of the rehabilitation story. It is a Category 2 spring creek that in past years has received intensive care, and was known for the production of native or wild brook trout. Then in May 1998 there occurred a catastrophic fish kill on 4.5 miles of the creek due to the application of liquid manure too soon before a substantial and not quite anticipated rainfall. The manure used up the oxygen, killing 3,500 to 4,000 brown and brook trout. Downstream in the Kinnie 4,000 brown trout were snuffed. Following the usual vigorous discussions concerning property rights versus the rights of the wider polity, and with the loom of lawsuits, a local farmer was modestly fined and required to allow for buffer zones along the creek; a promise was extracted to go and sin no more. A delicate compromise that we applaud.

THE ROCKY BRANCH
DeLorme 58

The Rocky Branch, or Rocky Run as it is known locally, closely parallels the Kinnie at the bottom of the second, long, steep, public trail from River Ridge

Road. That's at the sharp corner once graced by a NO TRESPASSING sign, now thankfully gone. This is approximately three-quarters of a mile downstream from Glen Park. Rocky Run curves away from the river for 100 yards, usually through a beaver pond or two, unless the DNR has removed them, then rejoins at Richard's Riffle. We named the riffle for Richard "Dick" Frantes, who is memorialized in the Tiffany Creek profile. Dick caught his tiger trout here, an infertile cross that has been described also as "giraffe-striped."

There are several stair-step pools upstream toward the origin near County Road FF. The wild brookies up there seldom exceed 7 inches, but they are pretty.

Comprehensive lodging and dining facilities at River Falls, at Interstate 94, and in Hudson. See the vertical Swensen sundial on the wall of the Kleinpell Fine Arts Building at the university. It's said to be the largest and most accurate vertical dial in North America.

THE RUSH RIVER

DeLorme 59

Several years ago a 13-pound brown was abstracted from the Rush River by Walt Anderson, a member of the Eau Galle–Rush River Sportsman's Club. On June 7, 1998, Siiri Carver, Loren's daughter, caught and released a 23-inch brown that was compromised by a little black fly, not otherwise identified. On another June day Al Farmes released a 22-inch brown at the tail of the "complex pool," fooled by a carpenter ant facsimile. The Rush, wholly within Pierce County, has produced outsized browns for many years, often caught on live bait; sometimes on "water worms," the larval stage of the giant crane fly. The adult crane looks like a predatory mosquito, the larva like a small, somewhat dirty banana. Jim Loga, a renowned big-fish fly-fisher, took his last 22-inch brown on his Wobble Ace, a streamer with a silver belly.

On August 1, 1996, we were standing back from the big pool at the dead end, hiding behind a screen of brush, when 10 large trout slipped out of the pool singly, or by twos or by threes, to take station in that run along the west bank. It was exactly 8:20 PM. The trout were easy to count when they crossed runnels of sand to swim from pool to feeding area. Imagine! when we duplicated the observation one week later. Rush River browns have been known to rise to olives or tricos during the day, but you are advised to fish when the sun is off the water, or fish into dark with headlight and net. In areas of broken bottom where crayfish scuttle, big browns laze away the day to pursue the equivalent of shrimp cocktail at evening.

In mid-May yellow crane flies, which come quickly off the water like helicopters, are duplicated by a soft-hackle Partridge and Yellow. The hack-

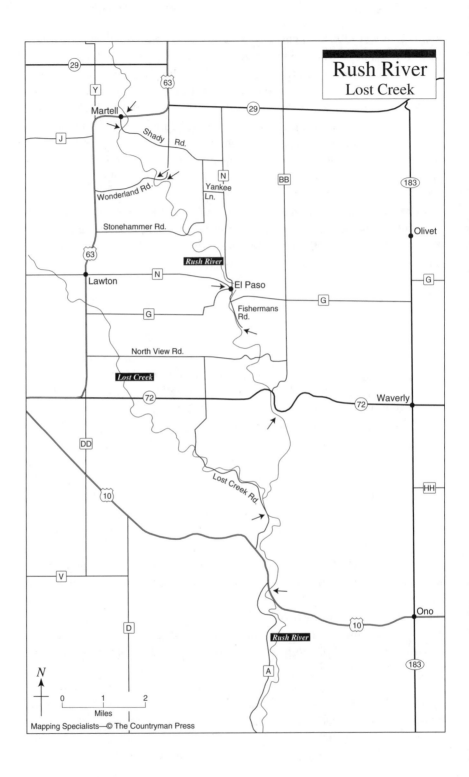

Rush River
Lost Creek

les should be long. Bill has been told that the lower river has a Hex hatch, somewhere around the middle of July. Because the Hex is a burrowing mayfly, look for it where there is compacted silt. Charlie Johnston, a notable fly-fisher, said that he puts on a hopper on September 1 and doesn't take it off. Al Farmes reported a break-of-dawn trip to his favorite crossing. He began with his D.B. (Dumb Bunny), really a #20 wound with a dubbing brush. The D.B. entranced a few fish. Then, at about 7:15, the PMDs (pale morning duns) emerged. Many refusals: The fish would rise, sniff Al's PMD, turn up their noses, and sink. Finally, around 8 AM, a huge fall of tricos appeared, again with many refusals. An experienced Rush River angler asserts that the fishing is "dead" prior to and immediately after a trico spinner fall. Nowhere will we say that the Rush River is easy.

Brown trout inhabit the river from a mile above the fishermen's parking lot on WI 29, 11 miles east of River Falls, downstream to 3 miles south of US 10, a river distance of 23 miles. It is Category 4 all the way: brown and rainbow trout 12 inches, brook trout 8 inches, and a bag limit of three. The fishing is considered excellent at several bridges, even through the villages of Martell and El Paso. Yes, El Paso. Can't you see some grizzled stage driver from the West coming home to die and naming this wagon crossing for a place out of his nostalgic past? A tiny park has been added to the northwest bank of the Rush in Martell on US 63. There is very little public land or posted easement on the river. The farmers are friendly—one of them even invites fishers but eschews horses and assorted trail machines—but the future for trout fishers is murky, because this premium land may be parceled for private estates.

Scot Stewart, a former fish manager for the DNR, since promoted, noted that the fish are not distributed uniformly; they are "clumped," he said, meaning that a fisherman may want to search for rising trout from a lookout on a bridge. About 2,500 trout per mile is average; and most of those, browns and rainbows, are planted. Recent studies infer that natural reproduction is occurring at an increasing rate. The Rush has all of the attributes of a broad, classic fly-fishing stream: deep pools, runs over rubble, limestone cliffs and shaded glens, a complex of hatches, and plenty of forage—sculpins, leeches, crayfish—to grow trout quickly and large. Although the Rush receives its water primarily from surface runoff down steep slopes rather than from groundwater seepage, summer water temperatures seem to be falling, which may indicate why there is some natural reproduction. The river is noted for the number and size of trout that overwinter into subsequent years. Both brown and rainbow trout are planted annually, a continuous project of the Sportsman's Club, whose members are friendly to strangers but fiercely protective of their river. No club works more diligently.

Trout habitat has been improved with funds from the state and substantial cash donations from both the Eau Galle–Rush club and the Ellsworth Rod and Gun Club, which has a clubhouse on the river. Both groups also donated hands-on help to install a rock chute and 18 lunker structures. Other work included the contouring of banks and the introduction of root wads.

Brook trout, which reproduce naturally in Cave and Lost Creek, drift into the main river early season and late when the water temperature hovers around their ideal 58 degrees.

June 16. Overcast sky, good for trout fishing, and Loren Carver promised to take me to "the Blue Hole" to show me the trout. As we wound down the hill from the onetime savanna into the steep, green valley, I said, "I remember this place!" Indeed, I had forced my way up that remembered difficult path to the long hole below the pasture many times, many years ago. The river ran full and ice-water clear under the bridge. The narrow path through shoulder-high Burning Donkey, skirting deadfall and ducking under fallen trees, was goose-goo slippery. Loren soldiered on, I slipping and sliding, and here is a fall with a thump. Is the Blue Hole worth it? Finally, the squeeze

Dr. Art Kaemmer on the Rush River above Martell

through a sideways stile and there we are. Lo! I have seen it all already; one of my favorites when I was younger and fitter. Loren caught and released five; I released one. The rocky bottom is stumble strewn; by July 1 the bankside jungle growth will be head-high, and coming out after dark a nightmare. Otherwise, a memorable day; except for Frustration Pool on the way out. That you could skip.

The Rush is subject to pesticide and herbicide runoff and to scouring by flash floods, and yet year after year it produces trophies for those who will take time to learn its secrets. In 1998 fishermen and residents opposed an 850-cow feedlot operation that would have straddled a dry wash into the Rush River. Opposition was strong enough to cause the lot to move elsewhere; however, the danger remains as population grows and development reaches into the countryside.

Twin Citian Steve Payne, Payner to NHL fans, had his heart stop during the early season on the Rush above WI 72. Steve spotted a 24-inch brown in a pool and tossed a #16 Hare's Ear. The brown took one halfhearted swipe in three passes, but no hook-up. On the fourth pass a 14-inch brown took the fly. As the little one struggled, the big brown attacked. Three times the cannibal charged and missed. Steve could have reached out and touched the lunker when he netted the 14-incher. Awesome, according to Steve. Maybe you should carry a net on the Rush River of Wisconsin.

It is 8:25 on "the complex pool." Again 10 trout crossed from pool to run. Just before 10 PM Bill catches a 15½-inch brown on a Prince Nymph. It is deep shadow among the trees and cold; Bill is invisible. But what a night! The Big Dipper is stitched boldly against a blue-black sky, and the North Star is as bright as a planet.

LOST CREEK

DeLorme 59

Lost Creek joins the Rush between WI 72 and US 10 and is crossed by Lost Creek Road. Several streamside easements also invite the attention of anglers. It is a tiny jewel of a stream worthy of an hour or two of precision casting with light lines and tiny flies for feisty brookies. There are two long, conjoined pools between the highways, but we choose not to pinpoint their location. They contain naturally reproducing brook trout that could be pounded to extinction in a matter of days. Not to be overshadowed always by the larger Rush, in June 2000 Lost Creek yielded a 22-inch, 4-pound, 9-ounce brown to Jacob Elsinger.

Facilities for visitors to both the Rush River and Lost Creek at Ellsworth and River Falls.

THE TRIMBELLE RIVER
DeLorme 58

The approximately 14 miles of the Trimbelle River lie wholly within Pierce County, Wisconsin, rising in farmland and pasture 8 or 9 miles south of River Falls and close to the village of Beldenville at the intersection of WI 65 and County Road J. For many years it was considered a second-class stream with little or no natural reproduction, requiring annual infusions of brown and rainbow trout. Humphrey's earlier experiences with the stream discouraged his further interest. In recent times Shogren has had some nice things to say about it. So here we are with this somewhat tentative endorsement.

While there is access at bridges on a couple of upstream roads, we recommend an exploratory on Posten Road 1, now known as 870th Street (!), where the DNR and the Trimbelle Rod & Gun Club have improved and sign-posted about half a mile of stream habitat. This location is a literal stone's throw west of County Road J. On older maps, by the way, Posten Road was known as Lovers Lane. The stream flow here is swift over large gravel, but shallow with some fishable pools at the bends.

Farther downstream there is habitat improvement at the Crosstown Road (570th Avenue) bridge, where the Eau Galle Rod & Gun Club members have also contributed hours of grunt work to improve your fishing. On a late-March day Jim spooked a pod of large fish when he peeked over the bridge railing. Sayonara. A day later a fleet of 30 or more planted browns ignored his presence. He couldn't raise one of those, either.

Downstream you'll find Leonard Park on County Road O at Peaceful Lane, and Trimbelle on US 10 where we have rousted some modest browns through the village park. Beyond that the river parallels and crisscrosses County Road O all the way to the Mississippi. There are numerous access points where you can hunt for larger trout that have located niches in which to lie and wait for finger food. Or they may be anticipating your Woolly Bugger.

The Trimbelle still needs substantial habitat improvement. In the upper reaches there are silt inflows from pastures, or sluggish current through tangles of fallen timber. At Leonard Park, for example, sand impedes the flow, although there were trout lazing in shade against the riprap. The DNR rates the Trimbelle as Category 4.

THE EAU GALLE RIVER
DeLorme 59

The Eau Galle is a wide river that is designated trout water for 14 miles, from County Road N south of Interstate 94 in St. Croix County, through scenic hills and precipitous valleys in Pierce County, finally to reach the Mississippi. It should be a frequent destination for trout fishers, and may become so if changes are made to the temperature of the waters released from the Army Corps of Engineers' dam at Spring Valley.

For years the Eau Galle above town was subject to flash floods from farm fields through hills and gorges, creating consternation and havoc in Spring Valley and downstream. The Flood Control Act of 1958 resulted in a rolled-earth dam on the north edge of Spring Valley that controls the runoff from a 64-square-mile drainage area. The dam also produced Lake George, now named Eau Galle Lake, and a substantial 630-acre recreational area.

Above the lake there are reputed to be natural brook trout and planted browns, but one of our sources suggests that the brook trout are "blown out" during the spring floods. Another source believes that brown trout will seek the cooler waters upstream of the lake during the summer months. In an adventure of discovery in the spring of 2000, Loren Carver (no relation, he says, to that famed explorer Jonathan Carver) and Jim Humphrey, and perhaps in pursuit of a chimera, probed the upper reaches above the lake. It was breathtakingly beautiful, alongside clear cold ponds under striated, vine-clad cliffs, and through occasional musical riffles. But the water, alas, appeared to be sterile, possibly due to fluctuating water levels. No rises, a brace of tiny minnows startled, no scuttling crayfish, and only microcaddis dotting the streambed rocks. There was evidence of recent high water. This is a place of dramatic beauty but few if any trout. If a pelting rain begins while you are exploring, get out.

Dick Frantes, an old friend, liked to fish below the dam right through town, but more of us prefer the downstream reaches where the scenery is natural. There are large trout in the Eau Galle that have wintered over and have fattened in a niche. You may want to try for them at the bridges downstream. The habitat down there is marginal, but some of our friends greet us with knowing looks when we denigrate the Eau Galle. A consortium of interests, public and private, is working with the corps to lower water temperature below the lake by manipulating water flow through the gates.

If you are interested in drawing your own conclusions, the stretch above the lake can be reached by taking County Road B south from I-94 to Boston Road, then east 1.5 miles to the northwest day-use area. Park immediately upstream of the slab bridge and go up. Good luck. Downstream of the lake there are numerous entries in Spring Valley and at the bridges on 170th Street and 770th Avenue.

Your map will show Lousy Creek on the upper east side of the lake. "Lousy" is an eminently accurate characterization, we think.

WILSON CREEK

DeLorme 59 & 60

There is a long stretch of Interstate 94, west of Menomonie, Wisconsin, that rises sinuously over ravines and between hills. And you tell yourself that down there in one of those hidden hollows, there must be a trout stream, or even two.

While I was otherwise engaged, my then partner would sometimes strike out for Wilson Creek to annoy the brook trout. Dick's 35-year record and rating of trout streams reveal that he fished it on 21 days, for 57 hours and a total catch of 258 trout, of which 243 were brookies. That is a remarkable 4.5 trout per hour. I wish that I could do as well. The last time we fished Wilson together I caught six, and he probably twice as many.

For all practical purposes, Wilson Creek begins about 2 miles east of the village of Wilson on US 12. The bridge is identified by an outcropping of limestone on the northeast side of the dead-end road that leads to the quarry. Don't bother exploring the road to the quarry; it curves away from the stream, which is probably unfishable up there anyway. You may fish down from the bridge through bottomlands, partly open, partly closed in. But the stream is quite small, shallow, and clear, suitable for pocket-picking. One of Dick's first stops, coming from the west, was at the bridge on 80th Street (Cherry Road), but the access is now posted. Ah weil, ah woe.

You may be tempted to examine the North Branch of the Wilson on the way east on US 12. Although there is a Public Hunting and Fishing Ground up there, the stream is too thin for fly-fishers. Our suggestion is to proceed east on US 12 to 250th Street (Valley Road), where you may work between the US 12 bridge and the Valley Road bridge. Downstream, a onetime DNR easement has been electrified for cattle. If you can wade under the bridge, you may be able to research that open section. However, only half a mile downstream you'll find a neat wayside on the riverside from which you may fish up or down. Our third preferred entry is at the County Road K bridge, where it is somewhat open both up and down. Downstream from County Road K at 690th Avenue and 390th Street the stream is mud-slick at the margins, indicative of excessive runoff. On my last trip the creek was martini clear upstream and slightly milky down. I should have had an angleworm.

If you examine your map, as we know you always do, you'll find Gilbert Creek, smaller than Wilson, which also joins the Red Cedar River at Menomonie. This pretty stream runs among spectacularly green and gentle hills, but we have not yet solved the problem of access, although the bridge on 377th Street (Brewery Road) is worth a try. Dick Frantes's record lists zero trout in three hours; hardly definitive.

ELK CREEK
DeLorme 60

Elk Creek, in Dunn and Chippewa Counties near Eau Claire, is a good example of what can happen to a degraded trout stream if it receives tender loving care.

When Bill first fished Elk Creek in 1950 the fishing was put-and-take. Since then this stream has recovered, and now features natural reproduction of both brook and brown trout. Cattle grazing and careless crop farming were a problem decades ago. Over the years these practices have changed. Habitat improvement by the Wisconsin DNR and volunteer sportsmen's clubs like the Ojibleau Chapter (Eau Claire) of Trout Unlimited have created a thriving trout population. The water temperature is perfect, and the insect hatches are abundant. Hendrickson, sulphur, and caddis hatches are predictable and plentiful.

This spring creek can be entertaining for the angler who likes to explore. Don't pass up the several feeder creeks.

The upper third of Elk Creek is crossed by WI 29, and the lower third by Interstate 94. You will find stream improvements immediately upstream of WI 29 on Elk Creek Road on the west side of the river, and below WI 29 on Elk Creek Road on the east side of the river. The state hunting and fishing area extends to about half a mile downstream from US 12. We do not recommend fishing much below County Road EE, although some anglers have reported the capture of trout below Elk Creek Lake Dam.

TIFFANY CREEK
DeLorme 71

In memory of the Acerbic Angler, Richard John Frantes, 1922–1993, friend, companion, and fly-fisher.

Over a five-year period, Dick Frantes, also known as Dry-Fly Dick, and I fished for trout together on more than 200 days in more than 50 Minnesota and Wisconsin streams. We outwitted big, rambunctious rainbow trout in a dozen trout lakes, too.

This most generous partner revealed all his secret fishing places to me, and I disclosed a few of mine. I gained on the exchange, because Dick had fished more midwestern streams than any other man, and by his own admission had been skunked more times on more streams than any other fly-fisher.

Dick was an indefatigable note taker. His monumental, detailed 35-year record counts more than 8,500 hours devoted to trout fishing on 271 different streams in the two states. Of the 10,576 trout he kept for the frying pan or released, 8,136 were brown trout, 1,855 brook trout, and 574 rainbows. There were also a handful of tiger trout and a splake. The tiger, a brook-brown cross, is marked like a zebra but unable to reproduce. If Dick were here, he'd remind me that until mid-1986 his record counted only trout that he kept to eat, so the totals are understated. By his calculations, Dick caught 1.4 trout per hour in Wisconsin and 0.8 per hour in Minnesota. Modern anglers are likely to report better catch rates, perhaps due to improved habitat.

Several spring feeders of the Tiffany converge near the town of Downing in eastern St. Croix County on WI 70. Although you can begin on one of the feeders at Glenwood City on WI 128 and fish all the way to Boyceville, where last fall trout were being taken behind the new high school, our favorite reach is from the Tiffany bridge on 130th Avenue, south of Glenwood City and just east of WI 128, to a mile or so below Downing. A promising entry is at the WI 170 bridge on the county line in Downing. Two of Dick's comments remain with me: Downstream from Downing was "tough going"; and "What a stream for hopper time!" Dick totaled, from 1975 through 1992, 56 days, 180 hours, 559 brook trout, and 1 splake.

The day passes, wind whispers in the trees, streamside grasses bend in concert with riffling water, birds pipe far and wee. The aspen are trembling, as usual. It is a wonderful day to wander the green and gentle land of western Wisconsin.

Facilities at Glenwood City, at Boyceville, and at Menomonie on I-94.

WAGON LANDING SPRINGS
DeLorme 71

Wagon Landing Springs in central Polk County, close to the St. Croix County line, is a tributary of the Apple River, downstream from Marquee Springs. Why they call it "springs" we do not know; we see only one, but there may be others in that short section of boggy creek into which the spring drains. Take WI 65 north out of Star Prairie to County Road C, then turn north onto 160th Street. Cross the creek and proceed perhaps 100 yards to parking opposite a well-defined trail to the spring.

The spring margin is gooey, so take care slipping or sliding to the spring proper. One of our friends took a hellacious fall there. If you make it, you will find a hard sand bottom straight out into deeper water. About bellybutton depth you'll hit silt. After that proceed cautiously, because it was here that Humphrey's pal, Dick Frantes, took one step too far, as was his wont, and had to be rescued from clinging black stuff. It was a question of going back to the car for a rope or Humphrey throwing that ubiquitous staff. Before Frantes disappeared, Jim threw him the staff, and Dick pried himself out with it. But that didn't stop us from playing tag with an assortment of pretty brook trout. On July 30 the water temperature was 54 degrees and tiny silver minnows scattered as we waded out.

This is a large spring pond, and the farther out we waded, the larger were the brookies. Ah! that far tail of the pond beckoned us, as it will you. Now, if only you have a belly-boat. Wade fish or belly, though, it may be wise to go in pairs.

MARQUEE SPRINGS
DeLorme 71

Wisconsin counts 443 spring ponds within its borders. Marquee Springs is one of but two ponds that we profile, mostly because Marquee is associated fondly with one of Jim's amusing fishing experiences. In the late 1950s Jim and Bud Lehmann and Bob Johnson were returning from a sales meeting at Balsam Lake. Naturally, they were exhausted from all the hard work, so they paused for coffee on the Apple River at US 8 in Polk County. Naturally, they had their fishing tackle convenient to hand. They climbed down to the pool and tail in the Apple below the bridge. Bud clambered onto a boulder and cast a Heddon Crazy Crawler. Bob and Jim sipped coffee. Bud slipped, whooped, and arose sputtering with a largemouth hanging from the plug. Following the appropriate festivities, Jim noticed flecks of light, or spackles, on the surface of the run. Could they be caused by small fish sipping? He loaded his 9-foot bass rod with a bluegill fly on the end, and amazingly hooked up on a brown trout, and more, and more. That began his affair with the Apple River and his love for trout. And that led to the discovery of Marquee Springs, which drain into the Apple downstream from Polk County Park on the river.

The Apple River here is not a designated trout stream and no longer offers planted trout in that half mile or so of pretty water below the US 8 bridge, but the river is an enchanting mix of runs, riffles, boulders, flats, et al. Find the park a quarter mile south of US 8 and between County Road H and WI 46. Stop for coffee and unfurl the rod. Who knows? A gigantic brown may have moved up under the dark of the moon.

Just west of the park you will find Marquee Springs and a public fishing area. There are two ways to fish the resident brook trout: Step carefully to the springs from the margins, or leap from hump to hillock like a gazelle; or walk to the outlet and wade up into the springs over a sand and silt bottom. Last time Jim was there, the wading wasn't difficult and the specs were cooperative, albeit not large. If you don't like Marquee, there are more than 400 other spring ponds, and some 180 trout lakes.

Although the Apple is primarily a warm-water river due to dams and its coursing through lakes, there are two places that we share with you where you will find trout, some very large because of their diet of forage fish. Chubs grow to trophy size in the Apple. Downstream from the County M bridge in the Sportsmen's Alliance park in Star Prairie is one that Humphrey has savored. And the second is in the village of Little Falls, downstream from the bridge at the intersection of County Roads C and PP. Easy access opposite the Little Falls Merc. Company, which is more Currier and Ives than Currier and Ives.

THE TRADE RIVER
DeLorme 82

The Trade River is a long, meandering stream that connects several warm-water lakes before it enters the Governor Knowles State Forest at the St. Croix River. Brook and brown trout are reputed to be scattered hither and yon in several locations, but you won't enjoy it upstream. Although we don't recommend the lower 5 miles as a direct destination either, you may want to try the bridge on 285th Avenue, about 3 miles west of WI 87, in the extreme northwest corner of Polk County. Or best, check out the Trade River Horse Trails area in the state forest on Evergreen Road. Park at the watering hole close to the bridge, or drive less than a quarter mile to a turnaround. Then follow the river trail.

This is one sweet-looking piece of water, and it may contain planted or wild browns. It is a photogenic reach down toward the St. Croix, some 3 miles away. If you encounter no trout, you might run into one of those acrobatic St. Croix smallmouths. Canoeists on the St. Croix may find a bit of trout fishing a pleasant diversion. We have not been able to find public access on Cowan Creek, a tributary that enters the Trade at Evergreen Road.

THE YELLOW RIVER
DeLorme 72 & 84

Many years ago Curt Dary, an entomologist and fly-fisherman, told me that the Yellow River produced substantial hatches of *Ephemerella* mayflies during June and July. I have not fished the Yellow often enough to find them, or perhaps I missed an evening hatch of one of the many species of that genus. You will run into the other usual suspects, though—caddisflies, stoneflies, scuds and crayfish, and assorted terrestrials.

The Yellow's trout fishery begins at County Road B in Barron County a few miles northeast of Cumberland, and ends at the Barron impoundment at US 8. Of the approximately 13 miles, the upper 9 are preferred. Downstream the river picks up more sand. It may have received its name from that sandy bottom. In any case, the farther down I go, the less esthetically pleasing it is to me.

Sometimes I begin at the first bridge north of WI 48 on 23¼ Avenue, but it is quite brushy in there. It would be a bit easier to strike it in spring before the foliage has filled out. Many anglers begin fishing at the DNR parking lot on WI 48. It was nicely mowed the last time I was there, and the footpaths were obvious. Curt Dary told me that he fished downstream from there over the hatches. Next stop: Go east on 48 to 12½ Street, then south to the corner with 21½ Avenue. (Ah, those broken numbers!) Note the sign: STREAM HABITAT IMPROVEMENT 1976–1982, and a narrow path. Those are old workings, but careful habitat improvements can last for decades. Next: From the corner, go east to 13th Street, then south past the Harmony Hills Tree Farm to the last corner. Turn west for half a mile to another DNR turnaround and a well-defined path down to the river. After that you are on your own; however, both Hickey and Engle Creek and Springs add cold water and brook trout to the mix. In fact, in recent years the brook trout have displaced the browns to some extent in the main stem, a phenomenon observed in a few other places in Wisconsin and Minnesota.

In addition to 6 miles of state-owned river frontage there are supposed to be 11 roads that cross or parallel the stream. A 1995 profile in *Wisconsin Trout* reported that the average width is 20 to 25 feet, that the water is mildly alkaline, and that midsummer temperatures rarely exceed the upper 60s.

There is a sign at the boundary with Harmony Hills that warns of bears in the neighborhood, but that's likely whenever you go into the backcountry, or up-country as they say. The state's bear population was estimated at 29,000 in 1999. On a lonely foray, whistle or sing to yourself. If you sing like me, the bruins will surely give you room to roam.

All facilities at Cumberland, or to the east at Rice Lake at the intersection of US 53 and WI 48. I usually manage to have dinner at the Tower House in Cumberland, a home-style Italian restaurant in a historic 1882 home.

THE SOUTH FORK OF THE HAY RIVER
DeLorme 71

The South Fork of Hay River rises in Barron County and flows southeasterly through northwestern Dunn County where it crosses WI 64 at Connorsville. It is paralleled on the east side by County Road K and WI 79. That tells you where it is, but what it is—is not so easy. We have patrolled and fished its approximately 18 miles from the top of Dunn County to the termination of the designated trout water at Highway 79 at Boyceville. On many of the streams we've profiled we have relied on the good offices of friends who report their experiences on a stream, as well as the results of our own forays. But not many friends have stepped forward to regale us with fabulous days on the Hay. One notably reluctant purveyor of information has admitted that the South Fork is "pretty good." Another newfound friend whom we met upstream in brook trout country said that the brookies were too small—except in spring, when 10- and 12-inch trout could hang up on the end of a worm. He thought the large brook trout were planted and promptly fished out. According to an older DNR report, the river supports natural reproduction of brook trout, but brown trout are planted. Marty Engel, area biologist and fish manager for the DNR, notes that wild brook trout are staging a comeback in many of the streams of the area, due he believes to improved farming practices and the set-asides of ag land under the Conservation Reserve Program. In our latest trip to the South Fork above Connorsville we caught feisty little brookies and one 12-inch brown.

The South Fork of the Hay continues to intrigue and confound us. In the

Friends on the upper South Fork of the Hay River

upper reaches there are visual delights from a number of bridges, and the lower river runs through marvelously green and verdant valleys. We will not give up on the lower river, because we know there must be large brown trout downstream from Connorsville in that slow-moving stream through pasturelands. Upstream on County Road K we will fly-fish specs in those seductive stretches at 1330 Avenue (Kuehnle Road), at 1390th Avenue (Hilson Road), at the abandoned bridge at 87th Street, and last at Thatcher Park, a memorial to Dan Amunson, 1951–1996.

You know that we have complained about the change from road names to numbers elsewhere, several times perhaps, but this one takes the cake: North of Boyceville on the west side of the river we find an intersection of 200th Street and 231st Street!

For brook trout, small and colorful flies are sufficient. At Thatcher Park we wowed them with a #18 Royal Coachman, much bedraggled; with an Adams and with a Hornberg, which was no doubt taken for a hopper.

THE SOUTH FORK OF MAIN CREEK
DeLorme 74

Main Creek and its several forks lie east of Ladysmith on US 8 in Rusk County. Take County Road B south from Glen Flora on US 8, or WI 73 south from Ingram. One bright day in September, Bill drove south from Ingram and took Nessa Road east to fish the South Fork. At the bridge he stopped to peruse the water. There were a few dimples, so he rigged up with a dry #16 Adams and released 20 brookies in short order. We have been told that these are native or wild trout. Our angler scouted more spots but, with little time, found nothing as good as the original bridge pool.

There is acceptable trout habitat at the WI 73 bridge south; and even better water along Walrath Road between WI 73 and County Road B. The stream here is wadeable up and down and is open wide enough for a fly-fisher to clear her backcast.

7 | Northwestern Wisconsin: Indianhead Country

If you view an outline of the state and let your imagination run, you may see the stylized head of an Indian chief in the northwest quadrant, complete with feathers represented by the Chequamegon Peninsula and the Apostle Islands. Hence the name Indianhead Country to lure and charm tourists, though perhaps it is not politically correct.

By any name, mundane or imaginative, this area will be attractive to fly-fishers and their families—with its rushing rivers, ice-blue inland lakes, waterfalls, state parks, national forests, the glorious Apostles and their sailing ships, and the spectacular southern coast of Lake Superior. It is an area rich in the history of the early exploration of the continent and the later exploitation of copper and tall pines.

Some trout streams are tributaries of the St. Croix, which empties into the Mississippi; more flow north into Lake Superior and contain runs of anadromous trout and salmon. We profile three widely different, or wildly different, rivers, and five less challenging streams.

THE NAMEKAGON RIVER
DeLorme 94

"Hurley, Hayward, and Hell." That's an old saying from the days of the river drivers, who knew they were the three toughest towns in the world, or out of it. A brash man could get an ear bitten off on a Saturday night in Hayward as easily as he could find a trollop in Hurley.

Hayward is now a neat, clean, welcoming, and conservative tourist town. But the historic Namekagon is still there, not much changed since the burly, bearded men in blanket coats came out of the woods on Saturday nights to get mean drunk and kick each other bloody in the streets. The lean

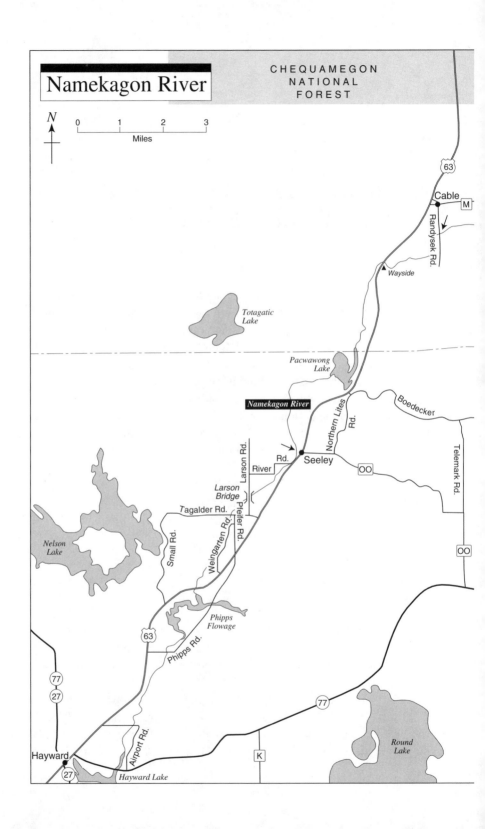

Namekagon River

CHEQUAMEGON
NATIONAL
FOREST

N

0   1   2   3
Miles

63

Cable   M

Randysek Rd.

Wayside

Totagatic Lake

Pacwawong Lake

Namekagon River

Boedecker

Northern Lites Rd.

Larson Rd.

River Rd.

Seeley   OO

Telemark Rd.

Larson Bridge

Tagalder Rd.

Pfeifer Rd.

Small Rd.

Weingarten Rd.

Nelson Lake

OO

Phipps Flowage

63

Phipps Rd.

77

27

Airport Rd.

77

K

Round Lake

Hayward

27

Hayward Lake

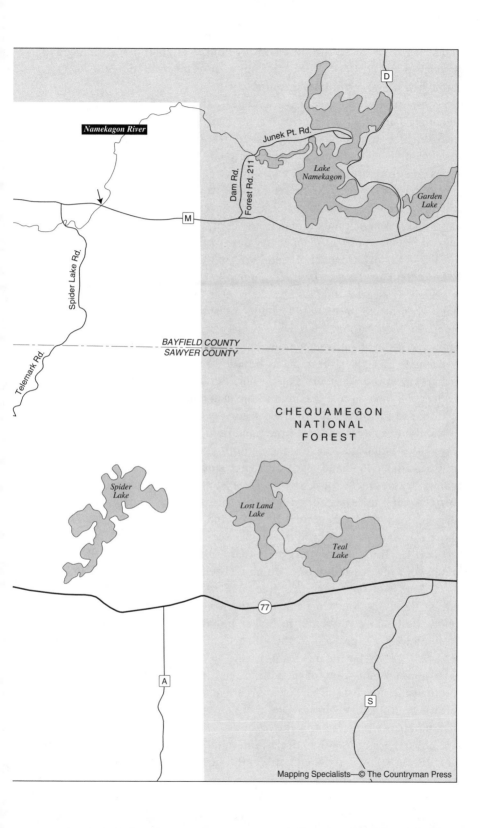

and stringy men went into the woods by donkey engine, shank's mare, and flatboats poled upstream. They came out with spring, whooping the log rafts through white water to the mills at Hayward.

Most of the iron men have gone, but the storied Namekagon flows smoothly, tamed not too much since the peak of the logging at the turn of the 20th century. It is still big water, riffling through narrows, gliding through pine plantations, spreading through the meadows of abandoned farms. The trout are there, too, awaiting the delicate fall of the fly. Only the species have changed. The native brook trout have retreated to the cooler waters of feeder creeks. In the few fast-water reaches you may strike an eager and acrobatic rainbow, hatchery-raised, but the golden dark, crimson-spotted brown trout has adapted and now owns the waters.

From County Road M 4 miles east of Cable and downstream from Namekagon Lake Dam in Bayfield County, to the Sawyer County line at the north end of Pacwawong Flowage, the river is Category 3. From Pacwawong Dam down to the lower US 63 bridge, a distance of approximately 9 river miles, the Nam is Category 5, with special regulations designed to maintain a stock of better-than-average trout. From Phipps Dam down to Airport Road it reverts to Category 3; then below Hayward Lake there is another stretch of Category 5 to the Washburn County line. Because of this mix of categories, anglers will have to pay attention to the many signs posted along the river.

Prior to the institution of the category system in 1990, the Department of Natural Resources had rated the Namekagon a Class II river: "Streams in this classification may have some natural reproduction but not enough to utilize available food and space. Therefore, stocking sometimes is required to maintain a desirable sport fishery. These streams show good survival and carryover of adult trout, often producing fish of better than average size." The application of Category 5 to two prime sections of the Namekagon above Hayward was designed to enhance the carryover and growth of larg-er trout. In all, the Nam offers more than 30 miles of unparalleled wading water, with the possibility of catching and releasing a spectacular trout.

If time is of the essence, confine your activities between Philippi land-ing on Randysek Road in Cable and the lower WI 63 bridge. In the riffle below the landing you ought to find some rainbow trout. In the village of Seeley on US 63, go west to the village hall and the private bridge (now removed). We prefer the upstream reach.

A quarter mile south of the village the Nam sidles up to US 63. Park at the roadside and fish up or down. We've had excellent fly-fishing in that most beautiful spot. Below Seeley there are numerous marked fishermen's parking areas within sight of the highway.

About 1.5 miles south of Seeley you'll find Larsen (aka Larson) Road. Go west a stone's throw and then north to the Larsen bridge. Cross the river and park in a grove of trees on the riverbank. Fish upstream into classic dry-fly water.

A quarter mile north of the Larsen bridge take River Road east to road-side parking at the elbow. Fish up among the old man-made islands or down through a long run that ends in a huge pool. We have had some of our best fly-fishing through the run, including success at matching a tremendous hatch of tiny blue-winged olives on the last day of the season.

Which reminds us of an experience. It was a hot day and the run hadn't produced as it should have. We waded up to the head of the run, where we met an angler from Duluth. He wasn't feeling too optimistic, either, although he allowed that he'd caught a couple, and the evening before he'd caught and released browns to 14 inches while fishing a Sulphur dry.

While we were chewing the fat, a frog came skipping across the run like a Jet Ski, squeaking all the way and chased by an 18-inch brown. Honest. Minutes later a different frog gave us a repeat performance. We pounded that run for the brown with everything we had in the boxes, but he disdained our offerings.

Bright in our memory is a day when our pal Eino Tutt, a master at swimming a lip-hooked minnow into the maw of an outsized brown, demonstrated his skill along McNaught Road at Cable. The auto trail ran between the house and the barn of a farm. Now the trail is bermed and the land is controlled by Telemark, a ski resort, and farther down by a gun club with warnings not to get in the way of the guns. Perhaps if you rent a condo at Telemark, you may be able to roll big browns as Eino did for us.

There is more good water between County Road M and US 63 than you can handle. We have our favorite places; you will discover yours, perhaps at the red cabin on Tagalder Road, at the end of the trail from the termination of Weingarten Road, behind the KOA campground, or in back of Turk's Inn, an extraordinary supper club a couple of miles north of Hayward on US 63.

In his book *Remembrances of Rivers Past,* Ernest Schwiebert tells of his arrival in Hayward during the peak of the muskie fishing, when the men and boys of the town decamped to the lakes and flowages to throw dead suckers or hardware at that largest of freshwater fighting fish. Mr. Schwiebert began his unharried exploration of the river at the old railroad trestle on the north end of the town along Airport Road. When last we were there the trestle was still rusting away and the tracks had been taken up, but the river ran dark and secret between the abutments. It's cleaner now than it was then. We have made some progress since the Clean Water Act of 1972.

During an evening of superlative fishing, Schwiebert recorded in his catch three browns, the smallest of which was 21 inches, and the largest at almost 7 pounds, all taken on an artificial representation of *Isonychia sadleri,* a large mayfly commonly known as the mahogany dun or maroon drake. This hatch may appear about the middle of June and again during the later part of August. The best fly-fishing is usually during the late-evening spinner fall.

As on most northerly streams, the notable hatches occur between opening day and the third week of June. Our local experts cite hatches of the Hendrickson, March brown, light Cahill, mahogany dun, and pale evening dun or sulphur. All season long, tiny blue-winged olives will be present, in early mornings during the early days of the season, and late afternoons in September. Tricos may show themselves late-June or early-July mornings in the flats below the weed beds. The brown drake, *Ephemera simulans,* #12, a Midwest superhatch, appears about the middle of June, or sometimes a week earlier. Late June or early July brings on the *Hexagenia limbata,* the largest midwestern mayfly.

Some of the hatches may peak before opening day. If so, hard luck. On the other hand, you may count your blessings. An earlier opener could put you into the middle of a northern Wisconsin spring blizzard. As Gus Kizer of the DNR at Hayward once said, "Fishing the Namekagon can be tough."

Our experience confirms that this large, semiwarm river can be difficult, particularly during the hot months. We recall all too vividly wading through more than a mile of entrancing water one day in late June without seeing a rise or enticing a somnolent trout to our searching Royal Coachman. Exhausted, we arrived finally at dusk at the private bridge at Seeley, where we sat to commiserate. And then the spinners appeared—three different species of mayflies. Curious, how they could sort themselves out!

The spinners were a #12 gray drake, *Siphlonurus quebecensis*—also a major hatch on the Wolf River—a #14 species of *Stenonema/Stenacron* (blue-winged olive, brown body), and a #16 *Ephemerella,* which was probably the fabled sulphur. After the adults had mated and the females had dropped yellow egg packets and died, the trout turned on, taking the spentwings in sips and swirls.

Water temperatures may rise to 76 degrees in quick, knee-deep water at midafternoon during a hot spell. The same water will read 10 degrees cooler by 7 AM the following day. So fish the early hours in summer and hope for a hatch of tricos or tiny blue-winged olives. But the confirmed fly-fisher will fish the pools of the Namekagon just before dark, and after, with a large Light Cahill for heavy-shouldered browns. If the trout aren't thumping the surface, dead-drift a big brown Woolly Worm or a weighted Muddler through the pool and along the surface coming back to the reel. John Goplin of the Twin Cities Chapter of Trout Unlimited recommends a crayfish pattern drifted deep. On Shogren's last trip in the special-regulations section he saw a 6-pound brown chase a chub, so you might experiment with streamer flies.

If you insist on fishing the daylight hours during warm weather because the river is so beautiful, flowing like tawny port around your knees, don't linger long in any one place. The water may be cooler in another location, or a thin hatch of caddisflies or mayflies may be localized.

The Nam is one of the easiest rivers to wade that we know, so some of us forgo blind casting entirely and simply wade upstream in search of one rising trout. Almost certainly it will be a good one. If you get in among the islands, you can slow down there and drop a terrestrial under the overhanging branches.

The Namekagon is part of the St. Croix Riverway and is protected under the 1968 National Wild and Scenic Rivers Act. Much of the riverbank has been acquired by the National Park Service, development is restricted, and riverside residences are being purchased as they come on the market. Access is easy from County Road M for as far downstream as you care to hunt. Although there are browns and rainbows below Hayward Lake, you are more likely to find northerns and smallmouth bass. Frank Pratt, senior fisheries biologist for the DNR, said that the growth rate for browns below Hayward is twice that of the growth rate above the city. Browns to 13 pounds have been taken, but they won't come easily. Mr. Pratt advised that the lower river performs best during cold weather. There is now a special open season for trout below Hayward, October 1 to the following first Saturday in May: no-kill with artificials only. In 1995, in a grand experiment, 1,400 fingerling sturgeon were planted below Hayward in an attempt to restore an indigenous species.

The Namekagon is mentioned favorably in Mary Orvis Marbury's 1892 *Favorite Flies and Their Histories,* where W. P. Andrus mentioned the Coachman and a mongrel Professor fly. He wrote, "The flies I used on the Namekagon, in June and August, are better adapted for use from about three to six P.M., after which a lighter color (Miller) is best." The Miller is still a first-class attractor for big browns at night on the Nam.

More than 30 years ago, before the need for special regulations, the accepted technique on the Namekagon was to fly-fish downstream, wading the middle, casting a trio of large and gaudy wet flies on a short, stout leader for big trout. Maybe that's not a bad idea today.

We can't say that the Namekagon is a superb trout fishery—some who count numbers of trout as important would even call it marginal because of warm water and lack of natural reproduction. Two other circumstances prevent the development of the river's potential: Beavers crowd the tributaries, and peculiarities in the Wild and Scenic Rivers Act prevent extensive habitat rehabilitation of the main stem.

The Nam is also a favorite run for the "aluminum hatch." Fishers will have to share that scenic thread of tawny water with canoeists. But they are usually off the water when the evening rise begins.

The Namekagon River at Seeley

In the Ojibway (Chippewa) tongue, Namekagon means "the place for sturgeon." That antediluvian fish has been speared and netted from the river. The long canoes of the voyageurs and the log rafts of the lumberjacks are only memories. But the Namekagon is a constant, golden tinsel through the forest-green fabric of Wisconsin. It is both promise and challenge to the peripatetic angler.

A wide range of overnight and dining accommodations is available in Hayward and Cable, at many lake resorts, and at numerous primitive campsites along the riverway. Children will enjoy Hayward's Fishing Hall of Fame, where they can overlook the countryside from the gaping jaws of a 144-foot muskie. Al Capone's hideout museum is located on the Lac Courte Oreilles Reservation near Couderay southeast of Hayward, close to the junctions of County Roads N and CC. The largest living white pine in Wisconsin will help you visualize this country as it was when the Frenchmen Radisson and Groseilliers first dipped paddles into its unmapped waters in 1659. The 300-year-old pine is 130 feet tall and 13 feet in circumference. It is located in the Flambeau River State Forest, 11 miles east of Winter on County Road W. The park service headquarters for the riverway, on US 63 northeast of Trego, offers a fine selection of maps and pamphlets. Turk's Inn is on the river 2 miles north of Hayward on US 63.

THE WHITE RIVER

DeLorme 94

The main stem of the White River flows for some 45 miles from the canoe access and park on Pike River Road near the village of Delta in Bayfield County to Lake Superior in Ashland County. It is Category 2 upstream of the Pike bridge; Category 5 downstream to White River Dam. Our profiled section runs from the park down to the village of Mason close to US 63, a river distance of more than 20 miles.

At the park on Pike River Road the White is quite small and clear, the haunt of naturally reproducing brook trout. There's a second canoe access at Kern Creek along White Road, then a foot trail from the end of the road. The river here is cold and deep, and can be difficult to wade during high water.

The real action for monster brown trout is that tortuous stretch through Bibon Swamp, almost invariably from a canoe, although there may be one or two trails to the river, the locations of which are secrets jealously guarded. The canoes put in at the Sutherland bridge close to the intersection of Town Line Road and Sutherland Road.

Some anglers claim that the swamp can be negotiated in a float of five to six hours, but recent experience suggests that is far too little time to fly-fish, either from the canoe or occasionally by standing chest-deep on hard bottom.

An additional complication is that the yearly heavy action is usually confined to a few weeks in late June and early July when the *Hexagenia limbata* is on the wing. On a recent trip into the upper end of Bibon Swamp, Bill Shogren was dropped off bankside during the early evening and picked up by canoe at 11 PM. Bill caught and released two brown trout of 16 and 17 inches; his partner, Pete Mitchell, connected with two 18-inch browns. On another occasion Bill walked the bank around the Sutherland bridge and picked up four browns while other anglers who walked deeper into the swamp came out with fewer.

If this whets your appetite for a most unusual experience, don't let us deter you, except to warn that the swamp water is exceedingly cold and very deep, the current swift, and the mosquitoes ferocious on midsummer evenings. Many fly-fishers have tested Bibon Swamp but once!

We should add something about the *H. limbata*. This burrowing species of mayfly has a life cycle, from egg to adult, of somewhere between 8 and 12 months, depending on the temperature of the water. During the nymphal

BILL SHOGREN

This brown fell to a big hex nymph pattern on the White River, just before the evening hatch.

period it must leave its U-shaped burrow in clay to molt—shedding its exoskeleton to allow for growth. The literature does not give us the number of molts, but each time it crawls out of its burrow it is vulnerable to predation. Therefore there should be weeks, or perhaps several months, prior to emergence when a large yellowish nymph laid over the silt should produce action. One major study of the Hex reported that trout get 60 to 70 percent of their annual food requirements from that mayfly. A recent report stated that the White has excellent water quality and good natural reproduction of brown and brook trout.

In some respects Bibon Swamp may be the most unusual, difficult, and challenging 20 miles of water in Wisconsin. It may be only a once-in-a-life-time trip, and we wish you joy of it.

For approximately 10 miles, from Mason downstream to the White River impoundment at the Ashland County border, the river flows faster through a succession of riffles and pools. We have it on good advice that this section contains cased caddis, in local parlance "stick caddis," along with sculpins; during May and June it is "crawling with 1-inch-long green crayfish." The brown trout are reputed to run larger than average. Anadromous trout and salmon are the main quarry below the impoundment.

Modest facilities and canoe liveries at Mason; complete accommodations at the city of Ashland on Chequamegon Bay, at Cable to the south, and at Iron River on US 2 to the northwest.

The Iron River Trout Haus in Iron River is a little out of the ordinary. This is one of two bed & breakfast retreats in Wisconsin that are wholly devoted to fly-fishing for trout. It offers fly-fishing schools, fly-tying sessions, and casting for rainbow trout in three ponds on the premises.

THE BOIS BRULE

DeLorme 93 & 101

Here, where the magnificent Bois Brule joins mighty Lake Superior, is a dramatic meeting of moving water and sand and sky and inland sea. It must have been so when Daniel Greysolon, the Sieur du Lhut, came to it one summer evening in 1680 when the sun was a band of bronze on the silver surface of the great blue lake.

The river was called the Misakota in the tongue of the Ojibway, Nemetsakouat in the language of the Dakota. Later it was known as the Burntwood by the British and Bois Brûlé by the French. Today it is printed as Bois Brule on the official maps of northwestern Wisconsin in Douglas County, but it is familiarly and affectionately known as the Brule to legions of trout and steelhead fishermen.

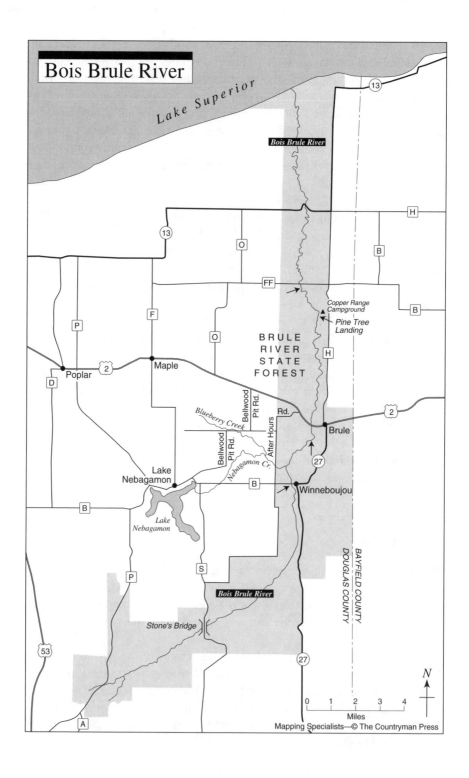

Bois Brule River

Lake Superior

Bois Brule River

Copper Range
Campground

Pine Tree
Landing

BRULE
RIVER
STATE
FOREST

Poplar

Maple

Blueberry Creek

Bellwood Pit Rd.

After Hours Rd.

Bellwood Pit Rd.

Brule

Nebagamon Cr.

Lake
Nebagamon

Winneboujou

*Lake
Nebagamon*

Bois Brule River

Stone's Bridge

BAYFIELD COUNTY
DOUGLAS COUNTY

| 0 | 1 | 2 | 3 | 4 |

Miles

N

Mapping Specialists—© The Countryman Press

In those ancient days it was a no-man's-land between the formidable Chippewa (Ojibway) out of the east and the indomitable Dakota, also called Sioux. Du Lhut's mission was to make peace between the tribes so that the fur trade could resume for the greater glory of the king of France and for the enrichment of the merchants. Du Lhut, a representative of the governor-general of New France, did not make poetry of the wild waters and rock ledges of the lower Brule or the meanders of the middle river between high green banks, nor of the dark slow upper third through bog country under lofty pines, where even now the eagles scream and brook trout rush to a gaudy fly.

In his terse military report du Lhut, or Duluth, said only that he entered the river, "where after having cut down some trees and broken through about one hundred beaver dams, I went up said river, and then made a carry half a league to reach a lake, which emptied into a fine river the St. Croix, which brought me to the Mississippi."

Since 1680 the Brule has been a warrior's path, an explorer's track into the interior, and a trade route. It has been logged, stolen, sold, and resold. Several miles of it have been tastefully embellished by summer homes and lodges of rustic elegance. In the 1870s commercial fishermen extracted brook trout by the ton from its spring ponds, packed the fish in barrels, and shipped them to Chicago. One of the ponds was appropriately named Fulton Market, after New York City's famous market. In 1907 the state of Wisconsin recognized its unique historic, scenic, and environmental qualities by establishing the Brule River State Forest, encompassing 52,000 acres. For all of this time it has offered superb fishing for the artful angler. The Nature Conservancy also holds 9 miles of river and 5,000 acres under easement.

The northward-flowing Brule is a river for three seasons, because of the mix of resident trout and anadromous salmon. The regulations are necessarily complicated and may change from year to year. In 2001 the river from County Road S, Stone's Bridge, to County B, Winneboujou, was open only during the regular season to Category 5, artificials only and restricted size and bag limits. The 30-mile downstream portion, from US 2 in Brule to the mouth, was open March 25 through November 15, Category 5, with restricted size and bag limits.

In addition to the split categories and variety of salmonids, the Brule offers three faces to the angler. The upper third is slow water over sand and silt, wandering through many spring ponds, rich in waterweeds and insect life. A shorter middle section has the characteristics of a meadow stream—deep pools at many crooked corners and overshaded runs that are sometimes too deep to wade.

The lower river is most like a freestone mountain stream—long glides, ledges, and rocky runs that will snick the bottom out of a canoe. Though the riverbed is hard, the banks are thickly forested over slopes of red clay that are subject to erosion, frequently leaving the water turbid. Around the Oxbow, a couple of miles from the mouth, we have seen long, deep fissures where the slope, trees and all, was sliding into the river.

There are five distinct types of trout and char that have graced the river for so long that they are thought of as natives: brook trout, resident rainbows and browns, and migratory rainbows (steelhead) and browns.

In addition, three species of Pacific salmon have established spawning rights in the river in recent years. Coho and chinook salmon were introduced into Lake Superior in 1966 and 1967, and have since spawned in the Brule. Pink salmon were introduced into the lake in 1956, but it was not till the late 1970s that they appeared in the lower Brule.

With all of these populations and species milling around and competing for spawning gravel, space, and food, naturally there is concern that some favored species will be hurt. A DNR Fish Management Report from 1984 is inconclusive: "The Pacific salmons, to date, have not demonstrated any obvious adverse effects on trout populations in the Brule River, since migratory brown and rainbow populations (numbers) were similar to those reported in past studies. Their effects, however, may remain to be seen if numbers of salmon spawning successfully were to increase significantly. Coho and especially chinook salmon have the potential to outcompete brown trout, spawning during fall, for available or preferred spawning sites, because of their larger size. Young salmon could potentially compete with juvenile trout for available food and habitat." The report goes on to state that pink salmon "may not compete to a great extent with trout while in the river because of life history differences." Anecdotal evidence since 1984 does not suggest that the fishery for browns and rainbows has deteriorated to any marked degree.

The movements of the various species in and out of the river are complicated and are worth a few paragraphs of explanation.

We quote from a Wisconsin DNR fisheries report: "Migratory brown trout begin to enter the river in July with the peak of the run usually in September. Some return to the lake after they spawn in the fall but others return rapidly as the ice goes out in the spring. These fish are wary and prefer deep, calm water. The best fishing is when the water is murky, on cloudy days, early morning, late evening, and at night.

"There are two steelhead (anadromous rainbow trout) runs each year. The fall run starts in September and these fish return to the lake after they spawn the following spring. The spring run starts in March and these fish return to the lake in May and June. Steelhead prefer faster water than browns."

Coho and chinook salmon spawn in fall and have found their way into at least one of the feeders, where the young may compete with the natives. Young chinooks have been found in Blueberry Creek, a tributary of Nebagamon Creek that joins the Brule from the west about three-quarters of a mile north of County Road B. The hunt for migratory steelhead and chinooks in the Brule is a separate story, and most of the action takes place north of US 2 during the spring and fall extended seasons. The techniques are different, as is the equipment—fluorescent yarn and micro eggs; or spawn sacs, heavy rods, and reels loaded with monofilament rather than fly line. A few diehard fly-fishers stick to sinking fly lines and large stonefly nymphs. The brook trout, which were the only trout (read "char") indigenous to the river in historic times, are now found primarily in the upper third.

From the headwaters to Winneboujou Landing on County Road B, some 15 miles, the Brule is almost impossible to get to on foot because of private land, although there is one long foot trail in from the west side, partly through private land. In the headwaters section most fly-fishers take to the canoe. The canoes go into the water at the Stone's bridge landing on County Road S. The 12 miles from Stone's to Winneboujou will consume about five hours, alternately paddling and drifting. If you want to take your limit of three brook trout, the trip may involve an hour or two more. A #5 line is preferred with a .005 leader, the butt end greased for surface fishing the pockets.

Approximately 5 miles downstream from Stone's, below Cedar Island, there are a few short, sharp rapids, none of which is rated worse than Class II difficulty for canoeists. Above Cedar Island there is a short section of unrated fast water. The novice may want to reverse direction at this point and return to Stone's against an easy current. Such an excursion would include the very best of the brook trout water, but you would miss some of the scenery through Cedar Island and the mirror waters of Big and Lucius Lakes, where the huge resident browns hang out. The ponds at Cedar Island look very like the water of the River Test at Whitchurch, England—green fronds of grass and clear runnels among them where the brown trout lie finning. A wise choice for the visiting fly-fisher is to hire a guide and canoe in Brule, see the whole show, and let someone else do the work.

Cedar Island is an extensive, gracious estate of some 4,500 acres, its buildings fashioned of cedar logs and shakes. Built in the 1890s and meticulously maintained since, it was visited and fly-fished by those distinguished presidents-fishermen Coolidge, Hoover, and Eisenhower. The Brule was also fished by Presidents Grant and Cleveland in the 1870s and 1880s.

Fishing the Brule should be at least a once-in-a-lifetime experience for every dedicated fly-fisher. The quiet fisherman will come upon the great blue heron stock still within a tangle of deadfall; he will see the eagles and hear them shout a raucous warning. He may see the soft-footed mink hunting along the bank. It is said that on some drowsy evening you may startle the rare Wisconsin moose feeding knee-deep in a spring pond, but that, we believe, is more poetic fancy than reality. Certainly you will watch the graceful white-tailed deer watching you.

The resident brown trout that inhabit the upper reaches of the river are like stream trout anywhere. In spring they will rise readily to a fly; on summer days they will sulk in cool and darkened places until they are teased out with repeated casts over their lies. In the evenings the browns will feed in the long flats, at the lips of pools, and on the placid surfaces of the upper lakes when the hatch is on. If you are so fortunate as to fish the Lucius or Big Lake section at sundown, remember that big flies take big brown trout. The resident rainbows are found in faster water and can be taken with Brown Bivisibles, Spiders, and attractors.

And that brings us to the exploration of a conundrum. We have never encountered good brown trout fishing below Pine Tree landing (which is north of Copper Range Campground) during the summer months, although the water is as promising as any you have ever seen. One theory holds that the lower river is so well known to steelheaders (every pool is marked on a map available from the Brule River Sportsmen's Club) that resident browns don't have a chance to grow to respectable size. Another theory posits that the residents are displaced from the best lies by the movement of migratory rainbows and browns.

We have had our best summertime wade fishing for resident browns and rainbows from County Road B down to the first rapids, around Copper Range Campground, and upstream and down from Pine Tree landing. An evening fly-fisher will enjoy easier wading upstream from Winneboujou landing at County Road B into the summer home section.

According to a former fish manager at Brule DNR headquarters, the best summer fly-fishing is in that stretch from 2 miles above and below the ranger station and Brule River Campground at Brule. Upstream is fast water to Little Joe and Long Nebagamon Rapids. Downstream there are softer meanders to US 2. Access to the river is at the parking lot at Winneboujou, in the campground area next to the ranger station (park entrance fee required), and on the west side of the river from a fire trail exactly 1.5 miles north of County Road B off After Hours Road. The fisheries expert also noted that migratory browns spawn near the ranger station, around the mouth of Nebagamon Creek, and below Cedar Island. Many of those fish will hold station in the Meadows section downstream from US 2 until the onset of spawning in October. So we could recommend the Meadows in August and September, but without any guarantees. Although the migrating browns, which average 22 inches and 4½ pounds, are not active feeders, they may be provoked or teased with attractors.

A hatful of small rainbows can be taken most days in the rapids and particularly through Brule River Campground, but they seldom exceed 9 inches. Most of them are migratory, so by the time they reach this length they are usually on their way to the lake.

The Brule is a cool river, fed by dozens of springs in the brook trout waters and by several cold-water creeks. In midsummer the water will read a steady 55 degrees between the Stone's bridge and Winneboujou. Two miles from the mouth the water temperature may reach 65 degrees on a bright summer day. A DNR study stated that the water is medium hard.

In a multifaceted stream like the Brule, the predominant mayfly hatches will vary among sections. Brown drakes, *Ephemera simulans,* and Hex, *Hexagenia* genus, will be found in the slow water from the Stone's bridge through the lakes and the summer-home section. *Callibaetis,* or speckled wing, a slow-water dweller, will be limited to the lakes and ponds. March browns, *Stenonema* genus, are reported to emerge late afternoons and early evenings June through early July in the rapids between Cedar Island and WI 2. Tricos should show early mornings beginning toward the end of July through September in the slower flats below fast water wherever there are sufficient weed beds. *Baetis,* tiny blue-winged olives, are present all season long. In the early months they'll appear in the morning; in September they'll often appear in late afternoon. Caddis will be intermittently present up and down the river all season long, as will the midges and stoneflies. The Hendrickson, *Ephemerella subvaria,* has been reported on opening day of the regular season, afternoon emergence, with sporadic hatches until the end of May. Sulphurs of the *Ephemerellidae* family appear occasionally afternoons through late evening from May through June.

On a river as complex as the Brule, with its diverse habitat, the various hatches are difficult to pin down. In general, the largest species, Hex and brown drake, are found in slower water where there is an accumulation of silt. Tricos and *Baetis* will inhabit the weed beds in the upper two-thirds; stoneflies are found among the rocks in well-aerated water. Caddis, depending on the species, will be found everywhere. It is best to be prepared to match the hatch with an artificial that reasonably approximates the natural.

There are numerous developed entry points to the river on the east side from Winneboujou to the mouth, but as mentioned before the lower third of the river will be tough going for traditional fly-fishers: The wading is difficult and the classic mayfly hatches scant and unpredictable.

The Bois Brule is a river of extraordinary beauty and historic interest. Since 1907 the state of Wisconsin has attempted to preserve its unique qualities through careful management, and to expand public ownership of its corridor by acquisitions and gifts. Today the devoted fly-fisherman must share this resource with canoeists during the lazy summer days. But when shadows form and peepers come out of hiding, when the quick water speaks in tongues, then the river belongs to the one who casts a fly. It is yours. Treat it well.

In 1994 DNR biologist Dennis Pratt installed a series of gravel bars in the upper Brule to provide prime spawning spots for native brook trout. The stream was narrowed to speed the current, and by October 75 redds had been constructed where only four trout spawned the year before. As many as 200 pairs of brookies have been seen on individual gravel beds during nuptials. On other beds as many as 20 brown trout were observed.

BLUEBERRY CREEK

DeLorme 101

Blueberry, a nursery for three species of trout, plus coho and chinook salmon, is a tortuous stream, open in some places, densely overgrown in others, but a marvelous place to spend a couple of summer daytime hours wading upstream and casting a small hopper to the edges. Access is at the Bellwood Pit Road bridge. Go north on After Hours Road, then west on Bellwood Pit Road. Immediately upstream of the bridge is a fine pool, but bog and brush beyond.

NEBAGAMON CREEK

DeLorme 101

Nebagamon Creek also contains all three species of trout. It drains Nebagamon Lake and is consequently somewhat warmer. Find it on County Road B west of Winneboujou and on After Hours Road three-quarters of a mile north of County Road B. Following a downpour, Nebagamon can double the volume of the water in the Brule, thus playing havoc with aquatic life downstream.

Overnight accommodations in the Brule area are not extensive. There are two motels, restaurants, a campground, a convenience store, and a fly shop with modern cabins. The Lumbermen's Inn at Iron River is a favorite stopover. Farther away there are facilities for sleeping and eating at Superior, and at Herbster and Cornucopia on the Lake Superior shore along WI 13. Canoe liveries are at Brule. Excellent maps are available at Brule River Canoe Rental and from the Brule River State Forest Headquarters, Brule, WI 54820.

THE CLAM RIVER AND THE NORTH FORK OF THE CLAM

DeLorme 83

The main stem of the Clam River flows north to a dam at Clam Falls, Wisconsin, in the northeast corner of Polk County. It collects the flows of several streams in a tangle of country above the flowage. Many years ago the main tributary, McKenzie Creek, earned a reputation as one of the best brook trout streams in the northwest quadrant. Its name is now given to a segment of the Ice Age National Scenic Trail: the McKenzie Creek Segment. You will find a turnaround and the beginning of the trail at the south end of 60th Street, a gravel road immediately east of the village. Follow the trail to a footbridge over the Clam and along the river. It will be possible to wade in places, and for several hundred yards the river has in the past received extensive rehabilitation. In other years we could fish an early-morning fall of tricos after June. On our last trip on September 11, under overcast and through a mist, alas, the mosquitoes drove us back to civilization, so called. This river is copper colored, mostly over sand; but deeper into the interior the flow will slow over silt. Brook trout are wild; browns are planted.

Both the Clam and McKenzie may also be fished from County Road W, about 2 crow-flight miles to the south. At that end we prefer downstream (north) fishing in the McKenzie reach, although roadside parking is dangerous. If memory serves, there is off-road parking a bit west.

Theoretically, it is possible to find trout downstream from Clam Falls, but we haven't been able to find suitable access; and anyhow, there probably aren't any trout down there. Which may be sour grapes.

The North Fork of the Clam is another kettle of fish—in this case, brook trout in a typical brook trout stream, where we fish—intimate, easy to wade, and more likely to produce small trout taken with delicacy.

You may wish to demonstrate your skill at Lunch Bridge Road where the North Fork is wide, open, silt over sand, and canoeable. Malone Road downstream is a possible entry where you might run into stocked brown trout. But we begin our adventure at the County Road H bridge a quarter mile north of Clam River Road and/or Heart Lake Road. There is a PUBLIC HUNTING & FISHING GROUND sign and off-road parking on the southeast. Next, drop down to Heart Lake Road and go east. You'll find two parking lots and easy access to a very wadeable brook trout stream.

This area of the North Fork lies in that odd square extension of Burnett County in the southeast corner. You can go east from Clam Falls or south from WI 70.

SAWYER CREEK
DeLorme 84

Sawyer Creek rises from springs close to Shell Lake, the name of a city and popular lake in Washburn County on US 63. This first-class brook trout stream wanders through public land and easements for 6 miles to the Yellow River. We include this minor stream because its story provides a perfect example of the creative ways that trout streams can be eliminated or diminished. Shell Lake is a 2,600-acre spring-fed lake that is nearly fully developed. A combination of runoff from the roads and green lawns, together with a rising water table, has threatened to inundate some private shoreline. Vocal locals suggested that the city install a siphon to take water from the lake and dump it into that oh-so-convenient Sawyer Creek. Fortunately, an administrative law judge ruled in favor of the creek, based on testimony from the DNR. Eternal vigilance is the price that we must pay if we want to protect our vanishing outdoor heritage.

Incidentally, the creek is close to Tozer Lake, which is annually planted with rainbow trout averaging 14 inches.

THE EAU CLAIRE RIVER
DeLorme 93

The Eau Claire River between Lower Eau Claire Lake and the flowage or impoundment at Gordon, Wisconsin, is a classic representation of a trout river—breathtakingly beautiful on the day I first saw it: clear and cool, moving around boulders, separated by islands, with emerald grasses at the margins and jade weeds rimming runnels of golden sand. Although my experience and instincts tell me that it must be a marginal fishery because of the warming effect of the lake, I must return. We are both hopeless romantics; and often the ambience of the place becomes more compelling than the promise of a rise of trout. Visit the Eau Claire and dare to say we are wrong.

Find it in the southeast corner of Douglas County on County Road G, east of Gordon and US 53. See it at South Lawler Road and at Lidberg Bridge Road. There it reminds me of the Brule River at Copper Range Campground, but of course not so wide or deep. My notes end with "Come Back!"

If you are in the mood to explore, and have the time, you may face either of two directions. Go east, a long pull, to the freestone streams of Iron County; or north and west to the wonders of Pattison State Park, the Black River and Big Balsam, and last to the Blackhoof in Minnesota, southwest of Duluth. Let us guide you, just a little, and forgive us if our prejudice shows.

THE FREESTONE STREAMS OF IRON COUNTY

The rugged streams of Iron County storm through a ragged wilderness of cutover country and vast swamps. The Rivers Marengo, Bad, Potato, Black, and East and West Forks of the Montreal all flow into Lake Superior. They are primitive, root-beer colored, and—according to John Ramsay, a guide based in Ironwood, Michigan—air-cooled. Which means they are not spring fed, that the water warms quickly, and that the trout are not widely distributed.

We have been advised to fish the Marengo, and we have heard of a 14½-inch brook trout taken from that stream in town; Bill took a 13-inch brookie from below Peterson Falls. But our brook trout came laboriously, with time between hook-ups. There are also impoundments that warm the waters and prevent the reproduction of trout.

Because the rivers are difficult to wade and the trout are scattered, footpaths along the rivers do not extend far from the bridges. Sometimes you have to imagine where the paths might be. In this corner of northwestern Wisconsin you'll find a spidery pattern of long freestone rivers racing north to Lake Superior. Expect difficult wading, pocket fishing, intermittent trout stretches, natural and planted brook trout, and some natural browns.

THE BLACK RIVER AND THE BLACKHOOF RIVER

In the other direction, go west on County Road A out of Solon Springs on US 53 in Douglas County, through farmland, tree farms, and cutover, to the Black River, which crosses or parallels WI 35 in several places, then flows north to Pattison State Park and the waterfalls. If you work at it, you may find access to the Big Balsam, but we weren't too successful on the occasion of our last foray into that backcountry. Certainly, the falls at Pattison are worth a side trip.

From there you may want to curve into Minnesota's Carlton County and test the Blackhoof River upstream from MN 23 into the Blackhoof Wildlife Management Area; or check another of Carlton County's 38 trout streams. We profile the Blackhoof in the "North Shore" chapter in the Minnesota section of this book.

II | MINNESOTA

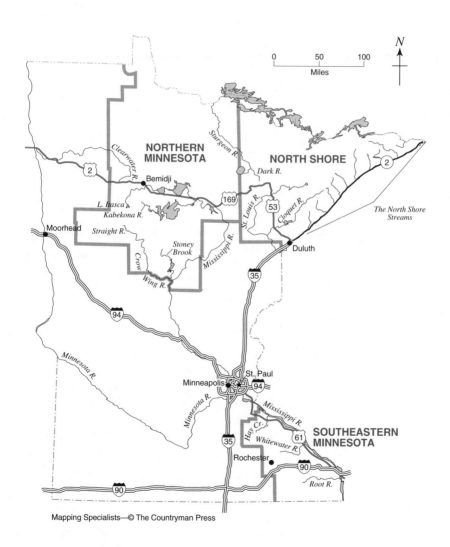

N

0   50   100
Miles

NORTHERN
MINNESOTA

NORTH SHORE

Clearwater R.

Sturgeon R.

2

Bemidji

Dark R.

2

L. Itasca
Kabekona R.

169

St. Louis R.

53

Cloquet R.

Moorhead

Straight R.

The North Shore
Streams

Stoney
Brook

Crow

Mississippi R.

Duluth

Wing R.

35

94

Minnesota R.

St. Paul

Minneapolis

94

Minnesota R.

Mississippi R.

35

Hay Cr.

61

SOUTHEASTERN
MINNESOTA

Whitewater R.

Rochester

90

Root R.

90

Mapping Specialists—© The Countryman Press

8 | Secret Streams of Southeastern Minnesota

Through brooding hardwood forests, ancient watercourses have worn their way down to the Mississippi, exposing weathered limestone cliffs and crenellated towers. Clear, cold springs rush from rock caverns, and watercress blankets a thousand seeps. Brook trout flit in crystal cups of tiny tributaries, and saffron-bellied brown trout prowl the pools as darkness falls. In some fast-water sections even the iridescent rainbow will clear the water in mighty leaps.

Each year, fishing for wild trout in southeastern Minnesota improves. Since 1984, 17 streams have been identified or improved and included on the map as designated trout waters. Several hundred miles of trout habitat have been added to pre-1984 streams. Under the ministrations of the Minnesota Department of Natural Resources, streambanks are riprapped, lunker structures are inserted, easements acquired. Fences and cattle crossings are installed. On a few streams, too few in our opinion, special regulations have been applied, sometimes over the fierce objections of a cadre of anglers and a couple of legislators from the southeast. The larger, long-term battle for improved water quality has yet to be won, but the energies of the state are being applied aggressively.

The huge, shaggy right triangle of Minnesota's southeastern eight counties encloses more than 600 miles of trout waters in more than 100 named rivers and creeks, from Red Wing on the north to the Iowa border. Three major stream complexes are protected by state parks. Other streams meander through patches of the 42,000-acre Richard J. Dorer Memorial Hardwood Forest. Wildlife management areas, totaling an additional 31,000 acres, adjoin or enclose segments of 10 streams. County parks and city parks are also thoughtfully located on the banks of several first-class streams.

Access to the streams of the southeast is easy at hundreds of bridges and across public lands. Where easements are not marked, a visiting angler should ask permission to cross the fields. Most Minnesota farmers are unusually generous with fishers who are polite, who close the gates, and who leave no trash behind. Many of those farmers also employ enlightened farming practices—not plowing or grazing close to the streambanks, installing cattle watering systems away from the streams, or leasing easements to the DNR. More than a few are active in local sportsmen's clubs and in chapters of Trout Unlimited. Cooperating farmers may also benefit financially from the lease or sale of easements and from the habitat improvements that enhance the esthetic and economic value of their properties.

Fishing for the three species of trout is very, very good—on many days, spectacular. Anglers who brave the rigors of a Minnesota winter may even raise browns and rainbows on approximately 50 miles of 12 southeastern streams that open on January 1 for catch-and-release with barbless hooks. In 1999 all the streams in eight counties of southeastern Minnesota were open early on April 1 for catch-and-release with barbless hooks. Special regulations are also effective on a number of streams during the regular trout season, from the Saturday nearest April 15 through September 30—although given all the extended opportunities to fish, the "regular season" may become a historical footnote in future books. As we have noted elsewhere, trout regulations are not static; read the states' publications carefully.

The Section of Fisheries of the DNR grades its trout streams as "Good," "Fair," or "Poor." The DNR is unduly modest. Many Good streams might appropriately be labeled "First-Class" or "Blue Ribbon." Many Fair sections are changing to Good, often with the hands-on help of local chapters of Trout Unlimited. Of the 600 miles, more than 250 are classified as Good or Fair—enough to exhaust the energy of even the most devout fly-fisher.

The DNR's Long Range Plan For Fisheries Management (1987) stated, "Brown trout are the major species present, although many streams contain brook trout and a few contain stocked rainbow trout. Trout standing crops are 100 pounds per acre on high quality streams and can be over 300 pounds on excellent streams. Thirty-four percent of the stream miles have wild trout . . . Fishing pressure is characterized as heavy on 23 percent, moderate on 25 percent, and light on 43 percent."

Trout numbers and sizes have improved during the last two decades. Bill Thorn, senior research biologist at Lake City, found that pounds of fish per acre of stream had more than doubled during the last 20 years to more than 100 pounds. Trout size also increased: "The average number of browns more than 12 inches long increased from 26 per stream mile in the 1970s to 55 in the 1990s." In-stream habitat improvement, improved farming practices, and increased catch-and-release have all helped, as has the scientific management and care that our DNR has devoted to our sport.

Water temperatures range from 32 degrees in winter to a summer high of 75 degrees in some sections, but the normal range encountered by fly-fishers is from the low 40s to the high 60s. Alkalinity ranges from 200 to 300 parts per million, a range desirable for the growth of aquatic life; pH is typically close to the neutral 7.0. The mayfly and caddis emergences of southeastern Minnesota vary from year to year in onset, duration, and intensity. Some species of aquatic insects will blanket the water of a favorite stream one year and be only a remnant presence the next. Spring floods may scour aquatic invertebrates from a watershed, while just over the hill another watershed, having been treated to normal precipitation, will witness the timely arrival of predicted hatches. Other variations in natural phenomena, such as drought or prolonged cold spells, may also affect emergences.

Where you find massed waterweeds and cress you'll find scuds. In the warmer sections, usually downstream, there will be leeches, forage fish, crayfish perhaps, and always a smorgasbord of terrestrials. Stoneflies are not common in the southeast.

Few of the streams profiled are wide and deep by western standards. None is swift like the Brule and Wolf of Wisconsin, and mayfly sizes generally range from small to minuscule. A 3- to 5-weight rod with a double taper or weight-forward floating line will serve. A favorite working tool is an 8-foot rod with a 9- to 10-foot leader tapering to .005 (6X) and .006 (5X) for #12 hoppers, and .007 (4X) for occasional forays after trophy browns with Woolly Buggers, Muddlers, or streamers.

Chest-high waders are useful in spring; hip boots are usually sufficient after the water levels recede. Wading staffs help you negotiate slippery banks and are mandatory during the winter season, when ice shelves form along the margins. Felt-bottomed waders or hippers must not be used during the winter; they're deadly on ice. One added warning: Be on the lookout for barbed wire. The old fences from abandoned farms have fallen, and the wires are snares for the too-eager angler.

The peculiar topography and geology of the southeast pose dangers for the future of trout fishing. In the middle sections many streams are cold, hard, spring fed, and perfect for trout. In their extreme upper reaches they may collect silt and multitudinous forms of pollutants from fence-to-fence farming, expanding communities, highway and bridge construction, and other ills.

Although the streams are buffered against acid precipitation by their passage through limestone, they nevertheless are fragile. A pulse of pesticides or herbicides could kill all aquatic life. A malfunction of a city or village disposal system could write finis to wild trout spawn. Occasional fish kills have been recorded as a result of the accidental or deliberate introduction of toxic substances.

Extensive cavities and subterranean channels have developed in this *karst* region. When acidic groundwater passes through limestone, fissures and channels develop and sinkholes open and close. Pollution in runoff can move quickly from surface to stream.

Fortunately, these potential disasters are being addressed by various agencies of the state and counties of Minnesota. Volunteer environmental organizations have formed powerful coalitions to protect clean air and clean water. Even farm organizations are concerned with the long-range effects of commercial agriculture on the purity of drinking water and the quality of life.

In the past 20 years the dedicated professionals of the Department of Natural Resources, often unsung, frequently underfunded, and probably overworked, have improved the quality of trout fishing in the area. Each year a few more miles of streams show up as trout habitat on the map. The unpaid workers of the Hiawatha, Wa-Hue, and Win-Cres Chapters of Trout Unlimited have donated thousands of hours and tens of thousands of dollars toward improvements.

Bill's comment on one of the streams profiled below should set the stage for your venture into the southeast: "It's just another one of these wonderful trout streams . . . so many of these streams are so similar. They all have their open meadows, brushy areas, wooded slopes, and pastureland. There's so much good, clear water; you see little pods of trout, clouds of midges, so it's difficult to individualize them." But we'll try.

The Northern Trio

These three streams are accessible from US 61, which parallels the west bank of the Mississippi. Hay and East Indian drain directly into the Mississippi; West Indian joins the Zumbro, a warm-water river.

HAY CREEK
DeLorme 34

Hay Creek in Goodhue County joins the Mississippi River at Red Wing, which is less than 60 miles from St. Paul and Minneapolis. The trout-fishing stretch may be reached from MN 58 or County Road 1 out of Red Wing.

The upper 7.5 miles, down from the gigantic fenced spring in Section 33, are rated Good. For any of you who sometimes feel that your individual action can't amount to much in the long and sometimes lonely battle to save your favorite stream, know this: It was through the single-minded action of Al Farmes, whom we gratefully acknowledge in the front of this book, that the spring was fenced to keep out cattle, an act that may well have saved all of the stream for trout. To find the trail to the spring, take MN 58 south from

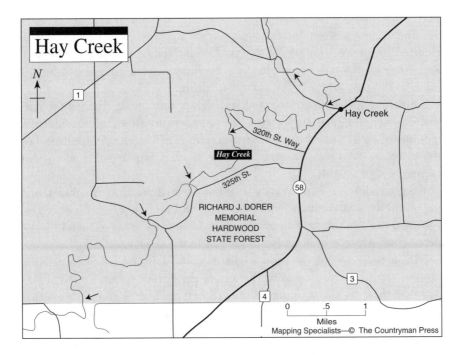

Red Wing for 6 miles through the crossroads village of Haycreek. Continue on this road for a bit more than 3 miles to a west-running dead end in Section 35. This is the first gravel road south of the junction with County Road 4. Park at the dead-end barrier and take the trail down to the spring.

Below the great spring the stream wanders through silent and mossy glades and under the remains of abandoned railroad trestles. At evening the setting reminds us of Edgar Allan Poe's "ghoul-haunted woodland of Weir"–dead, bone-white cottonwoods, dark and mysterious pools, the sour smell of decaying oak, the crazy, leaning trestle pilings like prehistoric dolmens.

Two river miles downstream from the spring is the first bridge. Between the first and second bridges, almost a mile through pasture has been improved by extensive riprapping and fencing. Two years ago Trout Unlimited chapters put up the funds for a watering tank and cattle fence about midway between the two bridges. The cattle no longer trample the banks or laze in the stream.

The pasture pools are a favorite winter haunt, especially in the area completely boxed in by DNR fence. We've been there as early as the first week of January under blue skies and bright sun, with air temperature in the 20s, casting a #20 Griffith's Gnat to trout rising in the pools. One recent March 3, finding tiny black stoneflies swarming on fence posts, we promptly switched to a #18 Black Ant and took trout. The pasture lies within a 3.9-

mile section posted to special regulations both winter and summer.

To find the pasture and the bridges, take the west-running road a mile south of Haycreek from MN 58. Or take County Road 1 on the north edge of Red Wing for 5.4 miles south to the schoolhouse; turn left and go about 3 miles to the first bridge below the great spring.

Stream improvement projects like fencing, riprapping, and special regulations are designed to increase the numbers of trout, or the biomass (pounds of trout per acre), or to produce trout of larger size. Biomass has increased on Hay Creek over the past several years, but size of trout has not increased significantly.

Hay Creek is the most heavily fished of the streams of the southeast, and yet on the second afternoon of a recent season I met only two anglers spin-fishing down from the big spring. By dusk I had it all to myself—and I wondered what was creeping up behind me from the shadows!

On a more recent occasion Al Farmes and I fished Hay between the hours of 11 AM and 5 PM. Oddly, there were more trout fishers on that Tuesday than there had been on the previous Sunday, which is an indication that not all fly-fishers storm the streams on weekends.

I fished up from the upper bridge in Section 27, starting at the huge pool under the decaying trestle, which is usually good for at least one brown trout. Later, after I'd skipped a number of runs and pools because absolutely nothing was happening, I came up behind a pair of fishermen trampling the banks ahead of me. They walked boldly to the edges of every pool to peer

A sign at Hay Creek near Red Wing, southeast Minnesota

in—surely no way to sneak up on a trout. I surmise that all of the water I explored fruitlessly had been "fished" in like manner.

Al, meanwhile, had hiked upstream a long way along the old railroad grade. Way up there he discovered a pool where trout were feeding actively on midges. Al crawled on hands and knees to the head of the pool, where, he says, he sat on his butt and with great care succeeded in catching and releasing 18 trout on a #18 soft-hackle, fished in the film. Al's theory is that the wind gusts were drowning midges before they could become airborne and that the trout were picking them off.

The morals of this story are two. Be prepared to walk away from the access points to find a section that hasn't already been pounded to death, and approach the stream with infinite caution—on hands and knees if necessary. Or slide your way into casting range on the seat of your pants.

Downstream from the village of Haycreek there are a couple of bridges, some deep pools, and about 3 miles of marginal trout water through public lands.

In recent years we have invested many days fishing Hay Creek through the pastures upstream from 320th Street Way, a gravel road south of Hay-Creek on MN 58. We have fished in January, during the summer, and during the last days of September. More than a mile has been improved with bank covers at considerable expense by the DNR. Bill recommends a 9-foot rod when the bankside weeds are high. During the winter a kneeling or praying position in the snow may bring up the trout. It is a revelation to walk this wonderful stream under a winter-blue sky when the wind is soft, the air temperature is in the 20s, and inquisitive chickadees signal their two-note commentary.

In July 1997 a toxic chemical was deliberately or accidentally loosed into a 2-mile section of the Hay. Some 7,800 trout perished. The source of the pollution was never discovered. Consternation and commiseration from the trout fraternity, and dire predictions for a tortuous recovery; but in January 1998 Bill and Jim caught trout in that devastated section, which speaks well for the resilience of the species (trout we mean, not humans).

The nearest city with overnight and dining facilities is Red Wing on US 61.

MAZEPPA CREEK
DeLorme 34

Mazeppa Creek has always intrigued me, partly for its exotic name. Turkish, or middle European, most likely. There are other reasons for my interest. On the west shoulder of County Road 1, a mile north of the village of Mazep-

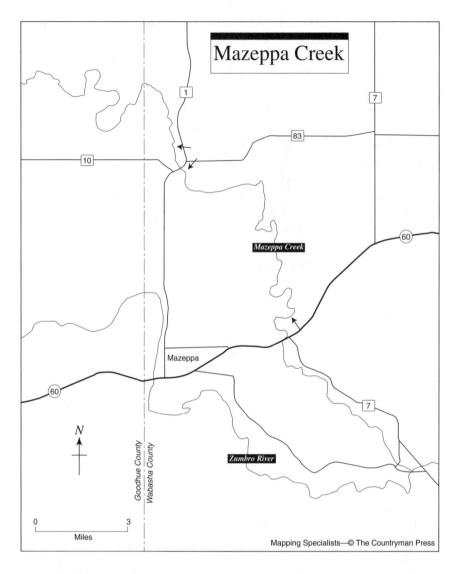

Mazeppa Creek

1

7

83

10

60

Mazeppa Creek

60

Mazeppa

7

N

Goodhue County

Wabasha County

Zumbro River

7

0   3

Miles

Mapping Specialists—© The Countryman Press

pa and beyond the bridge and the junction with County Road 83, you will find an off-road slot for one car, two in a pinch, and a wooden stile. Head over the stile and down a long, steep slope into pasture and the springs. One day, when the head of water flowing under the bridge was substantial and cold, I decided to circumnavigate the watershed to discover the source or sources of all of that free-flowing trout water. Every feeder creek was bone dry on that May 2 day. On my last trip, on the 5th of September, an angler occupied the space next to the stile. Parking on the shoulder allows only minimal space and is dangerous when the milk trucks power down around the curve, so I parked in the rough triangle just northeast of the bridge. Another angler had taken possession of that sweet stretch of stream, so I fished the pools around the bridge. There was a touch of color in the water and a remarkable temperature of 54 degrees! Under bright sky I could not coax a trout out of hiding. Downstream the creek is swift, narrow, deep, and weedy; in short, a perfect trout stream, at least for a way.

For reasons that escape me, natural reproduction is insufficient, so the DNR plants several thousand brown trout fingerlings each year.

The next bridge down from County Road 83 is well surrounded by farm buildings, although there appears to be a path downstream on the north bank. You'll have to ask for permission if you like the looks of it. I also fish the Mazeppa upstream of the MN 60 bridge east of Mazeppa. Fifty yards east of the bridge on the north side, find a stub gravel road leading to a turn-around. Although the creek there is wide and flows over sand and gravel, there are pools between the runs and riffles. It's quite open for fly-casting, and a spin-fisher will like it, too.

Downstream from MN 60 the river flattens, widens, and warms. I wouldn't waste my time, except for a short streetch below the bridge.

I haven't done extraordinarily well on Mazeppa, and I was told it was "blown out" a few years ago, meaning a catastrophic spring flood, but I continue to return. A water temperature of 54 at the beginning of September speaks well for cold-water fish life.

The creek is in southwestern Wabasha County and is a tributary of the Zumbro River.

COLD SPRING BROOK
DeLorme 34

The sign states that you must use barbless hooks, and you are limited to one brook trout of 12 inches or longer. A welcome sign to anglers who relish delicious brook trout streams with naturally reproducing populations. Yes, I said "delicious," the word that popped into my mind when I first saw it. If you travel east from Mazeppa on MN 60 at 60 miles per hour, you may miss Cold Spring Brook at Zumbro Falls. Take County Road 68 just before you reach town and turn north for 50 yards. Park there at streamside and say to yourself, "Delicious," or whatever adjective springs full-blown.

This short, cold, clear stream requires low-profile bank fishing in places; in other places wading upstream ever so slowly will not spook the trout. The margins are thick with cress; the bed is flush with weeds, which separate the runnels of sand and gravel. Upstream of the first roadside parking spot, not too far to walk, you'll find a magnificent corner pool. Fish this by stealth

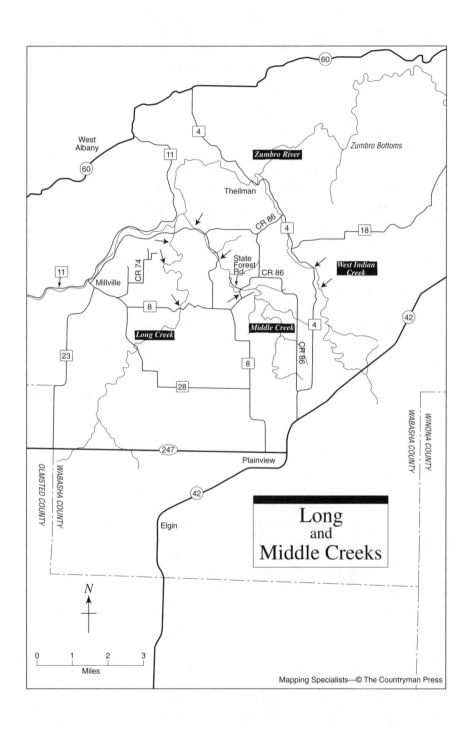

Long
and
Middle Creeks

Mapping Specialists—© The Countryman Press

from below. If you stand on the road in sunlight and paint the pool with a Royal Coachman, you will surely drive them deep. Wait until the evening sun goes down.

There are springs bordering the stream, and upstream there are seeps from the high bank on the west. The first bridge a mile up is about where I finish. And where I run out of superlatives.

LONG CREEK
DeLorme 35

Long Creek can be found by taking County Road 2 south out of Millville to County Road 8 and taking a left (going east) for approximately 1.5 miles to the bridge where there are DNR easements, upstream and down. This water is beautiful, with good runs, deep wide pools, and inviting little pockets.

Carl Haensel, friend, enthusiast and writer, reports fair catches of brown trout, but not great numbers of them. Actually, if you are up to it you can find more fish by hiking down into the valley, miles downstream from the County Road 8 bridge. Take County Road 2 south from Millville to County Road 74. Zigzag on this dirt road for 2.5 miles to the spot where the path and easement begin. Take this scenic stroll into a secluded valley. Fishing here is a bit spotty, but when you find a likely spot it will be loaded with brown trout, many of which are large. The pools are farther apart in this middle stretch and there is more sand, so you'll walk more. But if solitude is what you like and denser populations of trout appeal to you, you'll enjoy this area.

MIDDLE CREEK
DeLorme 35

Middle Creek in Wabasha County is small, clear, and ice cold. It is lined with watercress, and for much of the way the free-flowing center is only a couple of feet wide. For the accurate fly-caster who accepts a challenge, the rewards are native browns and brook trout that will dance all the way to hand.

Go east from Long Creek 1.5 miles to the downstream bridge on Middle Creek. Continue upstream along the creek road to the next bridge, where you will find some habitat improvement that was installed by private owners. Crib shelters, ramps, riprap, and newly created pools hold substantial numbers of trout. Permission here is a must.

You may prefer to continue upstream to fish in state forest land where there is public easement and habitat improvement. A state forest road connects County Roads 8 and 86, and there are two spurs off that. Gorgeous brookies taken with light tackle and a thoughtful approach are the quarry. A larger brown may surprise you.

There are many forest roads in the sprawling acreage of the Richard J. Dorer Memorial Hardwood Forest. Some may be difficult to negotiate with a passenger car. There may be deadfall across the trail or, more likely, low spots created by enthusiasts with four-wheel-drive pickups. If in doubt, send out a walker with a red flag ahead. Some of our hidden treasures require an approach by shank's mare. Sometime let us tell you about "Rainbow Creek."

WEST INDIAN CREEK
DeLorme 35

West Indian Creek, which lies east of Middle Creek and joins the Zumbro River, is 7.2 miles long and contains both browns and brook trout. Take County Road 86 to its junction with County Road 4 at a private campground. County Road 4 parallels the river upstream and joins MN 42 near Plainview. There are more than 2 miles of public land upstream, of which 1.5 miles have been rehabilitated with funds from the state's Reinvest in Minnesota program. Biomass of trout has increased by more than 300 percent due to improved overwinter survival. The improved section lies under and upstream of the upper County Road 4 bridge. Upstream from the bridge and immediately before the highway begins its uphill rise, look for an auto trail. Look sharp; it's not much of a trail. Although you can drive along the edge of a cornfield almost to the edge of the stream, where there is a small turnaround, we park at the first wide spot in the trail and walk the rest of the way. Sometimes the ground will be spongy or torn up.

Bill has enjoyed superior results in this section, which has been rip-rapped with huge chunks of rock. It fishes best when the bankside weeds are not yet head-high. Another favorite spot is the abandoned bridge some 100 yards downstream from the new County Road 4 bridge. Jim has invested many pleasant hours there, wading upstream next to cornfields. West Indian was once one of our all-time favorites, but one year spring floods devastated it. It bounced back; then, in 1998, 4,000 trout died as a result of a mysterious disease or spill into a 1.9-mile stretch. It has recovered from that trauma, too.

West Indian is known for robust browns—broad shouldered, deep bodied, and energetic. A devious fisherperson should do well with a nicely tied #16 or #18 Adams. Or a beadhead Pheasant Tail perhaps?

Excellent overnight and dining facilities at Wabasha on US 61. Outstanding country cuisine at the Anderson House since 1856. For a family lark, see Donn Kreofsky's L.A.R.K. (Lost Arts Revival by Kreofksy) workshop and toy store in Kellog, close to Wabasha. Children delight in his fantastic carousel. Adults, too.

EAST INDIAN CREEK
DeLorme 35

East Indian, which is appropriately a few miles east of West Indian, in Wabasha County, with access from County Road 14 off US 61, is a small stream containing naturally reproducing brook trout. Short rods, light lines, and small flies are recommended. Its upper reaches are being improved by the DNR with the aid of the Wa-Hue Chapter of TU.

The nearest city with facilities is Wabasha on US 61.

THE WHITEWATER RIVER COMPLEX
DeLorme 26 & 35

By the end of the 1920s the valley of the Whitewater had become the wreckage of a dream. Shortly after the 1851 treaty with the Dakota, which opened the land to settlement, land-hungry pioneers advanced up the floodplain of the Mississippi. They wanted free land. The Whitewater River and the folds of lush green hills seemed to be the end of the long journey north and the beginning of independence and wealth. Black-soil bottomlands and the alluvial shelves below high bluffs were there to be seized and ripped open to seed. The massed ranks of black walnut, hickory, and juniper were to be cut and burned. Life in the late 19th century would go on forever, it seemed—peaceful, fruitful, and profitable.

The pioneers hacked the trees without thought, planted the slopes, and burned deep-rooted grasses. Prosperity seemed just around the corner, but in 1900 the floods began. Heavy rains fell year after year, washing away the topsoil and filling the valleys with debris. Towns vanished in spring floods. Fields yielded less and less. The long dying of the valley had begun.

As farms were abandoned or foreclosed, the pioneers moved once more—north or west toward other promised lands. The clear trout waters of the Whitewater and dozens of other streams ran thick with mud. A handful of farmers who survived the ravages of ignorance and nature were finally finished off by the depression of the 1930s.

As early as 1919 the state purchased its first parcel of exhausted land to be included in the projected Whitewater State Park. Fifteen miles of the Whitewater and many miles of tributaries are now included in the park.

In 1938 Richard J. Dorer joined the Minnesota Department of Conser-

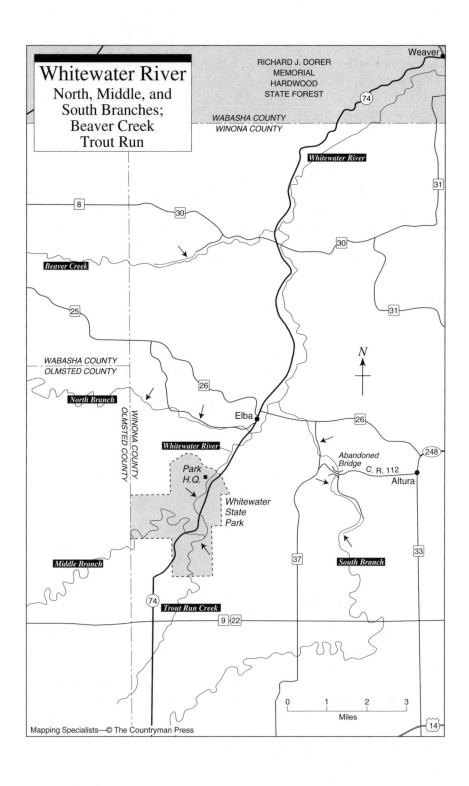

Whitewater River
North, Middle, and
South Branches;
Beaver Creek
Trout Run

RICHARD J. DORER
MEMORIAL
HARDWOOD
STATE FOREST

Weaver

WABASHA COUNTY
WINONA COUNTY

Whitewater River

WABASHA COUNTY
OLMSTED COUNTY

WINONA COUNTY
OLMSTED COUNTY

Beaver Creek

North Branch

Elba

Whitewater River

Park
H.Q.

Whitewater
State
Park

Middle Branch

Abandoned
Bridge

C. R. 112

Altura

South Branch

Trout Run Creek

N

0   1   2   3
Miles

Mapping Specialists—© The Countryman Press

vation, now the Department of Natural Resources, and began the visionary and painstaking work of rebuilding the battered valleys of the Whitewater. Gullies were blocked and filled, slopes were replanted, and grazing was halted in the watershed. Land was taken for back taxes or purchased for inclusion in the Whitewater Wildlife Management Area. The Whitewater River complex of three branches and three feeders embraces 55 miles of classic fly-fishing water.

THE NORTH BRANCH OF THE WHITEWATER
DeLorme 26

The North Branch on Fairwater Road, west of the village of Elba in Winona County, offers roadside access to 3 miles of respectable fly-fishing in spring but becomes less productive after the middle of May due to marginal water quality. This 8-mile branch, which is always a few degrees warmer than the others, originates in farmland on the savannas where fence-to-fence farming is practiced. It muddies quickly, clears slowly, receives less recharge from springs, and is subject to pesticide and herbicide runoff. Its middle reaches, through a heavily wooded and narrow valley, are not accessible to heavy equipment, so the DNR has not been able to reconstruct habitat. Most brown trout are stocked. Nevertheless, a fisherman who is willing to pick his way into the jungle above the last DNR parking lot will find solitary and picturesque pools.

One May day up there we autopsied a brown and found its stomach stuffed, sausagelike, with green, segmented midge larvae. We switched to midge nymphs and emergers. While we enjoyed a catch of small trout delicately inveigled from smooth runs, worm fishers were taking browns to 14 inches from the holes.

One of our friends claims to have fished downstream from Carley State Park, but we have not tried that yet.

Dining at Elba on MN 74, and public and private campgrounds on the middle branch of the river.

THE MIDDLE BRANCH OF THE WHITEWATER
DeLorme 26

Six miles of the Middle Branch snake through Whitewater State Park. It is as fine a reach of open water as we know. Browns are both wild and hatchery stock; sizable rainbows are planted annually to amaze the campers. Four- and 5-pound browns are taken every year and often displayed proudly at Mauer Brothers Tavern in Elba.

HENRY HALL

Jim Humphrey on the Whitewater

Approximately 4 miles, from the mouth upstream to the third MN 74 bridge crossing, are open January 1 through March 31 to catch-and-release with barbless hooks only. In one quarter-mile station, electro-fishing turned up 926 adult and 1,228 fingerling brown trout, of which 241 exceeded 12 inches.

Midges will be on the wing on most winter days. *Baetis* mayflies, blue-winged olives #18, may show as early as late February. Tiny early black stoneflies should be trit-trotting across the snowbanks.

On February 17 and 18 we found orange scuds among the weeds, and almost every decent run or pool was occupied by an angler. Surprising to find so many fly-fishers outside on a winter day, but it was a long dreary winter and the 48-degree air temperature on a Minnesota February weekend was evidently enough to pry them away from their vises—or vices.

Drift your weighted Orange Scud in the emerald-green pools and under the bridges.

There is also a 3.3-mile section posted to no-kill during the regular season. If you fish within park boundaries, you'll need a park sticker, winter as well as summer, but this is excellent fly-fishing water, so it's worth the price. Buy the sticker at park headquarters on MN 74 about 2 miles south of Elba.

In summer you'll likely find campers flinging spinners into the pools, but during the winter season you'll usually find peace and quiet, except in the Cliff Pool in Cedar Hill Campground. Not to fret; if the pool is occupied, go down about 50 yards to a second, insignificant pool. It doesn't look like much, but we've had our best success there. Still farther downstream, not far beyond the spot where the Dakota Trail crosses the river on a series of cast concrete blocks, is a long run. You might see it as a long narrow pool. No matter: It'll drive you crazy. There's another favorite long, curving pool outside the park downstream of the County Road 39 bridge.

Upstream, outside the park boundaries, the Hiawatha Chapter of TU has devoted years of extravagant care to habitat improvement, with excellent results in the production of larger trout.

And last, don't miss the live trout and stream display, partly funded by several chapters of TU, in the headquarters building at the north edge of the park.

TROUT RUN
DeLorme 26

The tributary to the Middle Branch of the Whitewater, Trout Run in the park, is a classic small spring creek—glass-clear, weedy, cold, with a mix of wild browns and brookies. Exceedingly light tackle may capture a minor masterpiece. But not all the residents are small. Mike Schad, of the Wa-Hue Chapter of TU, had been soft-footing along Trout Run for a couple of hours without notable success. He finally planted himself on the bank with boots in the water to take five. A very large trout swam out from under the bank between his feet and moved away leisurely, no doubt thumbing a fin in disdain. That's trout fishing for you, at least in southeastern Minnesota.

THE SOUTH BRANCH OF THE WHITEWATER
DeLorme 26

The 10 miles of the South Branch, or South Fork as it appears on some maps, are favored by dedicated fly-fishers. A preferred section for many years began at the abandoned bridge west out of Altura and continued up into the private pastures. You can find the bridge from Elba east on County Road 26, south on County Road 37, then east on County Road 112 past the hatchery. Or west out of Altura on County Road 112, if you want to follow the gravel road that parallels the river on the east side upstream toward the pastures.

This wild section, which averages 25 feet in width, offers an optimum of habitats—a few deep, jade pools, swift runs over gravel, classy flats over limestone rubble, and even some grassy verges where you can splat a grasshopper during the dog days. Large trout are taken with regularity up there.

Late one April evening, after the big pool above the abandoned bridge had been pounded all day, Jim created a fake hatch by drifting a Light Cahill among the branches of a sunken tree. On the umpteenth cast, or more, a brown surprised him. Three more browns to 13 inches, and a chunky rainbow, rose to the "hatch" in short order. You've read about creating a false hatch in the literature, no doubt. And no doubt dismissed it as the product of a romance writer. Try it some time, when the fish are obdurate.

There is winter catch-and-release, January 1 through March 31, on a 3.8-mile posted section from the mouth to 1 mile upstream of the abandoned bridge. There is a complex pool that we dearly love. Take the trail at the edge of a cornfield about midway between the County Road 26 and County Road 37 bridges. You'll return, too, if you can outwit a bright brown there on a gorgeous February day.

During the summer you might like to sample the open fishing through the pastures of the upper South Branch. If the gate isn't padlocked, open the gate and drive through and park under the trees. This is private land, so we do not guarantee access. At any time, property may change owners, or the present owners may get tired of picking up trash. Paul Krogvold, a fly-tier and writer, came from Norway to fish it with us. He had no complaints, kneeling and casting to scores of visible, rising browns.

THE MAIN BRANCH
DeLorme 26 & 35

Downstream from Elba, the Main Branch flattens and slows for 13 miles, partly through a wildlife refuge, to the Mississippi. A 1978 flash flood dumped enormous quantities of silt in this stem. The natural recovery process has been slow, but the 10 miles below Elba produce some large trout in huge pools. It won't be easy, and the action may be like watching a big-league pitcher go through his motions, but big-fish fishers may want to give it a shot. In May 2000 anglers appeared in goodly numbers on the Main Branch of the Whitewater, which signaled to us that the word was out: Significant trout were being creeled.

Fifty years ago a series of man-made dikes and ponds were constructed on the lower 3 miles of the Main. The system was designed to create waterfowl habitat. In a 1998 project, funded by the state lottery, the river was returned to its original bed and structures added, which should improve water temperatures and trout habitat.

There is a winter catch-and-release season on a 6.9-mile section from Winona County Road 30 upstream to the confluence of the Middle and North Branches in Elba. Barbless hooks are demanded.

We cherish three places on the Whitewater complex: the snag pool on the South Branch on a warm summer evening when the bats begin to fly; a split pool at the end of a walk through cornfield stubble to the South Branch on a shining day in February when the temperature is in the 20s and the air is still; not least, we find a challenge in those complex pools and runs that rub up against the cliffs where swallows dart.

BEAVER CREEK

DeLorme 35

Beaver Creek, which enters the Main Branch of the Whitewater 5 miles downstream from Elba, parallels County Road 30. Go west on County Road 30 from its junction with MN 74 for perhaps half a mile. Beaver is a small stream that in the past has harbored some very large trout, including the onetime state-record brown. There's a winter season on the entire 6.3 miles, for barbless hooks and catch-and-release. Look for a set of steel-gray barns just east of a signposted WW 10 TWP low-maintenance road. In winter it's better to walk in than to chance getting stuck. About 1.5 miles upstream you'll find DNR parking at a barrier.

We met a young fly-fisher there in February who admitted to having released eight browns on a Black Gnat. We suspect the Black Gnat was seen by the trout as a midge or winter stonefly. There are tons of small brown trout between County Road 30 and the barrier; we are advised that big browns come out at night. Farther upstream is brook trout water.

Beaver is a terrific stream for a novice who wants to learn how to fish small water and tight corners, and keep his fly out of streamside vegetation and trees. Bill described our fall trip lyrically: "If you perfect your skills, the native browns will cooperate. I caught two 9-inch browns, then two 10-inchers, on a #16 Hare's Ear. Intermittent showers enhanced the powerful aroma of the autumn hardwood forest. Butternuts were strewn across the gravel road; and to cap the memory, 27 wild turkeys crossed ahead of us. What a sight; what a day!"

The nearest city with overnight and dining facilities is St. Charles on Interstate 90. Cosmopolitan facilities at Rochester, about 25 miles west on County Road 9. Dining also in Elba.

GARVIN BROOK
DeLorme 26 & 27

Garvin Brook is a pretty stream—and maybe more. You'll find it about 10 miles west of Winona and southwest of Stockton in Winona County on US 14. It was and is a blue-ribbon stream, from "The Arches," a historic and photogenic double overpass abandoned when a railroad died, down to and through Stockton. In 1989 Stockton and Garvin Brook were almost wiped out by a flash flood. A few years later both were hit again. But both survived, and the brook is a joy to follow from arch to town perhaps even downstream from town, although we cannot vouch for that.

The stream through Farmers Community Park at The Arches is clear, cold, and shallow; "smiling" is the word for it on a bright summer day. A place to introduce a young one to the joys of trout viewing. Downstream from the park the brook winds through an overgrown meadow for about a mile. There is a very small parking lot close to the arches and two pull-offs on US 14 downstream, but you will be well served if you traverse the bank path down from the upper parking area and walk back via the highway when you tire. Garvin is reputed to contain "high standing crops of wild trout," both brook trout and browns.

Facilities at Stockton, and Winona on US 61.

PICKWICK AND LITTLE PICKWICK CREEKS
DeLorme 27

These two creeks lie in the point of the angle and about midway between Winona and LaCrescent/La Crosse on US 61. Take County Road 7 west from US 61 to Pickwick. Fish upstream along County Road 7 or along Little Trout Valley Road. On some maps the streams are labeled Big Trout Creek and Little Trout Creek, but Pickwick is a more romantic name. No doubt the village of Pickwick was named in the 19th century by an admirer of Dickens; at least we like to think so.

These two are true success stories. For more than 10 years the Win-Cres Chapter of Trout Unlimited has improved them, adding structures, debrushing, narrowing, and deepening the streams. Sometimes spring floods have torn out the works, but TU has persevered. Two once-degraded streams through precipitous country are now great fisheries, monuments to the work of dedicated volunteers, which should be encouragement to all of us.

Facilities at Winona and LaCrescent.

Bucksnort Dam on Trout Run Creek

TRIBUTARIES OF THE ROOT RIVER

The Root River is a mighty complex of forks and branches that drains much of four counties and includes more than 100 miles of trout streams. Trout Run Creek and Torkelson Creek are tributaries of the main stem; another group that follows swells the waters of the Main and South Branches of the Root. The four streams of Winona County drain into the main stem, and two other groups either cluster around the South Fork or enter the main stem. We have grouped them for the convenience of traveling fly-fishers.

TROUT RUN CREEK
DeLorme 26

Trout Run Creek, in southwestern Winona County and northern Fillmore County, a cold-water tributary of the main stem of the Root River from the village of Saratoga on MN 74 downstream, includes 13 miles classed as Good. There is public easement on about 12 of the 13 miles. It may be in a class by itself. Begin at the bridge about 1 mile south of Troy on County Road 43, where through pastureland it reminds us of dew-diamonded, emerald-green Ireland in spring. Not more than 1.5 river miles downstream you'll find the fabled round red barn, if you want to wade it all the way. To reach

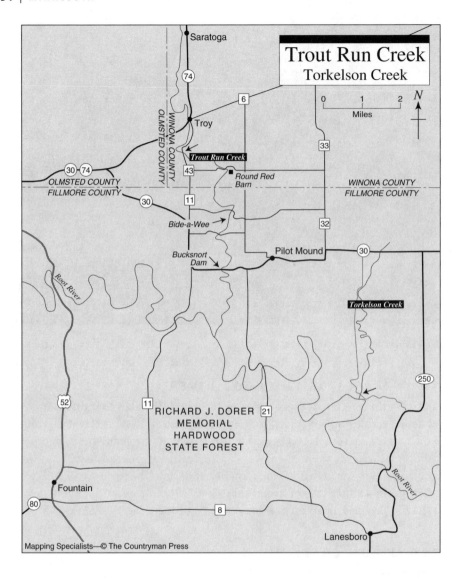

the red barn by road, take the first gravel road going east, approximately half a mile south of the bridge.

Upstream from the round red barn is tough going for a way under heavy overhang but with great potential for careful fly-fishers. We know the lie of an 18-inch brown. There are downstream paths on both sides from the barn bridge. Better yet, look for a trail on the west that climbs a ridge, then drops into an area that appears to be an abandoned campground flanked by shallow pools that will reward your skill.

If you keep going downstream, you'll arrive at a stretch of deep, dark, slow water. We take station on the forested west bank, where we watch big browns surface lazily to pick off an unsuspecting mayfly or midge. We must sharpshoot for individual trout and often we put them down, but it's the kind of challenge that we like. It reminds us of the technique necessary on some of the famous western spring creeks.

The next bridge down is Bide-a-Wee, in olden days a cabin and camping community, with a few remaining cabins upstream and superb fly-fishing down through three-quarters of a mile mile to the slab bridge, mostly through pasture. About midway between the Bide-a-Wee bridge and the slab is a long, deep pool with steep banks and a quick drop-off. Reserve this one for evening fishing, when substantial browns should feed on top. You may have to slide your boots into water and lean back against the slope to hold position. Don't be impatient, and keep your backcast high.

Next down from the slab bridge is Bucksnort Dam on MN 30. Above the dam is a long pool and Humphrey's "Devil's Seat," where he often sits at ease and waits for a bruiser brown to rise. Meanwhile, his pals fish downstream through riprapped pastures and riffles, where on one memorable day Dick Frantes raised 39 browns on a hopper while Humphrey got zilch. He did see, though, upstream and around the corner from the Devil's Seat, in the depths and protected by a snaggle tree, an 8-inch brown crosswise in the mouth of some great shadowy, fishy form. There are no northern pike in these icy waters; draw your own conclusions.

We recall vividly, and still with a shiver, an April opener above the slab bridge with Ken Hanson of the Kiap-TU-Wish Chapter, Dick Frantes, and a flotilla of dark Hendricksons struggling to rise through a sleet storm. Why they chose to emerge, and why we chose that bitter day to fish Trout Run, we do not know. To add insult to injury, Ken must have caught and released 20 browns to our somewhat fewer.

In three consecutive years of electro-fishing surveys, standing stocks of naturally reproducing brown trout varied from 2,500 per mile to a high close to 5,000—superior numbers for any stream, anywhere. Among them will be a few busters that exceed 18 inches. Look for them in impossible places. We can't guarantee the numbers on your visit, but we can guarantee a quality experience on Trout Run, if you take pains to maintain a low profile and cast the longest leader you can handle. Barbless hooks are required, and brown trout between 12 and 16 inches must be immediately returned.

Accommodations at St. Charles on Interstate 90 and at Lanesboro and Preston to the south.

TORKELSON CREEK
DeLorme 26

Torkelson, a tributary of the main stem of the Root, a bit south and east of Trout Run and a few miles due north of Lanesboro on MN 250, is a little jewel. Some places you can jump across, but follow it upstream on the unmarked gravel town road that angles northwest off MN 250 at green mile marker 5. Use the stiles and watch for rising trout. About the third meadow up it gets really good, and the valley scenery is spectacular. The DNR invested $30,000 in habitat improvement, so it must be something special.

Exceptional accommodations at Lanesboro to the south.

The South Branch of the Root River Complex

The South Branch of the Root and its feeders are about as good as it gets in southeastern Minnesota for fly-fishers who want to explore and experience a variety of waters. These seven streams include more than 35 miles of Good water. Adult browns, ranging from 9 inches to 12 pounds, inhabit the Root complex. A few rainbows are added each year, together with several hundred thousand brown trout fry. Naturally reproducing brook trout are in the tributaries. DNR surveys commonly find 2,000 to 3,000 trout per mile.

THE SOUTH BRANCH OF THE ROOT RIVER
DeLorme 26

A visitor can go west, upstream from Lanesboro in Fillmore County or from the city of Preston at the junction of US 52 and MN 12, or begin in and around Forestville State Park on the west. County Road 12 connects Preston and the park. Conveniently, 3 of the most productive miles lie within the park, a short stroll from fishermen's parking, from either of two campgrounds and a picnic ground. The park stretch is preferred by most fly-fishers, but that's not to denigrate many days of superior fishing downstream from the park boundary, where the Root widens and deepens, all the way into a beautiful riffle and pool right in Preston.

In August the Root through the park draws the trico crowd from far distances. Be prepared for some crowding early mornings. Trico fishers, however, aren't heavy-booted bank runners; they usually confine their downstream puddle or S-casts to relatively small areas of the stream.

John Schorn, a skillful fly-fisher from the Twin Cities who fishes the Root early and often, maintains that the trout there are peculiarly oriented to the surface. He says this is probably because the river through the park, and particularly along the picnic grounds near the Meighen Store, is shallow and shaded by mature oaks, so the fish are not driven deep by sunlight.

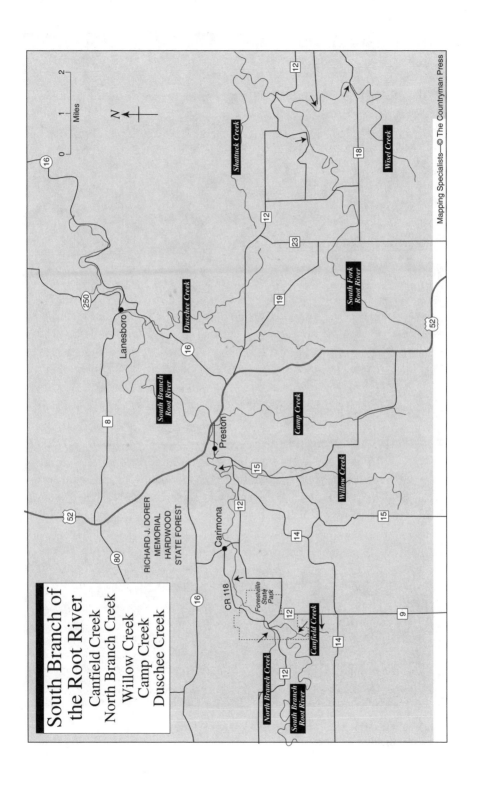

South Branch of the Root River

Canfield Creek
North Branch Creek
Willow Creek
Camp Creek
Duschee Creek

RICHARD J. DORER MEMORIAL HARDWOOD STATE FOREST

Lanesboro

Preston

Carimona

Forestville State Park

North Branch Creek

South Branch Root River

Canfield Creek

Camp Creek

Willow Creek

South Fork Root River

Duschee Creek

South Branch Root River

Shattuck Creek

Wisel Creek

Miles

N

Mapping Specialists—© The Countryman Press

Sandy Rolstad on the South Branch of the Root River in Forestville State Park. This area is known for prolific trico hatches.

We, too, have enjoyed excellent dry-fly fishing at the picnic grounds.

Along County Road 118 between the east boundary of Forestville State Park and the bridge south of Carimona, look for roadside parking at a stile. A fenced easement about 300 yards long leads to the river, where there are huge pools and sparkling runs.

One memorable day there comes to mind. As a spectator armed only with a camera on a May morning, I followed Jay Paulson, who released more than 20 browns, fishing upstream with a small dark Hare's Ear and a tiny fluorescent strike indicator. Among Jay's catch were a 16-incher, two 15s, and several I eyeballed at 14 inches.

Returning to Preston: Coming up County Road 12 from the south into Preston and just over the bridge, if you look you'll find on the left a rough road to a bankside picnic area with a spool table. Just a few hundred feet upstream is a jewel of a pool spreading over boulders, broken limestone, and sand. The pool has given us delightful hours over selective brown trout. On one occasion Al Farmes took a dozen without moving his feet.

Above the Preston pool is a half-mile-long horseshoe and a second bridge. We can't say that the horseshoe has been productive, but above the second bridge on a dirt road is fly-fisher's heaven. Roadside parking is up there, with a steep bank down to the stream. It's one of our favorites, particularly the upstream pool where we've enjoyed several mayfly hatches, notably the Hendrickson in May.

Between Preston and Lanesboro there are many places of access along the Root River State Trail. We have encountered 50 brown trout upstream of a trail bridge. Carry a pack rod on your bicycle.

At an auto bridge that crossed the state trail we watched a frustrated 19-inch brown attempt to separate a meal from a herd of minnows. No joy. Even the wily brown is not always as successful as we are.

CANFIELD CREEK
DeLorme 26

Canfield Creek, a tributary of the South Branch of the Root and labeled on the DNR map as South Branch Creek, springs from a cavern about 1.5 miles above its junction with the Root in the park. Small trout can be taken from this fascinating small creek, which contains untold numbers and varieties of Ephemerellidae mayflies.

Dick Hanousek, a world-traveling fly-fisher and writer, may hold the record for trout caught and released in Canfield—65 in a single day. But Dick's an expert with the long rod, fine leaders, and tiny flies. We wouldn't expect to do as well, but you might. Caddisflies are also abundant in both Canfield and the Root.

Another day on the Root complex is retrieved from memory to share with you. On a miserably cold day in April, when the water temperature was only 44 degrees, I watched John Rowell, a master steelheader on the Bois Brule of Wisconsin, take a half-dozen browns below Canfield on a "flymph," which could be described as a hybrid nymph/soft-hackle. Later I burned up a couple of hours casting to and spooking a pod of trout stacked up in a diversion channel where the water was warmer. I took a brace to prove that it could be done, while John went downstream and filled out his dozen.

NORTH BRANCH CREEK
DeLorme 26

Forestville Creek (labeled North Branch Creek on the DNR map), which enters the Root in the park near the historic Meighen Store (circa 1858), offers 2.6 miles rated Good. It's worth the investment of a couple of hours, since the DNR recently rehabilitated 2 miles of it. Bill avers it is really excellent since the habitat improvement.

WILLOW AND CAMP CREEKS
DeLorme 26

Willow and Camp Creeks are two feeder streams that join the Root River at Preston on US 52. Subsequent to our first edition, in which we praised them only faintly, both streams have been improved with substantial habitat structures. Jim likes that section of the Willow between County Road 12 and the junction with the South Branch of the Root through the streamside easement. The stretch of the South Branch below the junction and around the horseshoe into that tiny park in Preston is one we have described previously with more than faint praise.

Although Preston has overnight and dining facilities, Bill often stays overnight at one of the bed & breakfasts in nearby Lanesboro that have sprung up around that regionally famous tourist destination. He notes that Lanesboro supports first-class dining establishments and, not least, a sweet riffle and deep pools on the Main Root that produce a few big browns in the evening. His advice is to fill up on good food then take a leisurely stroll down to the river, booted and armed with a stout rod and outsized fly.

Camp Creek may be better than Willow Creek, or at least more pleasing to anglers. There is a winter catch-and-release season from January 1 through March 31 on a posted section from the mouth upstream for 3.5 miles. During the regular season browns between 12 and 16 inches must be returned within that same section. In both instances barbless hooks are mandatory.

A 2-mile section upstream from Preston has been improved by the DNR. River flow has been speeded, and riprap added to create hiding places. Farther upstream the creek is slower and wider, suitable for dry-fly fishing when the hatch is on. Blue-winged olives will begin disparate hatches as early as March. It is reported that the Hendrickson hatch begins during the third or fourth week of May. Caddisflies and terrestrials show season long.

In 1996 the DNR completed a bicycle trail, the Harmony Preston Valley State Trail, from US 52 in Harmony to the Root River State Trail in Preston. The trail parallels Camp Creek, so some anglers travel by foot or bike. Anglers are of two minds: Some welcome the ease of access; others resent the increased traffic. In either case there will be more fishers and bikers who will raise hell if the stream and the corridor comes under attack by mindless development.

DUSCHEE CREEK
DeLorme 26

Duschee Creek joins the South Branch of the Root River at Lanesboro. Take MN 16 south out of Lanesboro to the first road that parallels the stream. Below the fish hatchery the water may run murky. We've caught fish at the hatchery outlet and down toward the highway, but the many pools at the several bridges upstream are preferable. This 8-mile stream contains both brown and brook trout. One of our friends suggests that we go up into the pastures, but not to park our car on the small airstrip! Up there somewhere Bridget Hust caught and released a 19³⁄₈-inch brown. And that's not just eyeballed for size, as so many of us are wont to do. Duschee is a small stream that has been improved over the years through the public easements.

It is open to catch-and-release with barbless hooks, January 1 through March 31, on the 5.5-mile posted section from the mouth upstream.

GRIBBEN CREEK
DeLorme 26

A few miles east of Duschee you'll find Gribben Creek, crossed several times by County Road 23 going south from MN 16 at Whalan. Some folks would call Gribben tiny. Its 4 miles of Good water have been improved by the DNR, but during normal water levels the riffles are too shallow for practical nymphing and there are only a handful of pools. A friend has labeled it an "intimate" stream. But Gribben has been one of the most productive streams for wild brook trout around. An older electro-survey indicated more than 8,000 trout per mile and 350 pounds per acre—astronomical numbers that we can't promise now. Small streams are most likely to incur year-to-year changes.

Jay Paulson recalled with awe that five mayfly hatches once appeared in succession over the course of a single day, and he matched all five. We agree that Gribben is an intimate stream. A visitor should work slowly into the state forest unit to find his pool. Gribben yields its secrets most readily when the banks are full and there's a touch of color in the water. Incidentally, Tom Dornack said that there is a white fly hatch on the Root downstream from Whalan during the first week of August.

DIAMOND CREEK
DeLorme 26

A couple of miles east is Diamond Creek, east of Whalan on MN 16. Take the gravel road off County Road 107 in Section 11 to the site of the old schoolhouse; start fishing. Hit this two-branched stream early in the year, because the weed growth is amazing as the summer wears on. Early mornings are more likely to bring the naturally reproducing brook trout out of hiding. This 7-mile creek has been improved through an extensive state forest unit.

Four Streams of Winona County

These four streams lie immediately south of Interstate 90 in lower Winona County and add to the main stem of the Root.

RUSH CREEK
DeLorme 26 & 27

Rush Creek in Winona and Fillmore Counties is part of a complex of five streams that together total 33 miles. Possibly 25 miles are under public easement, and many of these miles have been improved with an assortment of habitat structures. A meticulous angler might spend a week in the area upstream from the city of Rushford.

There is a piece of Rush Creek north of Interstate 90 and west of Wyattville on County Road 25, but the stream is slim up there. Jim has leaned over a fence along the wayside on I-90, looked south down the steep slope into the valley of the Rush, and thought about zigging and zagging down to the stream. But better sense prevailed when he thought about having to climb back up at the end of a long day. If you are young, fit, and adventurous, do not let us dissuade you. Rush Creek is highly recommended by Bill Haugen, an expert fly-fisher and guide from Rushford.

In the abnormally low waters of one dry year, dozens of trout were

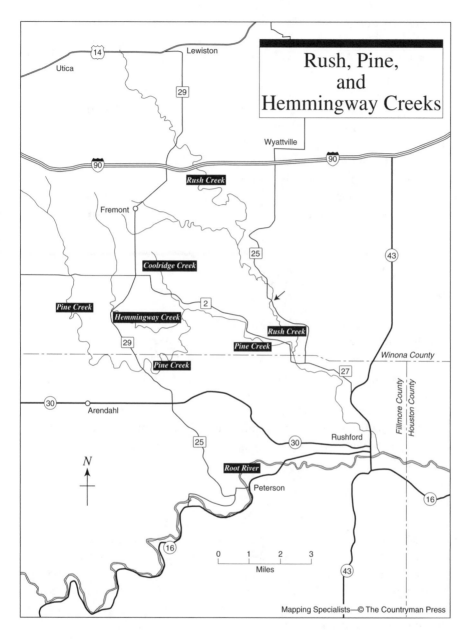

Rush, Pine,
and
Hemmingway Creeks

Mapping Specialists—© The Countryman Press

stressed and pooled above the bridges on County Road 25, but we didn't harass them. Sometimes it is better to observe and preserve. Between the bridges on a giant pool, a family with picnic baskets and coolers were enjoying a day out. The kids were drowning worms and keeping a few trout, but that's okay. Those kids will become the leaders of our next generation of volunteer conservators.

My partner and I did take a few feisty trout upstream, after asking permission of a friendly farmer to walk down his lane through the pasture to the spring creek. Through masses of watercress we took and released a dozen brook trout.

Bill records a phenomenal rise of light Cahills one early June afternoon: "Every 6 feet a Cahill came down, but many would complete the run successfully." It was a puzzle when they weren't all picked off by the numerous trout.

There has been extensive improvement behind a farm on the east side of the stream, and Bill has "billy-goated" down into the valley from the west, where at night you can hear the coyotes howl. On both east and west you will have to ask permission; and wherever you attack the hills, Bill says you must be young and fit to reach the stream.

PINE AND HEMMINGWAY CREEKS
DeLorme 26

Pine Creek, a tributary of Rush Creek from the west, is reached from County Roads 2 and 25. Town roads also cross the stream. It runs through hills, hardwood forests, and turkey country, and provides good brown trout fishing. Hemmingway, which is crossed by County Road 29, is a tributary of the Pine and one of the southeast's premier brook trout fisheries. To gain access to the interior reaches of Hemmingway, you may have to ask permission.

Both streams show terrific caddis hatches that render great numbers of trout. Pray for heavy overcast or slight drizzle. You'll appreciate it.

MONEY CREEK
DeLorme 27

Money Creek is a little junky, without much water movement, but it contains bigger trout. Bill kicked out an 18-inch brown from under a stump, and later broke off a 19-incher. In one pool a Pass Lake streamer was followed by three browns in the 14- to 15-inch range. Amazing! The two branches of Money Creek can be reached from County Road 19 in Winona County, a few miles south of Wilson on Interstate 90.

Complete facilities for the four streams of Winona County at Rushford in upper Fillmore County.

The South Fork of the Root River Complex

Six named streams are included in this complex. Feel free to explore several of them on your own. We profile two.

Schech's Mill on Beaver Creek

THE SOUTH FORK OF THE ROOT
DeLorme 26 & 27

Go south out of Rushford or north out of Mabel in Fillmore County on MN 43 to County Road 12, which is just north of Tawney and south of Choice. Take County Road 12 west to cross a new concrete bridge; follow County Road 12 west about 1.5 miles to a gravel road on the left near a rise in the road. Take the gravel road south to the South Fork of the Root; fish upstream. You can spend all day in this beautiful area. Pack your lunch and walk in. You know that you're dealing with deeper water and therefore bigger trout. It's our number one stream to return to next spring. Bill advises, "Lunkers have been taken out of this stretch, so I'm going to lose myself in this river." You can also find the stream by taking a west-running road out of Tawney or upstream from County Road 18.

Facilities at Lanesboro and Rushford.

WISEL CREEK
DeLorme 26

Wisel Creek, a tributary of the South Fork of the Root, is one of the quality streams of the southeast. Enchanting! There are both browns and brookies north and south of County Road 18 east of Henrytown and about a mile west of MN 43. South of County Road 18, which is upstream, you'll pass through a variety of landscapes—hardwood forest, pastureland, and open fields. There are several good-looking runs and dark pools. In the pools you must be patient. Drift your Pheasant Tail or Hare's Ear through them and you will catch trout, along with an occasional sucker. If you persevere, you'll hook up with a lunker brown, a reel screamer—that fish for a photo.

Facilities at Lanesboro, Harmony, Spring Grove, and Caledonia.

The Beaver Creek Complex

The Beaver Creek complex, 5 miles west of Caledonia in Houston County, includes East, West, and Main Beaver.

EAST BEAVER
DeLorme 27

East Beaver, a gem of a spring creek, lies wholly within Beaver Creek Valley State Park on County Road 1. Foot trails follow the stream from the parking lot near the east entrance for 2.5 miles of Good water down to the junction with West Beaver. There is a second DNR parking lot within a couple of minutes' walk from the junction, which is close to the bridge on County Road 10. From the junction at the footbridge the main stream widens to 40 feet and deepens to the dam at historic Schech's Mill. Along this slow, clear, deep stretch, wading is difficult; trout are visible but not usually responsive.

Going upstream from the footbridge by manicured trail along East Beaver, the fishing is primarily to pockets and pools. Several narrow, chest-deep runs are the result of older streamworks. Although the creek is narrow, the trout are of good size. They stack up along the bank, angling toward center stream, alert for drifting morsels.

East Beaver continues to receive the tender attention of fisheries biologists and park employees. Even if the fishing should be slow on the day of your visit, the surroundings are breathtaking—if you appreciate a crystal stream flowing softly through a rugged back of beyond. East Beaver through the park now offers catch-and-release with barbless hooks from January 1 through March 31.

WEST BEAVER
DeLorme 27

West Beaver may be a tough one. The last time we were there it was choked with fallen snags and pinched between thickets. An easement through a

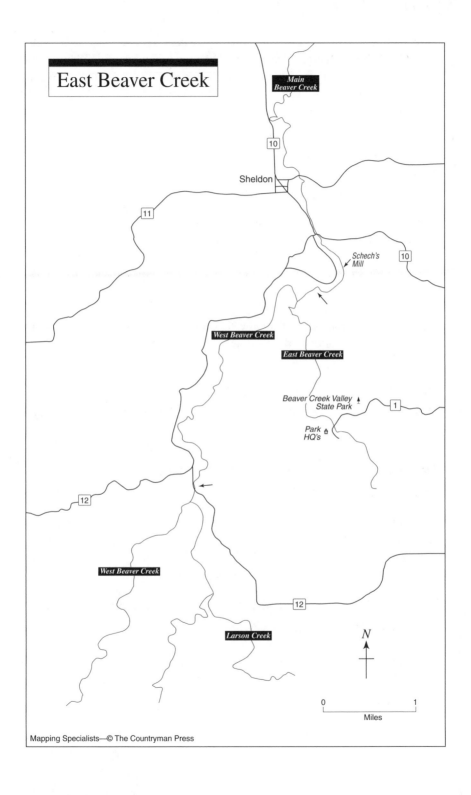

East Beaver Creek

Main Beaver Creek

10

Sheldon

11

Schech's Mill

10

West Beaver Creek

East Beaver Creek

Beaver Creek Valley State Park

1

Park HQ's

12

West Beaver Creek

12

Larson Creek

N

0   1

Miles

farm field and a bridge upstream provide access. West Beaver is not rated more than Fair, although it may have improved as a result of DNR habitat work on 2 miles. Bill's assessment is that it is really pretty good, especially far upstream, where he's run into a ton of brookies around the County Road 12 bridge.

THE MAIN BEAVER
DeLorme 27

Certain anglers of our acquaintance, among them Jay Paulson, whom we followed one fine day on the South Branch of the Root, sing the praises of the main stem below Schech's Mill at the County Road 10 bridge. They claim that the trout are large, even if not so plentiful. We've enjoyed the pasture and meadow fly-fishing within sight of that romantic old mill on several occasions, when we could attest to the fact that the trout were not plentiful. You should fly-fish upstream from the bridge and imagine that you're wading a pristine stream in the middle of the 19th century—or before. As we have said, there's more to fly-fishing than catching fish.

Facilities at Caledonia on MN 76.

Three Streams of the Southeast Corner
Some folks might characterize these three as minor streams, but they have the virtue of lying closest to travelers from outside the state.

THE NORTH FORK OF CROOKED CREEK
DeLorme 27

The North Fork of Crooked Creek in southeastern Houston County lies west of Freeburg on MN 249 and offers fine trout fishing. This creek can be susceptible to a swift spring runoff from melting snow or early thunderstorms. The fish may disappear for a while, probably downstream to deeper holes in the main creek, but they soon return.

There is extensive pastureland fishing, and you should see some scary-sized submarines cruising. Be careful in your approach and delicate with your cast. For big trout, nighttime is by far the best time.

Below Freeburg the main creek is all sand; not recommended.

Facilities at Caledonia on MN 249.

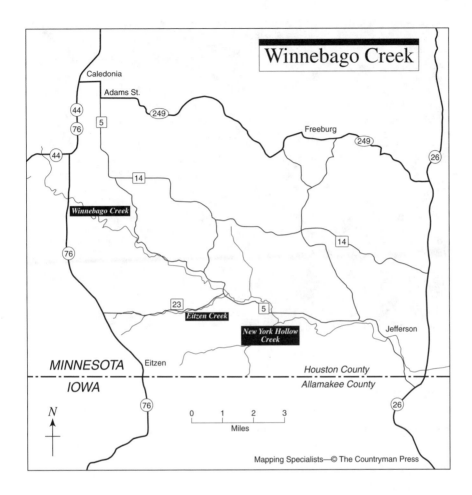

WINNEBAGO CREEK

DeLorme 27

Winnebago, in the extreme southeast corner of the state in Houston County, is paralleled by County Road 5. It includes a bit more than 8 miles of Fair water in the upper reaches. Access is limited, and the Winnebago doesn't get as much play as several more popular streams, but on at least one opening week it produced the best fly-fishing for brown and brook trout of any stream in the state. One disconsolate angler, Mark Beilke of the Twin Cities, had a 22-inch brown (eyeballed) break off on a Black Ant. I've seen dozens of trout stacked up in the pool between the buttresses of the abandoned bridge along County Road 5. I couldn't raise a trout, but that was before I had learned more about midge fishing with a Brassie or Griffith's Gnat (or a Black Ant). Below the bridge, in the riffles through a beef cattle pasture,

Chris Shogren on Winnebego Creek

I improved my average using the old reliable Gold-Ribbed Hare's Ear #16.

Facilities for visitors at Caledonia, and at La Crescent, Minnesota, and La Crosse, Wisconsin, on US 61 and Interstate 90.

BEE CREEK

DeLorme 27

Bee Creek on County Road 27 in lower Houston County can be fun! (The DNR trout map labels it Bee; the DeLorme labels it Waterloo Creek.) Go upstream from the quaint village of Bee or southeast from Spring Grove on MN 44. This is a nifty little stream that's not fished too much, but every year local fishers take some exceptional browns out of this minor treasure.

South of Bee village is the state of Iowa, where the creek is known as the Waterloo. Iowa also produces some excellent trout fishing, put-and-grow or put-and-take, in a small section of the northeast, but that requires an Iowa license and is a story for some other book.

Facilities at Spring Grove and Caledonia.

Southeastern Minnesota streams are user friendly and not dangerous, but watch for bulls and barbed wire. The streams are suitable for all ages, and you won't get lost. You are never too far from a road, field, farm, or other mark of civilization. There is a softness in the air, and the vistas are idyllic.

We never venture into that coulee country without fishing at least one new stream. We know where we can always catch trout, and will fish those familiar spots, but we always seek a new stream to explore. Put a sandwich, apple, and water flask in your vest and go pioneering. You'll never be disappointed. Explore! You may find your Shangri-la.

It is twilight on one of our favorite rivers of the southeast. Shadows stretch and fireflies wink on. Dark water from the chute slows on the pool and spreads, forming a conundrum of shining currents. I kneel, prayerfully, on the shingle beach and begin to cast a white-winged, cocky Cahill. A wild turkey gobbles in the fastness of the woods. Bats dance in that peculiar stuttering two-step. The last other angler has gone to home and hearth. Then the silvered surface blisters beneath the fly. The hook is lightly set, and there's a brown, palely gleaming green and gold in the last light. Will there ever again be such a night as this?

N.B. In April 1999 a 14-pound, 6-ounce brown was abstracted from a Fillmore County stream by Gary Medgaarden. It was not a hatchery brood trout, according to Jim Wagner, regional fisheries supervisor.

9 | The North Shore: Arrowhead Country

A gyre of gulls over the Knife River sounds like a basket of kittens mewling. An insubstantial mist drifts in from Lake Superior. This is the North Shore of Lake Superior, known also as the Arrowhead Country. With a bit of imagination you could swear that you are were on the Atlantic coast somewhere north of Boston. Nearly 200 miles of Minnesota shoreline fringe this gigantic lake, in area the largest body of fresh water in the world. Twenty-eight major streams and many smaller ones pitch down along this rugged shore from the Canadian Shield between Duluth, and Grand Portage, near the border with Canada. Up and over the crest of the escarpment, sometimes called the Laurentian Divide or the height-of-land, hundreds of remote interior streams await the exploring fly-fisher. The three Arrowhead counties, St. Louis, Lake, and Cook, contain 268 designated trout streams, most flowing toward the big lake from the height-of-land; others flow north into the Boundary Waters.

As a bonus, or more than that, brook trout, rainbows, splake, or brown trout are stocked in more than 100 lakes, which remain open through October 30. The splake is a cross between a female lake trout and a male brook trout. *A Guide to Lakes Managed for Stream Trout* is available from the Minnesota Department of Natural Resources.

Much of the fly-fishing action along the shore is for trout and salmon during their spawning runs from the lake to the first barrier falls or impassable rapids.

For those interested in fly-fishing for huge trout and salmon, the season is continuous for most species in Lake Superior and its tributaries downstream of the posted boundaries. The regulations for the several species of Salmonidae are complex and may change from year to year. A careful reading of the current year's *Minnesota Fishing Regulations* is necessary.

This area is so vast, so wild, and so productive of quality fly-fishing over a dozen varieties of trout and salmon that it's difficult to know where to begin—or where to end.

So let us begin with a look at a chart, the "Lake Superior Fishing Calendar," from the Minnesota DNR's *North Shore Fishing Guide*. It lists lake trout, brook trout, brown trout in streams, steelhead, steelhead in streams, Kamloops rainbows, Kamloops in streams, chinook salmon, chinook in streams, Atlantic salmon in streams, coho salmon, and pink salmon in streams. The "coasters" may even be making a recovery. That would be remarkable! The coasters were (are?) a subspecies or population of huge brook trout that fatten in Lake Superior and spawn in the rivers. Jim remembers boating a 5-pounder in the upper reaches of Lake Nipigon in Canada in the 1950s. Strictly speaking, that may have been not a coaster but one of a unique population of brook trout indigenous to Nipigon, but it foreshadows superb fly-fishing if the coasters return. Even smelt wiggle onto the beaches at the mouths of rivers in their spawning ecstasy, but they won't come to a fly. They're more often taken in dip nets, or even in golf bags!

Some of these species of trout and salmon are taken in deep water offshore, others in the first few hundred yards or first few miles of river below the barriers. But brook trout and brown trout in streams (and rainbows, too, in some sections) are the legitimate targets of this book.

Fishing for resident brown and rainbows in the upper reaches of the streams is rated Good by the DNR, although the brook trout usually run small. Thirteen- and 14-inch brookies are possible, even larger ones on occasion. There are few professional guides who'll take you into the backcountry specifically for stream trout, but at least one of them said that he'll take you to 14-inch brook trout "if I can blindfold you."

North Shore streams depend on runoff rather than on springs and seepage, so their flows are unstable, surging after a rain or snowmelt and dwindling to a trickle during a prolonged drought. On these spate streams a case can be made that beaver dams have some utility, holding water for a slower, later discharge. In slow, broad, middle sections of streams, a canoe or float tube may be useful. Shawn Perich, an author and fly-fisherman who lives on the Shore, tells us to look for wide, slow-moving water over a silty bottom. He adds that many of the best streams arise in lakes. See his *Fly-Fishing the North Country* (Duluth: Pfeifer-Hamilton 1995).

The streams of the North Shore and those over the height-of-land are deficient in the amount and variety of food for trout. The bedrock over which these streams flow has few of the water-soluble minerals necessary to maintain the alkalinity required for the development of a wide variety of aquatic insects. However, there are plenty of caddisflies, tricos in weedy sections, and emergences of *Hexagenia* in slower, silty reaches. Also, the streams remain cool throughout the year, and there are many deep and shaded runs where trout can hide.

In streams that provide only marginal habitat, the DNR stocks brown trout, which tolerate warmer water than do brookies.

As you travel northeast from Duluth along US 61, once described as "one of the 10 most beautiful drives in the country," you'd be hard pressed to deny it. The forested slopes in summer show every variation on the palette of green. In late September and early October the view is a romance of impressionist color. In all seasons dozens of waterfalls plunge precipitously, and rapids braid around boulders. County and state parks and waysides invite the photographer to record the view of lake and cliff and cascading water. The itinerant fly-angler may pause and study his maps.

If Duluth is your headquarters for initial forays into the interior, you might want to try your luck and skill on the broad waters of the St. Louis River in Jay Cooke State Park, in Carlton County, southwest of Duluth along MN 210.

Prior to World War II a few experts took sizable brown trout in the park and brook trout from a number of feeder creeks, including Big and Little Otter Creeks and Silver Creek, which meets the St. Louis in the park.

Then the St. Louis River fell on hard times from various nefarious forms of pollution and from the uncontrolled flow below a power dam. In 1979 a cleanup of the river began, but the problem of what constitutes sufficient water flow below a dam to support a trout fishery is still being argued.

The truth is that not many fly-fishers catch and release brown trout in the park today, so few that the St. Louis is not a designated trout stream. However, on one day in late May, Jay Paulson, whose exploits we have recorded elsewhere, and his wife were picnicking in the park behind the park office. Noticing an interesting eddy flecked with foam, Jay tied on a #12 Humpy and promptly landed two 19-inch browns. This is not a profile of a famous stream, merely an admonition to keep your rod handy and be prepared to experiment. Bill and Jim's fly-fishing lives are replete with such serendipitous adventures.

Going northeast along US 61 from Duluth, highway milepost markers can be used as guides for locating river mouths, state parks, and other points of interest. Every mile is marked with a green-and-white milepost marker. Gooseberry Falls State Park is at milepost 39; Split Rock Lighthouse at 46; Tettegouche State Park at 58.5; Crosby Manitou at 59; Temperance River State Park at 80.5; and Cascade River State Park at 100 miles.

As you head up from Duluth, the rivers change in character. Close to the city the rivers are short and lack substantial headwaters systems. Therefore, in spring they flood, then drain rapidly. In summer the flow is slow and shallow. Farther up the North Shore the streams are more complex, extending deeper into the interior. The watersheds are extensive and include lakes and marshes. Beavers have added thousands of small impoundments. For a comprehensive examination of the North Shore in all its glory, read Dr. Tom Waters, *The Superior North Shore* (University of Minnesota, 1987).

THE KNIFE RIVER
DeLorme 66 & 67

Without attempting to draw with too sharp a point, we'd say that the Knife River, which empties into the lake at the junction of St. Louis and Lake Counties, is the first major complex with excellent fishing for brook, brown, and rainbow trout in its upper reaches. The Knife is also the Shore's most popular steelhead stream. It is one of the few where the barriers are not imposing enough to prevent migratory rainbows from working their way up into the headwaters. The Knife is said to contain about 70 percent of the Shore's steelhead spawning water. Because of the quality of the steelhead habitat, special regulations apply. The river and its tributaries, from County Road 9 upstream, are open only from May 15 (the date may vary), rather than on the traditional Saturday closest to April 15. The closing date is September 30, as usual. A permanent fish sanctuary applies to the area from the US 61 bridge downstream to the cable below the fish trap.

The Knife is crossed by County Roads 9 and 11 west of Two Harbors, and by several county roads upstream. Upstream from County Road 11 is as good a place to start as any.

Lodging and dining facilities at Two Harbors, milepost 26.

THE GOOSEBERRY COMPLEX
DeLorme 67

The next major complex is the Gooseberry River at Gooseberry State Park, milepost 39, where the river rushes over three spectacular falls. This river is deceiving. In late summer the volume of water reaching the lake may seem too meager to support good fishing in the upper reaches. But go up and inland to find excellent fly-fishing for brook trout. According to Dr. Thomas F. Waters in his comprehensive work *The Streams and Rivers of Minnesota*, and in his lovingly written *The Superior North Shore*, water is lost downstream through seepage into fractured rock.

The barrier to anadromous penetration into the interior is 7.3 miles up from the lake; the main stem extends for another 25 miles and contains brooks, browns, and rainbows.

Bill Shogren with a brown from the East Branch of the Baptism River. The Pass Lake Streamer is a favorite pattern.

Your opportunities for stream trout lie upstream of County Road 3 and east of County Road 2, straight north out of Two Harbors.

Travelers' accommodations at Two Harbors and at Silver Bay.

THE BAPTISM RIVER COMPLEX

DeLorme 77

Past Split Rock Lighthouse at milepost 46—which is worth a stop to see the historic lighthouse and a brilliant panorama over the lake—and the town of Silver Bay at milepost 54, you'll reach the mouth of the Baptism in Tettegouche State Park at milepost 58.5. The first boundary is 5 miles upstream, and the main stem extends for only 3.4 miles above the barrier. Beyond that the Baptism splits into the East and West Branches, some 14 miles on each leg, where you'll find brook trout, browns, and some rainbows.

MN 1 parallels the West Branch upstream toward Finland for 4 or 5

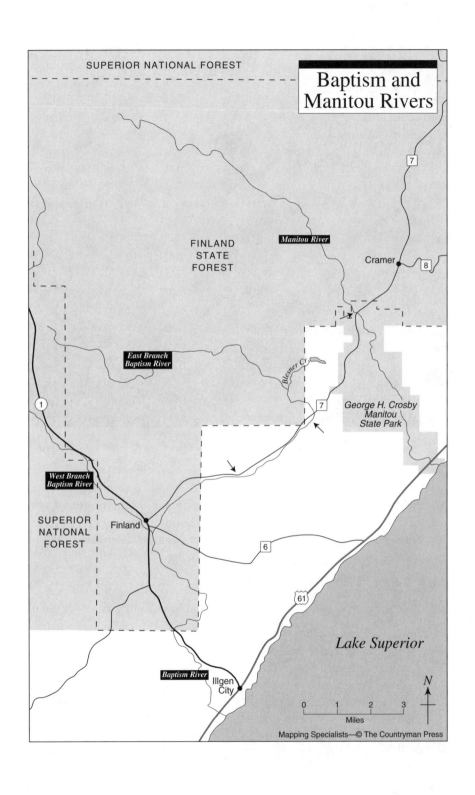

Baptism and
Manitou Rivers

SUPERIOR NATIONAL FOREST

FINLAND
STATE
FOREST

Manitou River

Cramer

8

7

*East Branch
Baptism River*

1

Blesner Cr.

7

*George H. Crosby
Manitou
State Park*

*West Branch
Baptism River*

SUPERIOR
NATIONAL
FOREST

Finland

6

61

Lake Superior

Baptism River

Illgen
City

N

0   1   2   3
Miles

Mapping Specialists—© The Countryman Press

miles, then crosses it upstream. At Finland the East Branch of the Baptism, which contains more naturally reproducing browns than the West Branch, parallels County Road 7, also known as Cramer Road. This is where we suggest that you test the river, as far upstream as Blesner Creek in Crosby Manitou State Park. There are wide, slow places on the East Branch where a canoe or float tube may be advantageous. This long stretch is easy to fly-fish and will produce better-than-average brown trout in the slow pools. Woolly Worms and Muddlers are suggested if trout aren't feeding on insects at the surface.

Downstream from Finland the Baptism is rocky and steep, dropping some 700 feet in 10 miles to the lake.

Facilities at Silver Bay and all along US 61.

THE BEAVER RIVER

DeLorme 77

If you enjoy long walks into the interior wilderness and can follow a trail without getting lost, this Beaver River is for you. Follow the directions closely and carry overnight survival gear—compass, matches, bug dope, a tested flashlight or two, food and water, and a stout knife, just in case. Always let someone know where you are going, in the event of a fall and a breakage of bone. Humphrey always recommends a wading staff to prevent falls in the wrong places. Shogren, being younger, relies on strength and common sense.

Take Heffelfinger Road, Forest Road 397, out of Finland (on MN 1) for 14.8 miles west to Forest Road 399. Go left for 4 miles to the orange steel gate. Walk in on the trail; keep to the main trail. In half an hour you'll find a bridge that crosses Little Big 39 Creek. Another 20 minutes should take you to the Beaver. There's a fine pool below the bridge and others above the bridge, where there has been some habitat improvement. Appreciate the fly-fishing over brooks, browns, and maybe rainbows, but give yourself time to walk out before darkness settles in.

Which reminds us of Bill's tale of woe. When obtaining directions from DNR personnel, Bill was told, "It's about 15 minutes in to a good section of stream." What they forgot to mention was that they were on an ATV, which moves faster than walking pace. It took Bill almost an hour to cover the same ground! Interrogate your sources and record their directions. DNR and national forest personnel are eager to help, and they always want to know how you fared on their recommended section. Report back, as we do. A postcard from your home will suffice.

You should also be able to find Forest Road 397 by going east from Jordan, which is on County Road 204, just off County Road 2.

Facilities at Silver Bay and at Tofte.

THE MANITOU RIVER COMPLEX
DeLorme 67 & 77

The Manitou River reaches the lake at milepost 59, just south of the border between Lake and Cook Counties. The first fish barrier is practically at the mouth of the river. The George H. Crosby Manitou State Park headquarters is located east of County Road 7 about 5 miles upstream from Lake Superior.

For those of you who prefer to mix camping with your fly-fishing, headquarter in Crosby Manitou and fish along the West Manitou River Trail as it drops 600 feet through the park. Both rainbow and brook trout inhabit the river through those 4 or 5 miles of flashing water. Campsites are located at a dozen locations close to the river.

Upstream you should fish the river at the County Road 7 bridge, primarily for brook trout. We have cast at Pass Lake at dusk to enthusiastic, dark, and beautiful brookies.

A third location is farther up in the Finland State Forest. Fish the North Branch of the Manitou downstream from the trail on Forest Road 361, via Forest Road 172 from Isabella (on MN 1) east to Forest Roads 362 and 361.

Facilities at Two Harbors and at Schroeder.

ARROWHEAD CREEK
DeLorme 77

Arrowhead Creek, northeast of Isabella on MN 1 north of Finland in the Superior National Forest, is a premier brook trout stream. Go east from Isabella on Forest Road 172 for 0.75 mile, then north on Forest Road 369 for 5 miles to a crossroads where Forest Road 173 comes in from the west. Take the east branch. Proceed less than a mile to the river, where the habitat has been improved. It's a little better downstream than up, through narrow and deep water around boulders, past plunge pools and lunker structures in a wild setting.

Dining and lodging at Silver Bay on US 61, and camping in the Finland State Forest and at campgrounds in the Superior National Forest.

THE TEMPERANCE RIVER COMPLEX
DeLorme 67 & 78

From here on up the coast every stream lies wholly within the boundaries of the Superior National Forest, within the Grand Portage State Forest, or within the Grand Portage Indian Reservation at the Canadian border. Conse-

Sandy Rolstad fishes the fast water on the Temperance River.

quently, there are few highways, but many unimproved roads and trails. A Superior National Forest map (see "Maps" in chapter 1) will be useful in this backcountry, as will the recommended survival gear and stout hiking boots. We pack our waders and survival gear in a knapsack and hike in to the streams.

There are many campgrounds in the Superior National Forest and superb facilities all along the coast highway, but towns and villages with overnight accommodations are sparse in the interior.

We might as well get the mossy old joke out of the way. The Temperance was, probably apocryphally, so named because it had "no bar at the mouth." Most North Shore rivers, but not all, form a sandbar at the mouth during the winter. In spring the snowmelt washes the bars away, and the anadromous species begin their migratory runs.

The Temperance fish barrier is at the lake. The main stem extends for 21 miles into the interior. The Temperance River joins the lake at milepost 80.5.

The Sawbill Trail, County Road 2 at Tofte on US 61, parallels the river upstream. As with the other river complexes, your targets are the sites where the river is wide and rocky, in this case around Temperance River Campground, and upstream via County Road 2 and several forest roads and trails. Any of the tributaries that cross County Road 2 is worth a cast for brook trout.

At one time the Temperance, a favorite with Jim Humphrey, was a firstclass brook trout stream. In recent years the river has warmed, for reasons that are in dispute. It may be that the many headwaters lakes and ponds have warmed due to logging and the consequent removal of shade; logging debris may also have drifted into the river. In any case, the brook trout have retreated to the feeders. To compensate, the DNR has planted browns in the main river.

The Temperance is one of the North Shore's longest rivers, having its headwaters in the Boundary Waters Canoe Area. In the middle sections it is a wide and rocky stream, the kind we love to fly-fish. And we admit to a prejudice: If browns become the dominant species of trout and char, we'll not be unduly distressed.

This may be a proper place to insert a word of warning. The last few miles of many of these North Shore rivers pitch down dangerously. The last 4 miles of the Temperance, for example, speed through an exceedingly narrow canyon. Anglers pursuing their quarry downstream into the canyons should be aware of the possibility of a sudden rise in the water level; it may be impossible to climb the rock face.

Travelers' accommodations at Tofte and all along the shore.

THE CASCADE RIVER COMPLEX
DeLorme 78

The Cascade, which drains an area of 120 square miles, begins in a complex of warm-water lakes and ponds in the Boundary Waters Canoe Area. The middle section is productive of brown trout; the tributaries contain brookies. County Road 45 crosses it about 4 miles above Cascade River State Park at milepost 100. We've fished it upstream at the Forest Road 157 crossing and farther up near the junction of County Road 57 and Forest Road 158.

The sections we waded are perfect for fly-fishing. The river is wide, with room to shoot the long casts so beloved of fly-fishers. The pools are big and the runs are deep and long, even during the low water of September. We filled out our self-imposed quotas of dark and chunky brook trout on streamers, Hare's Ears, Hornbergs, and Adamses.

The canyon downstream, above and through the park, provides spec-

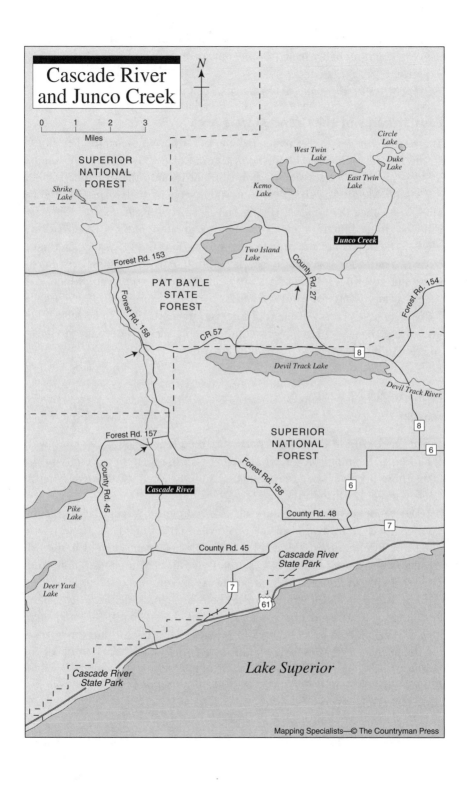

Cascade River
and Junco Creek

N

0   1   2   3
Miles

SUPERIOR
NATIONAL
FOREST

Shrike
Lake

Circle
Lake

West Twin
Lake

Duke
Lake

Kemo
Lake

East Twin
Lake

Junco Creek

Forest Rd. 153

Two Island
Lake

County Rd. 27

PAT BAYLE
STATE
FOREST

Forest Rd. 158

Forest Rd. 154

CR 57

8

Devil Track Lake

Devil Track River

Forest Rd. 157

8

SUPERIOR
NATIONAL
FOREST

6

County Rd. 45

Forest Rd. 158

Cascade River

6

Pike
Lake

County Rd. 48

7

County Rd. 45

Cascade River
State Park

Deer Yard
Lake

7

61

Cascade River
State Park

Lake Superior

Mapping Specialists—© The Countryman Press

tacular scenery but difficult access; if you do find a trail down into the canyon, you'll probably have to come out the way you went in. It's a unique experience for hardy souls.

Facilities at Tofte and Schroeder and camping in the park.

Four Streams of the Grand Marais Area

There are many wonderful rivers and creeks farther up the shore. The city of Grand Marais, milepost 110, at the beginning of the Gunflint Trail, County Road 12, is an excellent staging point for sorties into the interior.

Grand Marais is currently the northern end of the North Shore State Trail, also called the Superior Hiking Trail, a story in itself. *Backpacker* magazine has named the trail one of the nation's greatest, and one of the world's top 25. The trail is not yet complete from Duluth to Grand Portage, but more than 150 miles are serviced by seven parking areas, 14 shelters and campsites, and 40 bridges. It crosses more than 60 creeks and rivers, which give access to many interior trout streams.

Ninety-five percent of the trail traverses public lands, and because it lies away from the lake inland, it crosses the middle sections of many streams—where you'll find the best fly-fishing for trout.

JUNCO CREEK
DeLorme 79

Junco Creek rises in Circle Lake north of Grand Marais and flows southwest for 18 miles to empty into Devil Track Lake on the western extremity of the lake. There are two bridge crossings, at County Road 27 upstream and at County Road 57 close to the lake.

Our recommended adventure on this wonderful stream begins at the County Road 27 bridge. Fish up- or downstream. Bill says, "There is one good spot after another. You can fly-fish with ease over much of it, but roll casting is necessary in other places. You'll use all of your skills, going from one great spot to another. This stream beckons you onward."

The Junco has been improved with bank structures, deflector logs, half-logs, and even a Hewitt ramp. A path follows the left bank—Ah! and there goes a yearling bear across the path! Midges are in the air, but any attractor fly, such as the Mickey Finn, will bring these dark brook trout out of hiding.

A complete range of facilities for travelers, history enthusiasts, and fly-fishers at Grand Marais.

THE DEVIL TRACK RIVER
DeLorme 79

The Devil Track is close to Grand Marais. Take US 61 north to County Road 58; then go eight blocks to a parking area on the Superior Hiking Trail. Approximately two blocks on the trail takes you to the canyon section of the Devil Track. The climb down to the river is not easy; coming up is worse, but you'll be rewarded with complex pools and stocked rainbow trout. It's gorgeous here—the pools are 20 to 40 feet long and 4 feet deep. You might even encounter a moose at the MOOSE CROSSING sign, and that may be the most awe-inspiring memory of your trip.

Comprehensive accommodations at Grand Marais.

KADUNCE CREEK
DeLorme 79

Go north on US 61 to County Road 14; follow it north and east to the stream. Fish downstream or up at several Forest Road 140 crossings. The fish

The Canyon section of the Devil Track River offers long, deep, clear pools.

barrier on Kadunce is close to the lake; the river length is a bit more than 7 miles. This is a scenic brook trout stream with beaver dams and sparkling riffles upstream and a state wayside at the mouth. We like this one a lot, as does Sandy Rolstad, of the Twin Cities Chapter of TU. We three like it for its prolific brook trout and its manageable size, more probably because it is not so famous as the river complexes and attracts fewer fly-fishers. There is a fish sanctuary for about a quarter mile close to the mouth, where fishing is permitted from June 1 through August 31 only. Kimball Creek, a bit to the south, has produced "some nice brook trout."

Facilities and amenities at Grand Marais.

IRISH CREEK
DeLorme 79

Irish Creek is as far as we go up the North Shore on this trip, but it is one stream that you may want to reach for. Take US 61 along the coast toward Hovland. Go north on County Road 16 for 8.5 miles to Irish Creek Timber Road, then left for 1 mile to the bridge. We had a ball there, casting an Adams and a Royal Coachman streamer to 6- to 8-inch brook trout. There is a series of pools below the bridge where the brook trout collect at the surface. In the last several years beavers have taken over much of the stream and it is degraded. Check locally before exploring this creek. In 1996 The Nature Conservancy seized the opportunity to purchase 3,280 acres from Champion paper company in the Swamp River watershed, which includes Irish Creek. The area includes islands of old-growth forest that date to the mid-1700s. Subsequently, the Minnesota DNR bought the land from the Conservancy.

Facilities at Grand Marais and Hovland.

THE BLACKHOOF RIVER
DeLorme 57

Years ago, before we became serious, a fanatical friend rhapsodized over the virtues of the Blackhoof River in Carlton County, south of Cloquet. Because Maloney had the Irish gift of gab, the river was probably never as good as he willed it to be.

Years later Bill and Jim visited the Blackhoof separately, with expectations but more modest results. The Blackhoof offers a variety of trout and char—native brook trout and resident browns. Lake Superior produces spring and fall runs of rainbows (steelhead) and brown trout.

The river begins near Atkinson; downstream for 5 or 6 miles it is a warm-water fishery. Between County Roads 105 and 103 the river picks up springwater. These 3 or 4 miles are the haunts of brook trout. Downstream from County Road 103 you'll find browns and small steelhead that have not returned to sea.

The river comes by its name honestly. It is dark colored upstream of County Road 103, often twisting through steep valleys. It is still subject to erosion—which may be dangerous to unwary fishermen caught in a flash flood. An older DNR report noted "highly eroded clay soil, steep banks, and poor logging and farming practices," resulting in erosion and siltation. Bill notes that sinkholes are serious: Look for a stick in the middle of pockets to indicate caution.

In January 1987 the DNR purchased 1,617 acres between Minnesota 23 and County Road 103 for the Blackhoof Wildlife Management Area. An angler may hike in on several trails from MN 23, or fish up or down from the County Road 103 bridge. At County Road 103 there seems to be a natural division. Up from the bridge the river is narrow and slow; Jim remembers some days with feisty brook trout there. Down from the bridge the river is shallow and bouldery, more like a spate river designed for anadromous migrations. In this stretch Jim caught rainbow trout during the summer. Alas, there is now a house in sight of the bridge, and on a recent trip a power mower droned. If this does not please you, Carlton County embraces 37 other streams.

After our bouncing around all over the North Shore Arrowhead Country, our admonition to you is to confine your exploration to one watershed. Invest a week and get to know the main stem and its many feeders. Don't overlook the backcountry lakes that are managed for stream trout. Bring your float tube and canoe. If you must fly-fish for anadromous species below the barriers, bring your heavy-duty rods and reels and yarn flies.

You might even cast for a triple play: anadromous rainbows and chinooks at the mouth of a river, brook trout, browns, and rainbows in the middle sections, and stream trout in a hundred lakes. This may be one of the best areas for fly-fishers in the Lower 48—if you search for its secrets. It may be the wildest experience outside of Canada. Come and explore.

Maps of these wonders are available at many commercial establishments along the shore, in the coastal towns, at state parks, and in the Superior National Forest.

10 | Northern Minnesota: Paul Bunyan Country

This immense area was the domain of the legendary Paul Bunyan, the mightiest lumberjack of them all, and Babe the blue ox. Today representations of that pair can be seen in the environs of Brainerd in Crow Wing County, a gateway to the northern playgrounds of Minnesota. At the Paul Bunyan Center, junction of MN 210 and MN 371, the world's largest animated talking Paul tells stories from the lumbering days. Your children will love talking to Paul.

This is the land of 10,000 lakes, thousands of miles of rivers and creeks, hundreds of resorts, state and national forests, Native American reservations, the sprawling, empty Koochiching State Forest, and the wilderness of the Voyageurs National Park and the Boundary Waters Canoe Area. Many species of wild mammals inhabit the forests and graze in the glades. White-tailed deer are omnipresent; the ubiquitous beaver, which maintains a near-symbiotic relationship with humans, constitutes a pest on many trout streams. You may encounter a bear foraging for grubs or berries; if so, keep your distance. There are moose in the Boundary Waters and north of the Iron Range, and coyotes, bobcats, and lynx.

You may hear wolves ululate under a gibbous moon not far north of the city of Bemidji. Two thousand gray wolves range the northern forests; there is even a pack in the Mille Lacs National Wildlife Area, just 70 miles north of the Twin Cities. There has been no recorded incident of a wolf attacking a human, but you shouldn't let toddlers or young children wander far. Wolves are territorial; they particularly don't welcome dogs in their living room.

You probably will not see the secretive cougar, known variously as puma, panther, and mountain lion, but a few of them range down from Canada into the northern reaches. What appears to be a black panther has been seen north of the Twin Cities. What is it? Was it? Exotics do escape from private menageries, as we know from the frolicking hippo on the Mecan. We count our blessings that some small part of the original America has been saved for future generations.

Anglers come primarily to seek the tasty walleye, the elusive muskie, the deepwater lake trout, or the smallmouth bass in the primal waters of the canoe country. Other visitors come from around the world so they can brag

Bill Shogren on the Clearwater River

that they jumped across the Mississippi. Well, that's not quite true, but you can walk across the Mississippi on a series of stepping-stones at the outlet of Lake Itasca in Clearwater County north of Park Rapids off US 71.

The search for the source of the Mississippi is a fascinating tale of challenge, defeat, and ultimate success. As early as 1700 DuCharleville, a Frenchman out of New Orleans, turned back discouraged at St. Anthony's Falls in what is now Minneapolis. In 1805 Lieutenant Zebulon Pike, of Pike's Peak fame, reached Cass Lake. Close, but no cigar. In 1823 Count Beltrami, an Italian adventurer, declared a small lake north of Bemidji as the true source. Not quite. In 1832 Henry Rowe Schoolcraft, a geologist who hoped to help make peace between the Ojibway (Chippewa) and the Dakota (Sioux) tribes, arrived at Lake LaBiche, where he concocted the name Itasca by dropping the first and last syllables from the Latin *veritas caput,* meaning "true head." And you thought Itasca was a Native American name.

Fly-fishers who tire of boats, roaring outboards, and racing Jet Skis on the flat water of the lakes can don boots to wade more than 100 secluded trout streams in Paul Bunyan Country, far from the madding crowd. Crow Wing County alone has 13 trout streams, Cass County to the north encloses 17, and Hubbard to the northwest includes 15. Farther north, Beltrami County has seven streams, including the long Clearwater River, which harbors both brown and rainbow trout. Even Clearwater County, the site of Lake Itasca, has seven streams. St. Louis County, which is partly in the Arrowhead region of the state, contains 85 designated trout streams.

Although they are widely dispersed, there is a trout stream for every taste, from brook trout rivulet to wide-bodied water for better-than-average brown trout. We showcase four streams of differing aspects in this north central section. You can search out more trout streams on your voyage of discovery into the wilds of northern Minnesota.

STONEY BROOK

DeLorme 54

Stoney Brook rises in Cass County and flows for 19 miles to empty into Upper Gull Lake west of Nisswa. Although it is a long brook, only the last few miles through public land or leased easements have been extensively improved during the past decade. Much of the bull work on the stream has been performed, and partly paid for, by a handful of dedicated trout fishers from the Paul Bunyan Chapter of Trout Unlimited. Other Minnesota chapters have contributed funds for the annual projects.

To summarize the work projects: Hewitt ramps were repaired, banks stabilized, a log bridge constructed, runs deepened, bank covers and lunker structures installed, and riprap and brush bundles added. The list goes on, and the fishing for naturally reproducing brook and respectable browns is an example of the improvement possible through the cooperation of the Minnesota Department of Natural Resources and volunteers.

Stoney Brook is not a wide stream. Fly-fishers will need to move carefully, utilizing the utmost skill with short rods, light lines, and short, fine leaders under a dense canopy of trees. Although we usually recommend the longest leader you can handle, in brush you'll have to go short and fine if you want to keep your leader out of the trees. A poet might describe the experience as fly-fishing under the nave of a cathedral.

We suggest that you begin your exploration of the brook at the Fritz Loven County Park close to the shore of Upper Gull Lake. Take MN 371 north from Brainerd toward Nisswa past Round Lake on the east, then proceed west on County Road 77 to County Road 78. Cross Upper Gull and take the first road north to the park. There is additional DNR parking upstream where County Road 78, having turned north, parallels the stream. The park section is quite open; the upstream section, where much of the improvement work is visible, is the stretch that might remind you of a church.

We have participated in similar grunt work on the Kinnickinnic, the Willow, and the Rush Rivers of Wisconsin and Trout Brook in Minnesota, so it is always a special thrill for us to reap the rewards of the work of our fellow anglers on their cherished streams. Therefore, we always release our trout on Stoney Brook in deference to their labors; we hope that you will, too, out of the goodness of your heart. In September 2000 Mickey Johnson, working with a DNR crew, electro-fished eight fish of better than 25 inches (!) at one station.

Cass County has 16 additional trout streams, all brooks or creeks, except for the Shingobee River, which lies partly in Hubbard County. Inquire locally for information on their current potential.

All possible facilities at Brainerd, Nisswa, and dozens of lake resorts.

THE STRAIGHT RIVER
DeLorme 61

The Straight River, which for many years was considered the best brown trout stream in the state, with 4- to 6-pound browns being common, lies west of the city of Park Rapids, which is at the junction of US 71 and MN 34. The Straight flows from Straight Lake in zBecker County at Osage on MN 34 southeast into Hubbard County.

The Straight had fallen on hard times for more than a decade, but we believe it is coming back now due to the efforts of the DNR. We don't know if it will ever again attain that exalted title of the best trout stream, because

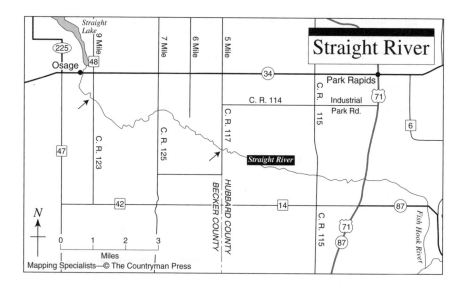

there are too many other streams that have been improved in the last few years, but it is a good one now.

Local anglers identify a location on the river by referring to distance from Park Rapids—that is "Two Mile bridge," "Five Mile," and so on. Visiting anglers should take a leaf from their books. County Road 117, the division between Becker and Hubbard Counties, is "Five Mile." County Road 123 at Osage is "Nine Mile."

Although this river flows from a lake, with all the potential that implies for warming water downstream, there are many springs to cool the water sufficiently for trout. Douglas Herman, an angler who has fished the river for years, notes that within half a mile or so of the lake outlet the Straight's volume has already doubled as a result of spring flow.

This river reminds us of the upper Kinnickinnic of Wisconsin. The banks are brushy and there's silt at the margins, but there is also a narrow wading path of sand and gravel down the middle. Anglers can enter the river at any of the bridges or culverts and from a number of paths that lead to the river between the bridges. The state owns blocks of land on the river, particularly upstream of Five and Six Mile entries, and has acquired easements above Nine Mile, and for most of the section between Three and Four Mile, downstream of Two Mile, and on the north side of the river between One Mile and US 71.

We can recommend the public lands above Five Mile where brown trout are known to reproduce (more than 1,000 trout per mile) and the half mile or more upstream of Six Mile, where Humphrey's fly-fishing pal Dick Frantes sold easements on 80 acres to the DNR. You can hike to the river from the dead end of Six Mile Road on the north. This is where Humphrey would fish if he were going out tomorrow. Bill Shogren has had excellent brown trout fishing upstream of Five Mile, very late evenings in June. Even though the Hex hatch did not appear on this latest June trip, due no doubt to a week of cold weather, his Muddler was good for a 16-inch brown. On his way out around 11 PM Bill exchanged notes with two young enthusiasts, Chad Hanson and Dan Grabow from the city of Detroit Lakes, who had released one 17-inch brown. They told Bill that the Hex hatch was just building.

On one of those sultry evenings Bill was standing belly-deep and casting upriver. Something caused him to turn and look downstream into the fading light. Two "things" were swimming upstream, a foot apart, flowing over any sweepers in the way. Not beavers, not otters. What? Bill drew his knees together. As would I; or you! The snakes separated and continued their swim upstream. Bill retreated, as would I. Or you. But don't let us discourage you: That's a once-in-a-lifetime experience. And in retrospect, it's a wonderful fireside story.

The large and juicy *Hexagenia limbata*, which has appeared on the river as early as June 10, probably accounts for the fact that the browns here can grow large. Look for the Hex during the latter weeks of June and the first two weeks of July. Try streamers fished deep in and around the logjams if there is no surface activity. Ed Atcas, a skilled fly-fisher from the Twin Cities, swims tarpon flies for outsized brown trout! We know big-fish anglers who throw black-and-silver Rapalas for huge brown trout, so why not tarpon flies?

An angler is more likely to find the Hex in the upper 3 miles of the river, which are slower and more silted; lower down there's more swift water and gravel. Huge browns are taken below Straight Lake, where there are easements above and below Nine Mile crossing.

Although, as noted above, there is good natural reproduction in only one section, browns have not been planted in recent years. The DNR's goal is to improve trout habitat to allow for natural reproduction, which makes sense to us.

In recent years the Straight River has been threatened by the possibility that a major potato farm will pump precious groundwater near the river, and thus deplete the cold-water seeps into the river. This is typical of the many threats to our trout resource. The battle may be temporarily won, but others lie ahead. As long as there is a dollar to be made by exploiting our natural resources, you may be assured that someone will want to cash in.

Becker County has 6 additional designated trout streams; Hubbard has a total of 15, including the Kabekona River, our next stop on this modest sample of northern Minnesota.

All facilities for travelers at Park Rapids and at many lake resorts.

THE KABEKONA RIVER

DeLorme 61 & 71

The Kabekona River rises in the Paul Bunyan State Forest in Hubbard County and flows southeast into Kabekona Lake near MN 64. US 71 and MN 200 intersect at the crossroads village of Kabekona, about two-thirds of the way up the river from the lake.

We recommend that you begin at the culvert on County Road 36, 0.5 mile north of MN 200 and 3 miles west of the town of Laporte. Fish upstream, taking the middle, and cast to every likely spot. Wear chest-high waders, move slowly while casting an attractor like the Royal Wulff, and you may have a fabulous day, as we did. Bill took the day's prize with a chunky, superbly painted 10-inch brookie taken on a Mickey Finn. "A phenomenal day!" said Bill.

As noted elsewhere, Bill can become ecstatic when wading up cold, deep, difficult, and demanding brook trout streams; Jim prefers brown trout taken from complex pools. Pulled in two directions, they cover the country and a spectrum of streams.

There is a second entry at the gravel road west of County Road 36. This section, which is 7 miles from the mouth of the river, according to a DNR report, "has mostly hard sand bottom, undercut banks, with brush and vegetation overhanging the stream." In a recent electro-shocking survey the brook trout ranged from 3.0 to 11.4 inches. Surveys on other sections recorded "quality-size" brookies, 8 to 10 inches, at all locations; "preferred size," 10 to 12 inches, at four of five locations; and "memorable size," 12 to 14 inches, at two of five stations. These are not large fish by the standards of some anglers, but then, an 11-inch brook trout is a rarity throughout its range, in spite of all the stories we hear about 12- and 14-inchers creeled routinely. In short, Kabekona is an excellent brook trout stream with a satisfactory mix of riffles and pools, and with the high probability of creeling a breakfast of sweet brook trout. If a solution is found to the overly energetic work of Paddy the Beaver, Kabekona will improve. Since 1990 the stream has been managed solely for naturally reproducing brook trout.

Other access points are at County Road 44 in the headwaters, at US 71, on MN 200, and southwest of Laporte on County Road 93. This lower section broadens, flattens, and slows.

Much of the land surrounding the stream is publicly owned, and easements have been leased through most of the remainder.

Some facilities at Laporte; everything at Bemidji to the north and Walker to the south.

THE CLEARWATER RIVER
DeLorme 71

The Clearwater River in Beltrami and Clearwater Counties is an exceedingly long and meandering river that drains eventually into the Red River of the North, and from there into Lake Winnipeg in Manitoba. Its several hundred snaky miles contain sections of cold-water fish, but warm-water species are more common. No one in his right mind would attempt to trace the wiggles of this complex river. We have fly-fished it but once north and west of Bemidji, Minnesota, near Pinewood. This is pretty rough, flat country, with miles of bogs to suck you down. Nevertheless, it stimulates the spirit of adventure. There are some wild places that call us to come back, if we dare. We will lead you to three spots, one of which has been improved by members of the Headwaters Chapter of Trout Unlimited, Bemidji, Minnesota; but we offer no guarantees.

First, go west from Pinewood on County Road 22 about 1.5 miles to a DNR/TU work site, where we found trout. Second, downstream on County Road 17 there's a gate to a pasture. And third, find the stretch below the railroad berm, north and west of Pinewood on an unmarked dirt road. Downstream from the railroad grade the stream is open through swamp. You should proceed cautiously in the black waters. Again, no guarantees. Most of our profiles bring you to places that are easy and open, but sometimes we will throw you a curve, accidentally, as others have done to us, perhaps deliberately. Ask Jim about "Rainbow Creek."

THE DARK RIVER
DeLorme 75

The Dark River, appropriately named for its root-beer coloration, rises in St. Louis County north and west of Virginia on the Mesabi Iron Range. It may be easier to get to the choice section of the Dark by going north out of Chisholm on MN 73. It flows for more than 20 miles to join the Sturgeon River, which in turn flows north into the Rainy River and some of the most remote country of the continent. After that, trace its ultimate destination, if you can.

According to a report by the Waybinahbe Chapter of Trout Unlimited: The Dark River is the premier trout stream north of Chisholm. In recent years the DNR and the forest service have worked jointly to enhance the fishery through extensive habitat improvement. Access has also been improved, by clearing a walking trail and creating casting room along the stream.

Most of the river lies within the boundaries of the Superior National

Forest or within the Sturgeon River State Forest. It is wilderness fishing, but accessible. Because the headwaters are close to iron mine settling ponds, which warm the water, we do not recommend the river upstream of Dark Lake. Below the lake the river can be reached from MN 73 (north of Chisholm) via Forest Road 272, County Road 65, and County Road 688 above the Sturgeon River. You will find other roads and trails to the river if you consult your DeLorme or St. Louis County maps.

The 10.5 miles from Dark Lake to the junction with the Sturgeon River were described in a DNR report: "The river flows from flat terrain covered with ash, aspen, birch, alder, willow, and grasses through a steep rolling forested area covered predominantly with jack pine, Norway pine, aspen, and birch. The soil is composed mainly of sand and rock." Ownership is 90 percent federal and 10 percent private.

The Dark River contains a thriving population of brook trout, with some brown trout reproduction. In an unusual turn of events that puzzles fisheries managers, the brook trout are taking over from the browns. Usually the brown trout drive out the brookies in water that is suitable for both. Large brown trout are more likely to be found close to the junction with the Sturgeon River.

Our preferred entries are at the County Road 65 crossing, and also

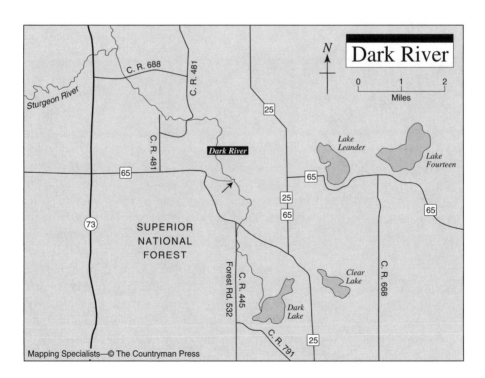

downstream from the trail where County Road 65 takes a southward turn. On a recent occasion we released browns of 15, 12, and 10 inches.

Beavers are a problem on the Dark, but a trapper has been hired to remove some dams so trout can move upstream to their preferred spawning areas.

Facilities at Chisholm and Virginia.

AFTERWORD

In this second edition we have led you to bridges and margins of more than 150 streams, and have hinted of others that you will discover on your own. Some of them are intimate, where tiny, silver trout flit in crystal cups. Some wander softly through greening glades or under the arc of autumn trees. A few will flash through chutes to fill dark and mysterious pools.

We have said that fishing for trout in our two states is better now than it was 30 or 40 years ago. Will it be as good 40 years from now? That depends on you.

APPENDIX A
FLY-FISHING SHOPS AND GUIDES

Fly-Fishing Shops

WISCONSIN
Lund's Hardware Fly Shop
201 South Main Street
River Falls, WI 54022

The FlyFishers
8601 West Greenfield Avenue
West Allis, WI 53201

Lunde's Fly Fishing Chalet
2491 Highway 92
Mount Horeb, WI 53572

Laacke and Joys
1433 North Water Street
Milwaukee, WI 53202

Brule River Classics
6008 South State Road 27
Brule, WI 54820

Fontana Sports
6670 Odana Road & 251 State Street
Madison, WI 53703

Madison Outfitters
7475 Mineral Point Road
Madison, WI 53717

Bob's Bait & Tackle
1512 Velp Avenue
Green Bay, WI 54303

Ace Hardware
500 East Northland Avenue
Appleton, WI 54911

Anglers All
2803 East Lake Shore Drive
Ashland, WI 54806

Mike's Service
Highways 64 & 55, Langlade
White Lake, WI 54491

Wild Rose Fly Shop
430 Main Street
Wild Rose, WI 54984

The Superior Fly Angler
310 Belknap Street
Superior, WI 54880

Bill Sherer's
P.O. Box 516
Boulder Junction, WI 54512

Rockin'K Fly Shop
P.O. Box 6
Coon Valley, WI 54623

West Fork Sports Club
Route 3, Box 176-B
Viroqua, WI 54665

MINNESOTA
Bob Mitchell's Fly Shop
3394 Lake Elmo Avenue North
Lake Elmo, MN 55042

Summit Flyfishing Co.
940 Grand Avenue
St. Paul, MN 55105

The Fly Angler
7500 University Avenue Northeast
Minneapolis, MN 55432

Bentley's Outfitters
582 Prairie Center Drive
Eden Prairie, MN 55344

Joe's Sporting Goods
935 North Dale
St. Paul, MN 55103

Fisherman's Corner
5675 Miller Trunk Highway
Duluth, MN 55811

Galyan's and Gander Mountain at many locations will have some fly-fishing equipment. Cabela's has retail stores at Owatonna and Grand Forks, Minnesota; at Prairie du Chien, Wisconsin; and in Nebraska, Kansas, South Dakota, and Michigan.

ILLINOIS
Fly & Field
560 Crescent Boulevard
Glen Ellyn, IL 60137

Roaring Fork Outfitters
2577 Waukegan Road
Bannockburn, IL 60015

Trout & Grouse
300 Happ Road
Northfield, IL 60093

Orvis Chicago
142 East Ontario
Chicago, IL 60611

Fishing Ambassadors
1416 West 55th Street
Countryside, IL 60525

G. R. Young Outfitters
221 South Waukegan Road
Lake Bluff, IL 60044

Great Lakes Fly Fishing Co.
2775 10 Mile Road
Rockford, IL 61101

The Great Outdoors Company
1001 University Mall
Carbondale, IL 62901

INDIANA
Jorgensen's
6226 Covington
Fort Wayne, IN 46801

Royal River Company
9504 Haver Way
Indianapolis, IN 46240

FlyMasters
8231 Allisonville Road
Indianapolis, IN 46250

Wildcat Creek Fly Shop
216 North 5th Street
Lafayette, IN 47901

MISSOURI
Feather-Craft FlyFishing
8307 Manchester Road
St. Louis, MO 63144

Puckett's Sportsman's Outfitter
906 East Broadway
Columbia, MO 65201

Rainbow Fly Shop
4706-D Shrank Drive
Independence, MO 64055

Show Me Fly Shop
1301-B Rayce Drive
Greenwood, MO 64034

NEBRASKA
Open Seasons
3673 North 129th Street
Omaha, NE 68164

OHIO
Mad River Outfitters
783 Bethel Road
Columbus, Ohio 43214

SOUTH DAKOTA
Dakota Angler & Outfitter
Rapid City, SD 57701

MICHIGAN
Little Forks Outfitters
143 East Main Street
Midland, MI 48640

Stream Guides

Most fly shops will be able to
recommend local guides.

SOUTHEAST WISCONSIN
Trout Bum, C.A.
John Langhout
621 Western Avenue
Plymouth, WI 53073
920-892-6356

SOUTHWEST WISCONSIN
Spring Creek Angler
Dennis Graupe
P.O. Box 283
Coon Valley, WI 54623
608-452-3430

Rockin' K Farms
Paul Kogut
P.O. Box 6
Coon Valley, WI 54623
608-452-3678
http://go.to/rocknk

Silver Trout
Spring Creek Fly-Fishing Service
Tom Ehlert
P.O. Box 11
Black Earth, WI 53515
608-767-2413

Dave Barron
Jacquish Hollow Angler
32491 Jacquish South
Richland Center, WI 53581
608-585-2239

NORTHWEST WISCONSIN
Western Wisconsin Fly Fishing
John Koch
W4345 850th Avenue
Spring Valley, WI 54767
715-684-2228

Andy Roth
Prescott, WI 54021

715-262-4556
Mondays, April, May, and June

Steve Therrien
1708 North 21st Street
Superior, WI 54880
715-392-4685

Brule River Classics
Chloe Manz
6008 South State Road 27
Brule, WI 54820
715-372-8153

Lorn D. Brown
2500 Spruce Road
Webster, WI 54893
715-635-7989

Anglers All
Roger LaPenter
2803 East Lakeshore Drive
Ashland, WI 54806
715-682-5754

NORTHEAST WISCONSIN
John Ramsay
N15414 Black River Road
Ironwood, MI 49938
906-932-4038

Ray D. Larson
601 North 40th Street
Sheboygan, WI 53081-1619
rlarson@excel.net
920-458-4021

CENTRAL WISCONSIN
Springwater Guide Service
Ron Manz
11710 South 64th Street
Wisconsin Rapids, WI 54494
Call after 3:00 PM: 715-325-5412
After 5:00 PM: 608-635-4700

MINNESOTA
John Edstrom
9667 103rd Place North
Maple Grove, MN 55369
763-493-5800

Bill Haugen
P.O. Box 221
Rushford, MN 55971
507-864-2867

Jim Kojis
5650 Odell Avenue South
Afton, MN 55001
651-436-2751
jikoj@aol.com

Troutchasers Ltd.
Bob Trevis
4540 Lenore Avenue
Eagan, MN 55122
troutchaser@msn.com
651-454-1397

Lone Wolf Guide Service
Dave Schaum
26201 Green Acres
Osage, MN 56570
218-573-3089

MICHIGAN
Bob Linsenman
Stream Fever
5875 Loon Lake Loop
Rose City, MI 48654
517-685-3161

APPENDIX B
RESOURCE TEXTS AND EQUIPMENT FOR THE STUDY OF
AQUATIC INSECTS

There's a jungle of information (misinformation, too) to plunge through before you can identify common mayflies and other aquatic insects, but don't lose hope yet. A handful of introductory texts will point the way. Number one on our short list is the *Instant Mayfly Identification Guide* by Al Caucci and Bob Nastasi (Comparahatch, Ltd., 1984), cheap and available at your fly shop. Two: *Naturals: A Guide to Food Organisms of the Trout* by Gary A. Borger (Stackpole Books, 1980). Three: *Aquatic Entomology* by W. Patrick McCafferty (Science Books International, 1981), available in softcover: a wealth of general information, including superb illustrations. Four: *Selective Trout,* in softcover, by Doug Swisher and Carl Richards (New Century Publishers, Inc., 1971). Appendix A of this one is a gold mine. Five: *Hatches II: A Complete Guide to Fishing the Hatches of North American Trout Streams* by Al Caucci and Bob Nastasi (Winchester Press, 1986). Six: *Nymphs: A Complete Guide to Naturals and Imitations* by Ernest Schwiebert (Winchester Press, 1973).

For those more technically inclined we recommend the monograph by W. L. Hilsenhoff of the University of Wisconsin Department of Entomology titled "Aquatic Insects of Wisconsin." It may be found in your library under the call letters QL 468.W62 or W595 7H, or purchased from Extension Publications, Room B8, 45 North Charter Street, Madison, WI 53715; 608-262-3346. It lists those aquatic insects that are indigenous to Wisconsin and possibly to contiguous states.

If you decide to go whole hog you'll want *The Mayflies of North and Central America,* the definitive work, by Edmunds, Jensen, and Berner. The first edition, University of Minnesota Press, is out of print but available from Books on Demand, Ann Arbor, Michigan. Or consult your used-book dealer. Dean Hansen's columns in *Midwest Fly Fishing* are a continuing source of information on mayflies.

In our opinion, identification of mayfly nymphs is more difficult than identification of duns or spinners, so in recent years we've equipped ourselves with a butterfly net, a small aquarium net hooked to the belt, and a couple of small plastic bottles. Sweep at least five specimens of the duns or adults out of the air or off the surface and transfer them to a bottle. They will be easy to examine at home under a bright light with an 8- or 10-power magnifier. Once you gain experience, specimens can frequently be identified on the stream with a 3-power loupe.

If you prefer to begin your studies by picking nymphs from stones or waterweeds, carry the white cover of a pillbox. Pop the nymph and a little water into the cover and you can count its gills and watch the sequential action of its breathing. A 2- or 3-power glass will be adequate for this examination. Wisconsin has strict rules on collecting. Even seining is forbidden, but a hurried exam in the cover of a pillbox is probably okay.

Specimens can be preserved for a year or two in a 50-50 mix of alcohol* and water. The positive identification of a handful of aquatic insects will add one more dimension to your art of fishing for trout.

*Ethyl alcohol is preferred but not generally available. Isopropyl alcohol works O.K.

APPENDIX C
DNR WEB SITES AND FIELD OFFICES

Wisconsin: www.dnr.state.wi.us
Minnesota: www.dnr.state.mn.us

Wisconsin DNR
101 South Webster Street
P.O. Box 7921
Madison, WI 53707
608-266-2621 or 266-1877

Partial list of regional or area
offices:
Northern Region Headquarters
810 West Maple Street
Spooner, WI 54801
715-635-2101

West Central Region Headquarters
1300 Clairemont Avenue
Eau Claire, WI 54702
715-839-3700

South Central Region Headquarters
3911 Fish Hatchery Road
Fitchburg, WI 53711
608-275-3266

Minnesota DNR
Section of Fisheries
500 Lafayette Road
St. Paul, MN 55155-4012
Minnesota: 1-888-MINN-DNR (646-6367)

Twin Cities metro area: 651-296-3325

Partial list of regional or area
offices:
Northeast Region
1201 East Highway 2
Grand Rapids, MN 55744
218-327-4415

Central Region
1601 Minnesota Drive
Brainerd, MN 56401
218-828-2624

Southeast Region
2300 Silver Creek Road, Northeast
Rochester, MN 55906
507-285-7427

Lake City Area Office
1801 South Oak Street
Lake City, MN 55041
651-345-3365

Lanesboro Area Office
Route 2, Box 85
Lanesboro, MN 55949
507-467-2442

Other important or useful addresses:

Trout Unlimited
1500 Wilson Boulevard
Suite 310
Arlington, VA 22209-2404
703-522-0200
fax: 703-284-9400
trout@tu.org
www.tu.org

Federation of Fly Fishers
P.O. Box 1595
Bozeman, MT 59771
www.fedflyfishers.org/

Flyfisher's Guide to Minnesota, Mickey O. Johnson (Wilderness Adventures Press, Belgrade, MT 59714), 2001.

Trout Country, Michael Furtman (NorthWord Press, Inc., P.O. Box 1360, Minocqua, WI 54548), 1995.

Trout Streams of Michigan: A Fly-Angler's Guide, 2nd edition, Bob Linsenman and Steve Nevala (Backcountry Guides, P.O. Box 748, Woodstock, VT 05091), 2001.

Fly Fishing Midwestern Spring Creeks, Ross A. Mueller (R. Mueller Publications, Inc., P.O. Box 296, Amherst, WI 54406), 1999.

Upper Midwest Flies That Catch Trout, Ross A. Mueller (R. Mueller Publications, Inc., P.O. Box 296, Amherst, WI 54406), 1995.

Favorite Flies and Their Histories, Mary Orvis Marbury (The Lyons Press, 123 West 18th Street, New York, NY 10011), 1892/2001.

Fly Fishing Minnesota's Trout Lakes, John Hunt (The Highweather Press, P.O. Box 211314, St. Paul, MN 55121).

Trout Fishing in Southeast Minnesota, John Van Vliet (The Highweather Press, P.O. Box 24624, Minneapolis, MN 55424), 1998.

Wildstream: A Natural History of the Free-Flowing River, Thomas F. Waters (Riparian Press, 2551 Charlotte Street, Roseville, MN 55113; 1-877-953-7487), 2000.

Trout Unlimited's Guide to America's 100 Best Trout Streams, John Ross (Globe Pequot Press, P.O. Box 480, Guilford, CT 06437), 1999.

Exploring Wisconsin Trout Streams: The Angler's Guide, Steve Born et al. (University of Wisconsin Press, 2537 Daniels St., Madison, WI 53718), 1997.

INDEX

ABOUT THE AUTHORS

Jim Humphrey, a native of Milwaukee and an intermittent resident of Minnesota, is active in the Twin Cities Chapter of Trout Unlimited. Before he quit his job to write, he was operations vice-president for a group of insurance companies. Twice he was the Minnesota state fencing champion; and he plays chess. He has lived in 6 states and fly-fished for trout in 16 states, along with Ireland, Wales, and Scotland. Jim lectures, occasionally guides, and has published more than 100 articles about trout fishing under the name J. R. Humphrey.

Bill Shogren has lived all his life in Wisconsin and Minnesota, except for short stays in Cincinnati, Ohio, and Chicago, Illinois. He has been active in Trout Unlimited, holding the positions of president of the Twin Cities Chapter, president of the Minnesota State Council, and board member of both organizations. Bill fly-fishes for all the freshwater species and has fished for trout in the Midwest, the West, and South America. Recent years have brought Bill and his fly rod to the salt flats of Florida and the Caribbean for bonefish, permit, and tarpon.

Books from The Countryman Press
and Backcountry Guides

Arizona Trout Streams and Their Hatches, Charles Meck and
   John Rohmer
Bass Flies, Dick Stewart
Building Classic Salmon Flies, Ron Alcott
The Essence of Flycasting, Mel Krieger
Fishing Small Streams with a Fly-Rod, Charles Meck
Fishing Vermont's Streams and Lakes, Peter F. Cammann
Flies in the Water, Fish in the Air, Jim Arnosky
Fly-Fishing with Children: A Guide for Parents, Philip Brunquell, M.D.
Fly-Fishing the South Atlantic Coast, Jimmy Jacobs
Fly-Tying Tips & Reference Guide, Dick Stewart
Fundamentals of Building a Bamboo Fly-Rod, George Maurer and
   Bernard Elser
The Golden Age of Fly-Fishing: The Best of The Sportsman, *1927–1937,*
   ed. Ralf Coykendall
Good Fishing in the Adirondacks, ed. Dennis Aprill
Good Fishing in the Catskills, Jim Capossela
Good Fishing in Lake Ontario and its Tributaries, Rich Giessuebel
Great Lakes Steelhead, Bob Linsenman and Steve Nevala
Ice Fishing: A Complete Guide . . . Basic to Advanced, Jim Capossela
Mid-Atlantic Trout Streams and Their Hatches, Charles Meck
Modern Streamers for Trophy Trout, Bob Linsenman and Kelly Galloup
Tailwater Trout in the South, Jimmy Jacobs
Trout Streams of Michigan, Bob Linsenman and Steve Nevala
Trout Streams and Hatches of Pennsylvania, Charles Meck
Trout Streams of Southern Appalachia, Jimmy Jacobs
Trout Streams of Northern New England, David Klausmeyer
Trout Streams of Southern New England, Tom Fuller
Trout Streams of Virginia, Harry Slone
Ultralight Spin-Fishing, Peter F. Cammann
Universal Fly Tying Guide, Dick Stewart

We offer many more books on hiking, bicycling, canoeing and kayak-
ing, travel, nature, and country living. Our books are available at book-
stores and outdoor stores everywhere. For more information or a free
catalog, please call 1-800-245-4151, or write to us at The Countryman
Press, P.O. Box 748, Woodstock, Vermont 05091. You can find us on
the Internet at www.countrymanpress.com